P9-BYI-182

STRESS

FOR

SUCCESS

STRESS
FOR
SUCCESS

**The Proven Program for Transforming
Stress into Positive Energy at Work**

James E. Loehr

THREE RIVERS PRESS
NEW YORK

Copyright © 1997 by James E. Loehr, Jack L. Groppel, and Pat Etcheberry

All rights reserved. No part of this book may be reproduced or transmitted in any form or by any means, electronic or mechanical, including photo-copying, recording, or by any information storage and retrieval system, without permission in writing from the publisher.

Published by Three Rivers Press, New York, New York.
Member of the Crown Publishing Group.

Random House, Inc. New York, Toronto, London, Sydney, Auckland
www.randomhouse.com

THREE RIVERS PRESS is a registered trademark and the Three Rivers Press colophon is a trademark of Random House, Inc.

Originally published in hardcover by Times Books in 1997.

Printed in the United States of America

Library of Congress Cataloging-in-Publication Data
Stress for success / by James E. Loehr.
Includes index.
1. Job stress.   2. Stress management.   3. Employee motivation.
4. Success in business.   I. Title.
HF5548.85.L63   1997
158.7—dc21   96-38020

ISBN 0-8129-3009-6

10   9   8   7   6

To my three sons, Mike, Pat, and Jeff,
who have always been the
wind beneath my wings.

Foreword

I have known Jim Loehr for two decades as a renowned sports psychologist, as an author, as a valued consultant to many of the superstar athletes my firm represents, and as a friend.

I first heard of him when he was doing groundbreaking work on toughness training with tennis players. At the time, Jim Loehr was way ahead of the tennis community emphasizing that players need a well-conditioned mental game to go with an arsenal of pretty strokes. Jim noticed that during the course of a two-hour match, a tennis player was actually running around the courts playing the ball—that is, being exposed to stress—for maybe 25 minutes. What was going on in a player's mind the rest of the time, when he or she should be recovering from stress? By keying in on this huge chunk of time between points and games and developing exercises and routines that helped players use this "down time" beneficially, Jim was able to have not just a significant but a *radical* impact on the performance of superstar athletes. And the sports world took notice.

Jim's impact on the business community has been no less radical than the one he's had on the sports community. Businesspeople who have absorbed his ideas have seen their performance rise to new heights.

Jim's key message is that stress is not the enemy you think it is. How many times have you heard so-called stress gurus say that you've got to get stress out of your life? "Eliminate stress," they say, "and you'll be more productive and be a healthier person."

I want to tell these "experts": "Reexamine your data!" Listen to what Jim Loehr has to say. The problem is not the stress itself but failure to oscillate between stress and recovery. The reality is that stress is the stimulus for all growth in our lives. There are very few people with a more important message for the business community—a message that will enhance not only your performance but the harmony of your entire life.

Stress for Success is Jim Loehr's magnum opus. In it he distills all the research he started two decades ago and transforms his findings into a singular book of wisdom and common sense for all of us. It does not offer a quick fix. So don't dive into its middle pages looking for seven secrets that will change your fortunes. Start at the beginning, as I did. You will be rewarded handsomely—for life.

Mark M. McCormack
Chairman and CEO, IMC

Acknowledgments

First to my parents, Mary and Con, for providing the foundation of *Stress for Success* in my life. To my partners Jack Groppel and Pat Etcheberry and to Nick Hall, the director of our research foundation, without whose support and insight, this book would not have been possible. Jack's concept of the "corporate athlete," Pat's insight into the dynamics of physical toughening, and Nick's insights into mind-body relationships were invaluable. Special thanks to Nicolas de Bourgknecht, our European partner. To Renate Gaisser for her unwavering support and belief in me. To John Mahaney, my editor, for his assistance, insight, and patience in the preparation of this manuscript. To Rebecca Murphy for the endless hours she logged in typing this manuscript and for her eagerness to help in any way possible. To Elizabeth Backman, my longtime friend and agent. To Jim Ellison and Warren and Kitty Jamison for their assistance in writing and interviews. To Jeff Balash for his insight, encouragement, and help with the entire project. To Ginger Garrett for protecting my writing time and keeping me focused. To Becky Johnson, David Striegel, Bernie Jensen, and all the LGE staff. To Tim and Tom Gullikson, Dan Jansen, Mike Richter, and all the athletes who have touched my life and formed the basis of this book. Their struggles, their pain and their triumphs provided a living laboratory for understanding the dynamics of stress. To Kathy Toon for her help in building and clarifying the Toughness Training model. To all those who have provided help and support for this project—to mention just a few: Victoria and Bob Zoellner, Gordon Uehling, Tony Schwartz, Debra Pines, Betsy and Mark McCormack, John Heffernan, Rob Knapp, Phil Hayden, Erik Henriksen, Gerry Griffin, Augie Nieto, Charles Peifer, Troy Shaver, Tom Loehr, Margaret Pyles, John Puerner, Billy Weisman, Rick Reichel, Steve Schwarzman, Ilene Lang, David Leadbetter, John Hawks, Kristen Lindelow, Jim Stern, Jane Evans, Phebe Farrow Port, Paul Roetert, Kathy Indermill, Barry Elson, Larry Biederman, and Dennis and Pat Van der Meer.

Contents

INTRODUCTION   Everything You Know About Stress Is Wrong   **3**

PART I   THE CORPORATE ATHLETE

1   **"In Today's Corporate World, You Either Perform to the Max or Don't Play"**   **13**
Learning How to Be Tough

2   **"Without Balance, We Shut Down Our Ability to Perform"**   **29**
Facing the Truth

3   **"It's the Heart, Guts, and Determination"**   **46**
Emotions Run the Show

PART II   PERFORMER SKILLS AND THE TOUGHENING PROCESS: TARGETING THE STRESS RESPONSE

4   **"Keep Things Simple and in the Same Routine"**   **67**
The Rituals of Success

5   **"It's Showtime Every Day"**   **95**
Learning to Create Emotion on Demand

6   **"It's About Being Right Upstairs"**   **118**
Getting a "Head" Start on Your Day

PART III LIFE SKILLS AND THE TOUGHENING PROCESS: TARGETING STRESS EXPOSURE

7 **"The Things That Pushed Me the Most Were the Things That Helped Me the Most"** 143
Becoming a Stress Seeker

8 **"Taking High-Quality Breaks"** 166
The Art of World-Class Recovery

9 **"Every So Often I Go Over the Edge"** 198
Riding the Waves of Stress and Recovery

10 **"Fatigue Makes Enemies of Us All"** 213
The Need for Energy

EPILOGUE Coming Home 223
A Daily Journey Without End

APPENDIX A Face-the-Truth Profiles 231

APPENDIX B Sample Daily Ritual 233

APPENDIX C Five-Day Energy Audit Form 238

APPENDIX D Meditation Resources 244

NOTES AND RELATED READINGS 245

INDEX 255

STRESS

FOR

SUCCESS

Everything You Know About Stress Is Wrong

IN CORPORATE AMERICA, stress gets a very bad rap. It's the basis for a mythology that has been building for years. Here are my candidates for the 10 most damaging myths:

Myth 1.   Stress is bad and should be avoided whenever possible.

Myth 2.   Freedom from stress will bring you great happiness.

Myth 3.   Stress undermines your health.

Myth 4.   The less stress in your life, the more productive you'll be.

Myth 5.   If you can't handle the stress, get out of the fast lane!

Myth 6.   Stress capacity is inborn.

Myth 7.   The greater the stress in your life, the less happy you are likely to be.

Myth 8.   The older you get, the more you need to protect yourself from stress.

Myth 9.   Stressing your body and brain eventually wears them out.

Myth 10. The level of stress in your life is a direct reflection of how many bad things have happened to you.

Stress for Success is based on my experience and research and has an entirely different perspective on stress:

Stress of all kinds—physical, mental, and emotional—is good for you.

Not only will I debunk the myths about stress, I'll also show you how to get revved up by stress, instead of fatigued and anxious from trying to eliminate it.

The most important aspect of stress from this perspective is the difference between *stress exposure* and *stress response*. Stress exposure is the most powerful stimulus for growth in life. People invariably grow the most in areas in which they've been pushed the most. Stress exposure expands stress capacity.

The ultimate impact of stress in your life is determined not by the stress exposure itself but by your response to that exposure. The endless traffic jams, the job loss, the failed merger, the nightmare bosses, the incompetent employees, or the costly product recalls are not what tears you apart; rather, your *emotional response* to those events does a number on your whole person. Emotional response and stress response are nearly synonymous. For 22 years, I've been in the business of helping performers of all kinds deepen their capacity for a highly unique response to stress through a vehicle I call Toughness Training©. By "toughness," I *don't* mean brute force and sheer willpower. I mean a relaxed, highly focused performance energy that has come to be known as the *Ideal Performance State (IPS)*.

My ideas about toughness developed and evolved from my work as a sport psychologist. For more than 20 years, I (and my colleagues at LGE Sport Science) have worked with hundreds of world-class athletes. They include: tennis greats Jim Courier, Pete Sampras, Sergi Bruguera, Monica Seles, Gabriela Sabatini, and Arantxa Sanchez-Vicario; boxer Ray Mancini; golfers Mark O'Meara, Nick Faldo, and Katrin Nilsmark; hockey players Mike Richter and Eric Lindros; 1996 NFL pro bowl quarterback Jim Harbaugh; and many Olympic athletes, including Dan Jansen, the Olympic speed skating gold medalist. My objective is to toughen professional and serious amateur athletes so they can go to the next level and exert whatever competitive force is necessary to emerge victorious.

From these experiences, I have learned that stress is never the real enemy. Protection from stress never took these athletes where they wanted to go. To the contrary, success was always linked to the same two things—stress exposure and stress response.

About 10 years ago, I realized that what we were learning from sports about stress and pressure applied to *any* high-stress performance arena. In the mid-1980s, I began applying Toughness Training to performers in business. I call them "corporate athletes." You may hate to sweat and you may hate all sports, but you're a corporate athlete nonetheless. To fulfill your dreams, you must concentrate, expend energy, break new personal records, and perform on demand in precisely the same way athletes do. You are, in fact, a big-time, high-stakes athlete, and *Stress for Success* will help you learn to prosper in a stressful and fiercely competitive world.

For most people in business, sport science sounds worlds removed from the day-to-day activities of, say, running an office, making a sales call, or meeting performance goals. However, the outcome in sports has a simple clarity: you either win or lose. If your preparation for performance is inadequate, the result is very clear. In real life, it takes a lot longer to figure out what is real and what is nonsense, and the answers are sometimes harder to find. Corporate athletes need to (1) deepen their capacity to tolerate stress of all kinds and (2) increase their ability to respond to stress in ways that bring full performance potential within reach. The corporate world is becoming more and more like the sports world; you either win or lose. *Stress for Success* gives you the tools to help put you in the winner's circle.

The foundation of *Stress for Success* is balance. Health, happiness, and performance are all part of the same mosaic of life. Going to the next level of performance means going to the next level of health and happiness as well. Real, lasting solutions are systemic and clearly acknowledge the dynamic interdependence of mind, body, and spirit.

I've applied the ideas and methods you'll find in *Stress for Success* to corporate athletes working in a whole range of industries, from finance and investment banking (Merrill Lynch, Morgan Stanley), to information systems (IBM), consulting (Price Waterhouse), cosmetics (Estée Lauder, Clinique), health care (Kaiser Permanente, Eckerd Corporation), and pharmaceuticals (Bristol-Myers Squibb).

In several companies, participation in our Toughness Training programs is not limited to people at management and executive levels. Westwood Squibb, for example, had everyone at its corporate headquarters, including senior management, administrative staff, and manufacturing, go through the program—a recognition that high performance and the stress that goes with it can affect every member of the corporate team. Moreover, because one of the core ideas of Toughness Training is balance, many companies (Merrill Lynch, for example) have included spouses in the program. That's a recognition that stress doesn't start and end at the office.

I've also applied these ideas to people who make life-and-death decisions: physicians and surgeons, elite SWAT teams of the FBI, and pilots. If a surgeon gets the "yips" at the operating table, or a SWAT team member chokes, or a pilot gets confused, people may die. Like corporate athletes, these professionals have stress that isn't going to disappear. They need to focus it and recover from it to perform at the highest level.

Stress for Success is a step-by-step program. The Toughness Training Road Map (page 7) provides an overview of how each chapter relates to the program as a whole. Part I of the book defines toughness, provides tools for assessing your own toughness, and explains why emotions are at stage center. Part II details three specific performer skills that empower individuals and teams to achieve their Ideal Performance State (IPS) on demand. Part III focuses on four specific life skills that expand stress capacity and increase the sense of harmony and balance in one's life. The ultimate goal of *Stress for Success* and Toughness Training is the achievement of maximum levels of productivity, health, and happiness, regardless of circumstance.

Stress for Success is based on a 30-day training program. It requires from you a commitment to train in a new way for four weeks—the amount of time it typically takes to form new habits and to begin to see and feel positive results.

For the next 30 days, think of yourself as an athlete in training for the Olympics. Like an Olympian, use a daily training log to guide your efforts and keep you focused and on track. The sample training log on page 8 organizes the most important training categories. Here is how they connect to the book's chapters.

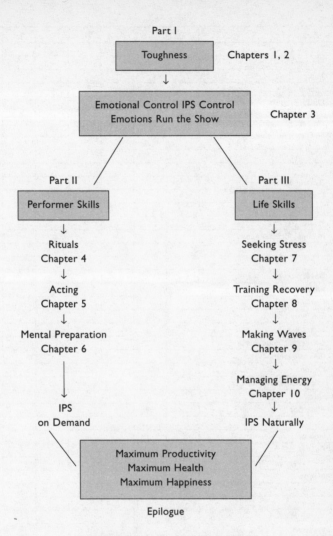

Part I

Toughness   Chapters 1, 2

↓

Emotional Control IPS Control
Emotions Run the Show   Chapter 3

Part II   Part III

Performer Skills   Life Skills

↓   ↓

Rituals   Seeking Stress
Chapter 4   Chapter 7
↓   ↓
Acting   Training Recovery
Chapter 5   Chapter 8
↓   ↓
Mental Preparation   Making Waves
Chapter 6   Chapter 9
                                           ↓
                                      Managing Energy
                                         Chapter 10
                                           ↓
IPS   IPS Naturally
on Demand

Maximum Productivity
Maximum Health
Maximum Happiness

Epilogue

The Toughness Training Road Map

Daily Training Log	Mon	Tue	Wed	Thu	Fri	Sat	Sun
1. Theme 1:							
2. Theme 2:							
3. Theme 3:							
4. Theme 4:							
Daily Rituals							
5.							
6.							
7.							
8.							
9.							
Acting Skills							
10. Disciplined Thinking							
11. Disciplined Acting							
12. Music Workout							
Mental Preparation							
13.							
14.							
Seek Stress							
15. Interval Stress							
16. Curl-ups							
17. Strength Training							
18. Stretching							
19. Challenge Emotionally							
20. Challenge Mentally							
21. Other							
World-Class Recovery							
22. Sleep							
23. Nutrition							
24. Exercise							
25. Humor							
26. Rest (Active)							
27. Rest (Passive)							
28. Needs							
29. Family							
30. Other							
Wave Making							
31. Physical							
32. Mental							
33. Emotional							
Manage Energy							
34. Time in High Positive							
35. Time in Low Positive							
36. Time in High Negative							
37. Time in Low Negative							
38. Got Tougher Today							
39. High Emotional IQ							
40. High Performance							

Sample Training Log

Items	Topic	Chapter
1–4	Themes	2, 3
5–9	Daily Rituals	4
10–12	Acting Skills	5
13–14	Mental Preparation	6
15–21	Seek Stress	7
22–30	World-Class Recovery	8
31–33	Wave Making	9
34–37	Manage Energy	10

Enter a plus (+) for each day you made a conscious effort to follow the suggested training procedure in that area. For example, if you went to bed and got up at your targeted time, give yourself a plus for that day. If you did anything to reinforce a daily theme, did your curl-ups, exercised for recovery, or worked to improve your emotional IQ for the day, give yourself a plus in the corresponding daily space on the log. The more pluses you earn, the better. (After reading the book, you'll be ready to design your personalized log so that it incorporates the essential training components of each of the chapters.)

Over the next four weeks, you will begin to sense a powerful transformation taking place within you; you'll start performing at levels you never thought possible. You'll have more energy, more stamina, and more resiliency throughout all phases of your life. Your capacity for absorbing the storms of life and of business will deepen significantly. You will get stronger mentally, physically, and emotionally, both on and off your corporate playing field. And you will clearly become a better, more intelligent fighter in the business battles you face each day. A new kind of warrior spirit will take form inside of you. You will be more in control, more confident, more precise. And, perhaps most importantly, a new sense of balance and harmony will enter your life. The demands of work, family, and community will become more manageable. The payoff is dramatic and real; you will reach new frontiers of productivity, health, and happiness.

PART I

THE CORPORATE ATHLETE

"In Today's Corporate World, You Either Perform to the Max or Don't Play"

LEARNING HOW TO BE TOUGH

WHEN I BEGAN speaking to audiences in the business world several years ago, I made a fascinating discovery. The people I met were facing demands and stresses far greater than those faced by any world-class athlete I have ever known. If your life is anything like those of the thousands of people who have gone through my Toughness Training program, you are working longer hours, and getting less sleep than any athlete, making more difficult decisions under greater pressure, and facing more potentially serious consequences.

CHAPTER 1

If a tennis player loses a crucial set there may still be a way to win the match. If a baseball player strikes out in the bottom of the ninth inning, the odds are high that his team will lose the game. Yes, that is stress, maybe even high stress; but in sports, the slate can be wiped clean. There is almost always another game tomorrow, a chance for the player to make amends.

When a surgeon makes a mistake, a patient may die on the operating table. When a law enforcement officer makes an error
under pressure, the officer's own life may be lost, or the error may
cause the death of innocent people. For those of us who aren't in
life-and-death professions, a bad decision can still have a devastat-
ing effect on the company we own or work for, or on our career.
Even apart from major stress moments—for example, the upcoming sales conference you're chairing, which will make or break
your company's next six months financially—the competitive pressure of everyday life in corporate America today is more intense,
demanding, and debilitating than ever before. It's characterized
by long hours, frequent travel, a constant need for high levels of
concentration, endless competitive pressure, and the ever-present
threat of downsizing.

We are all expected to accomplish more with less. Companies
are being forced to streamline their operations, and streamlining
affects everyone involved. We must work longer hours and achieve
higher productivity without burning out, abandoning hope, losing
the corporate vision, or breaking down personally. We have to
learn how to excel in a game that has constantly shifting rules. We
are asked to find ways to perform at our absolute maximum in
high-stress arenas and to summon whatever genius we have for accomplishing our goals—not only today or next week, but for years
to come. In today's corporate world, you either perform to the max
or you don't play. There's always someone waiting in the wings to
jump in and take your place.

FACING REALITY

I am standing in front of a roomful of 50 executives from a major
insurance company. I ask them a series of rapid-fire questions:

> How many of you are concerned that the level of stress in your
> lives is so great that it is seriously threatening your health?
>
> How many of you have no time for yourselves?
>
> How many of you are too exhausted to truly enjoy your families
> when you are with them?
>
> How many of you are feeling frustration, fear, and even anger
> about your job—and your future?

Almost without exception, every person in the room raises his or her hand in response to each question I pose. Now, I get more specific:

How many of you sleep eight hours a night? (No hands.)
How many six hours? (Two hands.)

The majority of people raise their hands at five hours—they survive on at least two hours' less sleep than experts say is necessary to be fully rested. Another considerable percentage volunteer that they sleep as few as four hours a night.

Based on my last few questions, this sleep shortage comes as no surprise. How many of you, I ask, feel that you are currently being pushed to your *absolute* limit? This time, every hand goes up. How many, I then ask, would have said the same thing a year ago today? Once again, all hands go up, accompanied by a ripple of laughter. How many of you, I finally ask, suspect you'll feel the same way next year at this time? The laughter turns to a collective shudder.

During the past two years, this experience has repeated itself 300 times when I've posed the same questions to well over 30,000 people we've trained—financial consultants, attorneys, executives from the cosmetic and pharmaceutical industries, law enforcement officers, and physicians. Their grim responses come as no surprise. Between 1987 and 1995, more than 50 percent of the companies in the *Fortune* 1000 downsized. According to the American Management Association, two-thirds of the companies that downsized are likely to do so again in the near future. A networking group called Execunet recently surveyed its currently employed members, who make up about half its clientele. They found that an astonishing 60 percent of those earning more than $100,000 annually believe they will be forced out of their jobs within a year. How can I make it any clearer that the pressures of corporate life have never been greater?

And these stresses at the office are not the only ones you're struggling with. Everyone we consult with now either has children and a working spouse or, more challenging yet, is a single working parent. These challenges add immeasurably to the level of everyday stress. And the new communications technologies, far from making life easier and increasing our leisure time, have mostly extended the workday and workweek. Here is how Augie Nieto, president of

Life Fitness, describes how increased competition and the new technologies have changed his life:

> Ten years ago, your drive home was your personal time to relax. Now, the car phone is an extension of the office. When you're competing in the marketplace, you have to use technology. That means you're always on stage, always on call. Two years ago, when you were on a jet, all you could do was make a call—now, you can receive one. You're always on at home now, too, because 18 percent of all homes have fax machines. In the old days, you'd wait at least one day for FedEx, but now you get instant feedback and proposals. I call my voicemail at night from home, and I have six or seven messages. Answering them takes up more of my leisure time. My day starts at 6 A.M., talking to my office in Europe, and doesn't end until 10 P.M. If I was the only one doing this and my competitors weren't, I'd feel OK about it. But I don't have a choice.

Does Augie's situation sound familiar? What's the answer for this kind of performance pressure and stress? How he deals with stress is going to determine how well he runs his business in the future.

A PARADIGM SHIFT

The conventional wisdom when it comes to managing stress is very simple. Reduce it! Don't work so hard, get home earlier, go on more vacations, just veg out. Many stress management experts offer the same advice on how to change the way you think: Just be more positive and upbeat and optimistic, and you'll be happier and more successful. Others suggest relaxation techniques as the solution—deep breathing, meditation, yoga, or even dietary changes, such as omitting coffee, sugar, and high-fat foods. And of course there's the classic coach approach. Tough it out. Buck up, suck it up, push away your fears and vulnerabilities and get the job done, whatever it takes. Unfurl the "No Pain, No Gain" banner.

The fact is that each of these answers contains a piece of the truth. But because each focuses on a single sphere of life, they are all ultimately quick fixes that produce short-term results, at best. The solution is not to discard these ideas, but, instead, to begin to look at them as pieces of a larger, more balanced, and more comprehensive puzzle. Positive thinking *is* useful. Relaxation techniques *do* provide a mechanism for recovery. Diet *does* matter. Setting aside negative feelings *can* be useful. None is a solution by itself, but by putting them together you can develop an approach in which the sum is greater than the individual parts.

The pressures of life in corporate America are not about to go away. If anything, they show every sign of increasing. High pressure is now a fact of life and a way of life. The only way to survive—and thrive—in today's workplace is *not to get rid of stress but to deepen your capacity to handle stress.* That can happen only by exposing yourself to new levels of stress, developing a new response to stress, and establishing a very special kind of mental, physical, and emotional balance, which will be discussed in later chapters.

Let's take a look now at a man who was stressed to the point of no return, and see what lessons we can learn from him.

DAN'S DILEMMA

Dan Jansen was the best speed skater in the world, as the Calgary Olympics approached in 1988.[1] He was the prohibitive favorite to win a gold medal. But, at 11 A.M. on the day of the 500-meter race—his best event—he learned that his sister Jane, perhaps the person closest to him in the world, had died of leukemia. He decided to skate anyway, knowing that is what his sister would have wanted for him. Halfway into the race, Dan slipped and fell. Four days later, racing in the 1,000-meter event, he fell again. It was scarcely surprising that Dan Jansen was unable to skate his best while feeling overwhelmed with grief. Still, it was heartbreaking, not just for him but for millions of sympathetic television viewers around the world.

Over the next four years, Dan went on to win numerous World Cup races. Twice, he broke the world record in the 500-meter event; he skated the second record-breaking time only three weeks before the 1992 Olympics. But no sooner did he arrive at the Olympic Village in Albertville, France, than he was besieged by reporters.

"Can you forget Calgary?" they demanded.

"Are you still haunted by the death of your sister?"

"Will you fall again?"

Overwhelmed again—this time by the memory of his past failure and the huge pressure to finally live up to his billing—Jansen came up short again. After finishing fourth in the 500 and 26th in the 1,000, he left Albertville bewildered and devastated.

Determined to figure out what prevented him from performing at his potential on the Olympic stage, Dan Jansen came to me. It was obvious that he had all the physical skills necessary to be the best in his sport. Except for his Olympic performance, he already *was* the best. But it was also clear that these physical skills alone weren't enough.

INCREASING CAPACITY

As a sports psychologist, I have spent the past 20 years trying to figure out, in measurable terms, how world-class athletes manage to perform at optimal levels under the most intense competitive stress. In the process, my partners and I have developed a comprehensive program aimed at helping athletes to get stronger physically, mentally, and emotionally.

We call these capacities *toughness,* but in doing so we have completely redefined the word. Traditionally, toughness has been equated with building will and strength with the capacity to push relentlessly and never quit. What we discovered is that optimal performance—true toughness—depends just as much on training the capacity for true, measurable recovery.

Think for a moment of weight training. To build strength, it is necessary to expose the muscles to increasing amounts of weight. Too much weight, though, can damage muscle tissue, and too little can break down muscle tissue and undermine strength. In other words, too much stress and you burn out; too little and you don't grow. The key to a successful weight-training program is to find a balanced relationship between stress and recovery. Our first breakthrough was the discovery that optimal performance depends on achieving this balance in every aspect of an athlete's life.

> The mental, physical and social parts of life must be emphasized in equal measure if the goal is to empower athletes to do great things.
>
> Norway's training philosophy for the 1994 Winter Olympics in Lillehammer. The performance of its athletes was unprecedented.

The ancient Greeks used the term *areta* to refer to this harmony of mind, body, and spirit. The first competitive sports, the earliest Olympic games, were a celebration of this harmony and balance as demonstrated in heroic feats of performance. The Greeks understood that setting new performance standards demanded not just brute strength but a purposeful blend of stamina, determination, and courage. Only then is it possible to respond to the highest levels of stress with flexibility and resilience—and to do so predictably and consistently.

For two decades, I have used the world of sport as a living laboratory, a place to measure precisely how athletes respond to stress. When they adopt our toughness philosophy and strategies, athletes perform better in competition. Our goal is not to change their techniques or mechanics but rather to transform the way they think, what they feel, and how they act. And nearly every discovery that we've made on the athletic venues has proven applicable to the modern corporate workplace.

DAN'S PROGRAM

We began with Dan Jansen the way we do with all athletes, undertaking a comprehensive mental, physical, and emotional evaluation. We looked first at his pattern of energy expenditure and recovery, which reflected his most basic needs. What did he eat, and when? When did he go to sleep and wake up? What was the quality of his sleep, and how many hours of sleep did he get each night? Next, we examined how much time he was giving himself for relaxation, play, and fun—the core elements of recovery. Our goal in this initial stage was to create a carefully balanced pattern of stress and recovery in all parts of his life—beginning with the basics of sleeping and eating.

We then created an interval training program for Dan, so that he could begin to alternate high-intensity workouts with less strenuous ones, building in time for recovery. We also added in naps, as well as periods of rest and relaxation in the course of his training day. The next step was to do motivational work with Dan. We know, from research, that whatever athletes are feeling has a direct impact on their physiology, and therefore on their capacity for performance. In Dan's case, the key issue was that he had never fully recovered from the death of his sister. For example, when we first met, I asked him to visualize winning the 500-meter race at Calgary. He literally was unable to do so. He couldn't bring himself to achieve his greatest dream—even in his imagination—on what had been the saddest day of his life.

Over time, we helped Dan to become more aware of these feelings so that he could work through them and could gain more conscious control over them when they did arise. Optimal performance, or true toughness, we have learned, requires a capacity not only to understand one's own emotional needs but to selectively summon specific feelings and to set aside others. Your goal is to gain greater insight into your feelings so that you can exert more control over them—no matter how difficult the circumstances.

We have learned that people don't perform well when they're feeling angry, or tense, or fearful, or worried. Conversely, optimal performance is clearly correlated with specific positive emotions, such as calmness, relaxation, confidence, focus, and openness. These states are not simply subjective; each of these emotions is connected directly with certain physiological responses. Calmness, to use just one example, is reflected in a very patterned, harmonious form of brain activity that can be seen on an EEG (an *e*lectro*e*ncephalogram is a measure of brain waves).

DAN'S BREAKTHROUGH

Our challenge was to help Dan become capable of accessing what we call the Ideal Performance State (IPS), no matter how intense the pressure.[2] After balancing his stress-recovery cycle, the second part of our program was to train the skills necessary for high performance. Our tools included visualization exercises, inspirational music, preperformance rituals designed to anchor desired thoughts and feelings, positive forms of self-talk, and physical postures that help prompt the biochemistry of high performance. For more than two years, Dan kept a training journal in which we tracked 27 variables in his life every day. A sample frame from the journal is shown on page 21.

One of the most powerful tools for him was an imaginary "war room" we helped him to create—a place in his own mind that he began to visit before every race. He equipped the room with

FRAME

35! Love The 1000!

DAILY MONITORING CHART
FOR DAN JANSEN

Rest

	Mon	Tues	Wed	Thurs	Fri	Sat	Sun
Interval Exercise (Time)	60'	—	—	—	60'	—	45'
Aerobic Exercise (Time)	—	sprints	—	2½ hrs.	—	90'	30'
Strength Training (Time)	90'	30'	—	—	90'	—	—
Diet (A–F)	B	C	B	B	B	A	B
Number of Meals	3	3	3	3	3	3	3
Sugar No. of Times	2	2	2	1	1	1	1
Quantity of R & R (Time)	4 hrs.	4 hrs.	All Day	4 hrs.	4 hrs.	6 hrs.	5 hrs.
Quality of R & R (A–F)	B	B	B	B	B	A	A
Time to Bed/Time Up	11:00/5:00	11:00/7:00	10:00/8:00	11:00/8:45	11:00/6:30	11:00/6:30	12:00/9:00
Hours of Sleep	6	8	10	9¾	7½	7½	9
Quality of Sleep (A–F)	B	B	A	A	B	B	A
Nap (Yes/No)	No	No	No	Yes	Yes	Yes	Yes
Positive Attitude (A–F)	A	A	A	A	B	B	A
Confident Fighter Image (A–F)	B	B+	—	A	B–	B	B
Concentration Today (A–F)	A–	A	—	A	B	B	B+
Confidence Today (Yes/No)	Yes	Yes	Yes	Yes	Yes	Yes	Yes
Motivation Today (A–F)	B	B	—	A–	B	B	B
Had Fun Today (A–F)	B	B	B	B	B	B	B
Relaxation Exercise (Time)	—	—	—	—	—	—	—
Feel Energy (A–F)	B	B	C	B	B–	B	B
How Well I Performed (A–F)	A	A	—	A	A–	B+	A

A Sample Page from Dan Jansen's Training Journal

everything that made him feel happiest and most positive: images of his wife and tiny baby, trophies from important races, the music that he found most inspiring.

Leading up to the 1994 Olympics at Lillehammer, Norway, Dan won World Cup races five times and broke the 36-second barrier in the 500-meter event three times—the equivalent of running a mile in less than 3 minutes, 40 seconds. Still, Lillehammer remained the ultimate test of his newfound toughness. At the age of 32, Dan knew that he was competing in his final Olympics. When he narrowly missed a medal in the 500, the pressure to perform at his peak became greater than ever. He wasn't even the favorite in the 1,000-meter race, but this time out—his last chance for a gold medal—he managed not only to win the gold but to set a new world record. Dan Jansen had demonstrated what every great performer must realize—grace under pressure is rarely inborn or God-given. The only way to meet the challenge of optimal performance is to train—mentally, physically, and emotionally—every day of your life.

Dan had the physical equipment to excel long before he won his gold medal, but the medal could not become a reality until he began daily training not just of his body but of his emotions and mind as well. We all have our Calgarys, when pressures and stresses bring us down. To face the highest levels of pressure while performing at the height of your potential on the job, you have to know who you are. You are a corporate athlete and you have to begin to think like one. That means training every day, just like an Olympian, and learning how to: (1) balance the stress in your life with equal doses of recovery; and (2) consciously cultivate the skills of performance so that you can summon your Ideal Performance State (IPS) on demand.

ACCESSING YOUR IDEAL
PERFORMANCE STATE

When your mind, body, and emotions are truly in balance, oscillating flexibly between stress and recovery, you have set the stage to summon IPS on demand. This is what athletes refer to when they talk about being "in the zone," or "in flow," or "treeing." It is a state typically free of conscious thinking, and it is characterized by feeling calm, confident, challenged, positively energized, re-laxed, and capable of producing whatever a given situation de-mands.[3] You may have been in IPS while playing sports, composing music, delivering a speech, climbing a treacherous mountain, or closing one of the biggest deals in your career.

One of the most remarkable discoveries is that it is possible to access this state consciously whenever you need it. Just as you can increase your physical strength by lifting progressively heavier weights, so it is possible to systematically train your mind and emo-tions for the maximum Ideal Performance State. The training tech-niques I will show you are all variations of those we used with Dan Jansen and other athletes.

The ideas I'm describing are new to the worlds of business and sport. Few world-class athletes have ever been exposed to this kind of systematic training of mind and body. Most of them discover the skills of optimal performance instinctively, or through the happy accident of trial and error. It is unlikely that any coach ever told the young Jimmy Connors that strutting like a bantam rooster and wag-ging his finger at the crowd between points, or doing his swivel-hipped victory dance, or grinning and pretending to swallow his racket handle after a bad shot, helped prompt the physiology that best served his performance. Likewise, no business school trained CEOs such as Bill Gates of Microsoft or Michael Eisner of Disney in the sort of disciplined positive thinking that consistently enhances performance.

THE ATHLETE OF ALL ATHLETES

You may be wondering why I am repeatedly calling you a corporate athlete, particularly those of you whose longest stretch of daily ex-ercise is the walk to the garage to get into the car that takes you to work in the morning. But ask yourself this: How much time, in the normal course of a training day, does a professional athlete spend putting out energy and performing? The average is 4 to 6 hours. How many of you work 4 to 6 hours and then call it quits? How many of you work more than 8 hours a day on average? How many of you work 12 to 14 hours a day, day after day after day? It's a safe bet that everyone reading this book has to drive energy more hours in each day than the busiest, most dedicated professional athlete. And if you make a mistake during your 12th workhour, because of extreme exhaustion, or if you fumble the corporate ball, do you get some slack for it? Does someone say to you, "Oh, that's all right. You've been working 12 hours without a break. No problem. Yes, you cost us time and money, but not to worry. I understand and sympathize." Is that what your boss will say to you? Of course not. No one cares how many hours you put in. You're still expected to knock in the winning run or make the crucial basket down the stretch. No excuses.

Corporate athletes in today's downsized business world often work 7 days a week, and many have the feeling they never stop working. Stop and ask yourself whether that's the case with you. Are you literally "on" all the time? Do you have pagers and faxes and cellular phones contacting you constantly? Do you have any downtime? Do you really *ever* stop working? Rarely is a professional athlete captive to pagers and cellular phones and such paraphernalia. What is plugged into an athlete's ear is a Walkman™—for music, for relaxation.

Now ask yourself this: Who has to drive more energy, for longer periods of time, without mistakes? I will tell you. No athlete we've ever studied in all of our 20-plus years in sport has anywhere *near* the kind of demands placed on his or her time or energy that you do. In this sense, you're more of an athlete than any athlete we've ever met. The demands of energy expenditure are infinitely greater for you. You are expected to work for 10 to 12 hours at a stretch while keeping your focus, making no mistakes, and never fumbling. Then you repeat the same routine for 10 to 12 hours the following day. So who has more pressure—you or a professional athlete? No contest. That is not to say that there isn't a lot of pressure in professional sports. But what happens when a good athlete can no longer make it in a sport? Where does he or she go? Into real life—the broadcast booth perhaps, or the spokesperson role for a sponsor, or the public relations staff for a former employer. Now compare that situation with yours. If you don't make it in the corporate world, where do *you* go? How many of you have the option of playing a professional sport? If you had that option, you'd have taken it years ago. You don't, so the life you're living today is not a dress rehearsal for a future life. It *is* your life. It's all you *have*. If you don't make it in this arena, you've got nothing else to fall back on.

How many people depend on you to maintain your spirit, to stay in there and fight, to approach every day with an unquenchable desire to succeed? What are the consequences if you don't survive; if you can't handle the pressure and fold like an accordion; if you just throw up your hands and say, "I've had it, I can't take it any more!" You are not a professional athlete who can quit and enter real life. If you quit in real life, the consequences are enormous, and you know it; and because you know it, you realize you have to keep on fighting.

In team sports, you have to be a team player. What happens in your world, if you can't get along with people? How important is it that you be a team player, that people feel good about you, and that you're able to make them feel good about their relationship with you? How crucial is that kind of team play in your work world? What if you *don't* get along with people? Are you going to be traded or put on waivers? No; in the first wave of downsizing, all those folks who couldn't get along are gone. "Thank God we got rid of Sam. What a pain!" Yes, Sam was competent enough, but he was no team player; when there was an opportunity to get rid of him, he was history. The corporate athlete has to be a remarkable team player and has to remain one for 30 to 40 years. The professional athlete's career is 5 to 7 years, on average. How much more important is it for you to play your game right? You perform or you're out of there. I perform in this book or you drop it on the table and never open it again. It's as simple as that. If you screw up, if you botch the presentation, if you manage to alienate your coworkers, the problem is yours. No excuses.

The storms of business are always brewing and raging, and what works today may not work tomorrow. We literally have to run just to stay in place; there is no personal time. I sometimes wonder what happened to those soothsayers who used to tell us that the greatest problem we would ever have is knowing how to fill in the leisure time that would be created by a high-tech culture. If you find them, shoot them. They set us up for a big-time fall. How many of us are forced to take on more and more responsibilities with fewer and fewer resources? Does anyone know of a team roster that has gotten bigger? Budgets are shaking out every last drop from the milk container. There is nothing left. How much tougher is competition today than 10 years ago?

And, compared to any time in the past, how much tougher a corporate athlete do you have to be today to stay the course? The competition is unbelievable; the global market is expanding, and people are literally on top of you, ready and eager to push you aside. It took you 20 to 30 years to get where you are, and now others who are younger, command lower salaries, and have a better grasp of the high-tech world, are breathing down your neck. The rules of the game are constantly changing; and they never were fair.

Can corporate athletes take advantage of what professional athletes have learned about preparation? What vehicle do professional athletes use to prepare themselves for the brutality of their playing fields? The answer is simple and direct: THEY TRAIN FOR IT! The most fundamental tenet of Toughness Training is that you must train every day to get stronger, more resilient, more responsive and flexible, just like athletes do. An example is Joel Schumacher, director of two giant movies simultaneously—*A Time to Kill* and the next Batman sequel. At 56 years of age, he puts it this way: "You have to be like an athlete to direct movies, because the hours are so strange, and you work in all kinds of weather." Joel gets up at 5:30 every morning, goes for a run, and works out with a personal trainer until 8:00 A.M. He's also very careful what he eats. For Joel, thinking of himself as an athlete helps him to thrive on stress and to take his daily training seriously.

NO PROTECTION

You must understand a very important caveat. Some athletes and businesspeople come to us seeking protection. They are broken in half and close to burnout, and they want us to make the path easy for them. The first thing we explain to everyone starting the Toughness Training program is that we offer no protections. Instead, we take the client back into the stormy sea of stress, which is exactly what the client wants to avoid. We know that's the only way to stop the slippage and defeat. If your life demands, in a metaphorical sense, that you run a mile in seven minutes—the pace you need to maintain, in order to keep your job—and you're only capable of a nine-minute-mile pace, what are we going to do to help you? First of all, we listen. You say, "I *can't* do a seven-minute-mile pace; I can only do a nine." You've got all the signs and signals of overtraining—you're upset,

> We took a multidimensional approach to improve our company's toughness. We created a task force of 20 to recommend changes. Recommendations were made at several levels. We changed our cafeteria selections to make it easier for our employees to eat more nutritious, better balanced meals. We upgraded out athletic facilities—we put in basketball courts, rowing machines, free weights, StairMasters™! And the facilities are accessible to everyone. We even created our own Sentinel Olympics, with the winners being the teams that compiled the most minutes of exercise over a three-week period. We even had our own Olympic closing ceremony. The results have been very exciting. The paper's rate of absenteeism is down dramatically. Our employees are healthier, happier, and more productive than at any time I've been with the paper. We're definitely tougher than we were in the past. I'm proud of what our organization has done.
>
> John Puerner
> Publisher, Orlando Sentinel

angry, and depressed. You're beaten up, you're just losing out every which way. You're bitter because all your friends have been chopped off at the knees in the latest downsizing directive. You don't trust anybody anymore. A seven-minute-mile pace is expected of you from this moment on—no two ways about it—and your job security depends on your doing it—and not just once in a while, but every day. So you come to us looking for protection. If we were to protect you, you would never do better than a nine-minute-mile pace; and if we protect you *too* much, you won't even be able to do that for very long. You'll slip farther and farther behind. By exposing yourself to stress and training every day, until you can run that metaphorical seven-minute-mile pace with ease, your productivity, health, and happiness will increase. You will literally thrive in the chaos of modern corporate life.

CONCLUSION

As we began working in the business world, we discovered that the physical, emotional, and mental responses to stress are remarkably similar for corporate executives and world-class athletes. For both, when stress becomes intense, heart rate increases, muscles tighten, and the stress hormones that prompt anxiety are activated. The stress response of the athlete typically disappears when the game is over, but the competitive battle in business never ends. Many of the corporate executives we work with are caught in a vicious cycle. They overwork their mental and emotional capacities and severely undertrain physically. The result is an imbalanced pattern of stress and recovery that compromises performance and, over time, erodes their precious health and happiness.

In sports, the consequences of this imbalance are very graphic. We have seen players with extraordinary athletic skills fail in contests against less talented competitors. Some simply hadn't trained hard enough, physically, to handle stress. Others, like Dan Jansen, were suffering intense emotional crises and lacked the awareness and the skills necessary for recovery—in the form of healing. Still others hadn't trained their minds to the fullest extent possible, and they lost the will to win under pressure. What they had in common was failure to perform at their best when it counted most. They choked, not for mysterious and unfathomable reasons, but because in one way or another they lacked the Performer skills necessary for control or the Life skills needed to ensure proper balance. In all likelihood, the same is true with you. Whatever your current capacity for performance under pressure, I would argue that it could almost certainly be better—and that your life could be more satisfying.

"Without Balance, We Shut Down Our Ability to Perform"

FACING THE TRUTH

IF I CALL you *tough,* I pay you the supreme compliment. It means you don't just simply possess talent and skill; you have the ability to bring your talent and skill to life, UNDER PRESSURE. You can CONSISTENTLY EXECUTE, regardless of circumstance. It also means you will never surrender your spirit. When the storms of life and business descend, you will stand firm. You won't collapse. When everyone else is looking for a place to hide, you're raising your hand and asking for the floor. I can lean on you, depend on you, believe in you. You absolutely will not go away emotionally when things get tough. You can handle stress. You simply deal with it; at times, you appear to actually thrive on it. Somehow, you've developed a deep capacity for continuing to fight until real answers are found. You can exert great force and resist great force— mentally, physically, and emotionally. You don't become defensive, rigid, or inflexible as the storms intensify. Nor do you become calloused and insensitive to the forces of life. On the contrary, you remain grounded, connected, engaged. You are fully alive to the conditions and people around you. Every cell in your body is driving toward the target. And, perhaps most importantly, you can take a hit. You bounce back quickly from failure, learn from your mistakes, and resume the fight more resilient than ever.

How important is this capacity to respond to stress in such a unique way? The destinies of nations, of cities, of the companies we represent, and of our own lives rest in the balance. Fulfillment of dreams, realization of personal happiness, and preservation of health are fundamentally rooted in personal strength and a deep capacity for stress.

I can think of no better example of someone who is stressed for success than John Heffernan, who had to learn this skill in order to survive in the modern business climate. John manages the day-to-day operations of a branch of a large pharmaceutical company, and his workweeks are 91 hours long—13 hours a day, 7 days a week. John is the very model of the modern corporate athlete; as a result of downsizing, rightsizing, and merging with another drug company, his functions, under a share-services system, are almost too many to count. John says:

> I guess you could say I'm the head of the daily grind, and I spend my time running from fire to fire. When companies merge, interdivisional cooperation and coordination become absolute musts. One of my principal jobs is making sure the left hand knows what the right hand is doing. Right now I'm V.P. of Sales, but that's only one of my jobs. I guide 125 reps, I'm director of the field sales force. It's up to me to make sure that sales promotional materials are on target. I'm also responsible for expense reporting, meeting planning, subscriptions, record retention, sales reporting systems, incentive plans, sales goals, field sales force training, management development—and basically running the sales department on a daily basis.
>
> That's why the ideas underlying *Stress for Success* are so crucial in today's world. Before we merged, I used to have a personal staff of 22. Now my staff is 2. And yet my workload is greater than it ever was! I'm not alone in this. It's par for the course in today's business world.
>
> About four years ago, I sensed that I was burning out. The idea of having a job for life was no longer guaranteed. Everything every businessperson worried about was coming true. You couldn't depend on loyalty or continuity. You had to depend on yourself, on your own

toughness to see you through. I took a good look at myself and didn't like what I saw. I was 46 years old and I felt and looked older than my age. I was out of shape, I was eating poorly, and my job was driving me crazy. When I was in the army, I had achieved the rank of captain—I was lean and tough in those days, but I sensed I was losing it.

The key to coming to grips with stress for me was making significant lifestyle changes. I had to find a way to sustain high productivity without undermining my health or happiness. I was looking for balance. Without balance, we get a shutdown of our ability to perform.

I worked on eating better, losing weight, exercising more—and then began a campaign to show others in my company the value of achieving balance. I knew so many executives who were in the same trouble I was, and I was convinced they could benefit just as I had. And it wasn't just an individual problem, but involved the entire company culture. Our company—like so many today—was fueled on anxiety. We had these tremendous reductions in the workforce—entire layers of management were being eliminated. There was also the "survivors' syndrome" problem, with those left behind having to take up the slack. We all felt the need for increased productivity despite the cuts in staff—all the things you read about when a company restructures. Many problems, dependent on tough solutions.

It's hard to say just what effect learning to deal with and recover from stress has had on our entire workforce, but I can see some big changes. For one thing, people seem more respectful of others in meetings. They seem to listen better. I guess you could say people are getting out of their boxes and spreading themselves, flexing their mental and emotional muscles. The company nurse says there are fewer people coming in complaining of aches and pains, sleeplessness and depression. Also, the corporate gym is suddenly the place to be. Fruit has replaced the fatty munchies at meetings, and healthy snacks are available. This is a revolution of sorts—a positive revolution that empowers all of us as we slug away in the corporate ring.

As for me, my life has taken on new meaning and new glow, thanks to Toughness Training. I make time to go to the gym three times a week—for both weight and cardiovascular work. I eat better, and I've lost 15 pounds, even though I eat more than I used to.

The symbol of toughness, for me, is all tied up with the Philadelphia airport. When you fly in there and have to change planes, you land at a far exit on one side of the airport and have to walk to the extreme other end of the airport to board the plane to your destination. You have about 35 minutes to get out of one plane and into the other, which, to say the least, is cutting it awfully close. Over the years, I've figured out the odds. Eighty percent of the time, I'll make it; the other

20 percent, I have to wait for the next plane out. Before Toughness Training, I used to lunge out of the plane, sweat popping out on my face, already breathing hard from anxiety and tension, and stagger along with my baggage as the seconds and minutes ticked away. As I say, I made my connection 80 percent of the time. Now, I get off the plane and walk briskly but without fear down the corridor. I know the odds are that I'll make it; but I also know that if I don't, it's not the end of the world. Ironically, because I'm in better condition these days, my odds have gone up from 80 to almost 100 percent. And I even have a minute or two along the way to browse in the airport bookstore!

Today is Friday—not exactly the end of the week for me because my workweek doesn't really end. But tonight I'm meeting friends at 7:30 at a very good French restaurant. We'll have some excellent chardonnay and a wonderful meal, and by 11:00 I'll be home in bed, fully recovered from a grueling day. Tomorrow—Saturday—I'll be back at work (in my office at home), but fully refreshed. I have a motto I keep on my desk: "Be conscious of fun stuff. Be conscious of work stuff. Love them both and recover!"

ARE YOU TOUGH?

The most important step in the Toughness Training process is confronting the truth about your own level of toughness. I learned early in my career that if I couldn't get an athlete—whether corporate or Olympic—to fully embrace the reality of his or her most profound weaknesses, everything we did from that point on was a waste of time. If you want this program to work for you, you've got to open up the hood and take an honest look at what's really underneath it. No hiding. No denying. We get so good at concealing our weaknesses from others, we actually start believing they don't exist. Opening up to personal truth can be both scary and painful, but the payoff in growth can be tremendous.

The questions posed in this chapter are intended to make you think about your own toughness, to get you to start peeling back the onion skin so you can see what's really inside. The objective is to identify the four most profound weaknesses that are currently blocking your path to greater productivity, health, and happiness in your life. Once identified, the weaknesses will be converted into positive daily goals. They will become themes in your life for the next 30 days.

Here's how it works. Let's assume that after completing all the profiles in this chapter, you conclude that your four weaknesses are:

Weaknesses

1. Insecurity
2. Defensiveness
3. Rigidity and inflexibility
4. Pessimism.

You are now to convert those weaknesses into strengths and make them important themes in your life. Here's what the conversion should look like:

Weaknesses	*Themes*
1. Insecurity	→ Confident
2. Defensiveness	→ Open
3. Rigidity and inflexibility	→ Flexible
4. Pessimism.	→ Optimistic

The next step is to create your own daily training log, following the model shown below. Enter your four positive themes in the space on the left side.

Sample Daily Training Log							
Daily Training Log	Mon	Tue	Wed	Thu	Fri	Sat	Sun
1. Theme 1:							
2. Theme 2:							
3. Theme 3:							
4. Theme 4:							

Whenever you do anything that reinforces one of your themes during a given day, give yourself a plus in your log for that day. Tracking your themes on a daily basis brings them to life. And when you get the right themes going in your life, major life-changing breakthroughs invariably follow. The key is to identify the right themes and then to keep them alive on a daily basis until new habits and perceptions are formed.

PROFILING THE TRUTH

To help you identify your most compelling areas of weakness, four different tools are presented here. Each tool addresses your toughness from a slightly different perspective, but there is considerable overlap. The first series of questions focuses on your emotional control skills. The connection between emotion and toughness will be explored in Chapter 3.

Tool 1. Assessment of Emotional Intelligence[1]

Peter Salovey believes that emotional intelligence is composed of five major factors that are at least somewhat independent of one another:[2]

1. Knowing one's emotions.
2. Managing emotions.
3. Motivating oneself.
4. Recognizing emotions in others.
5. Handling relationships.

1. Knowing One's Emotions.   Awareness of feelings as they come and go in our lives is the keystone of emotional intelligence. The ability to know our own feelings, discriminate among them, and draw on them to guide behavior is fundamental to self-understanding and self-direction. People who have great certainty about their feelings are good pilots of their lives; they have a sure sense of how they really feel about personal decisions.

The following statements are designed to assess your abilities in this area. Check (✔) true (T) or false (F):

T ___ F ___ 1. I use both negative *and* positive emotions as a source of wisdom about how to navigate my life.

T ___ F ___ 2. Negative feelings help me to address what I need to change in my life.

T ___ F ___ 3. When the time is right, I face my negative feelings and work through what the issue is.

T ___ F ___ 4. Negative feelings are helpful to me.

T ___ F ___ 5. I have the ability to monitor my feelings from moment to moment.

T ___ F ___ 6. Knowing my true feelings is crucial to my well-being.

T ___ F ___ 7. I'm aware of my true feelings most of the time.

T ___ F ___ 8. I can generally express how I'm feeling at the time.

Totals: T _____ F _____

More than two *false* answers is a red alert.

2. Managing Emotions.   This is an ability to handle emotions so that they are appropriate. Examples include being able to soothe oneself and being able to shake off rampant anxiety, gloom, or irritability. People who manage their emotions well can bounce back quickly from life's setbacks and upsets. As before, check whether each of the following statements is true or false for you:

T ___ F ___ 1. I've learned to control negative thinking.

T ___ F ___ 2. I am in charge of how I feel.

T ___ F ___ 3. After something has upset me, I can regain my composure quickly.

T ___ F ___ 4. I have control over my thoughts, feelings, and actions.

T ___ F ___ 5. I am calm under pressure.

T ___ F ___ 6. I do not dwell on negative emotions.

T ___ F ___ 7. I am capable of soothing myself after an upsetting event.

T ___ F ___ 8. I can quickly shake off negative feelings when I need to.

T ___ F ___ 9. I never fear that I'm losing control over my thoughts, feelings, actions, or memory.

T ___ F ___ 10. I can change from a negative emotional state to a positive emotional state when necessary.

T ___ F ___ 11. I feel emotionally stable.

Totals: T _____ F _____

More than three *false* answers is a red alert.

3. Motivating Oneself. Motivating involves marshaling emotions in the service of a goal. The capacities needed include summoning emotional self-control, delaying gratification, stifling impulsiveness, and being able to get into one's Ideal Performance State. People who have this skill tend to be productive and effective in whatever they undertake. Answer each of the following items true or false:

T ___ F ___ 1. I am able to motivate myself to try and try again in the face of setbacks.

T ___ F ___ 2. I don't give up when I don't get results quickly.

T ___ F ___ 3. When I do a boring job, I think about less boring parts of the job and try to enjoy being in the moment.

T ___ F ___ 4. I try to be creative with life's challenges.

T ___ F ___ 5. When I need to perform, I get very calm, focused, and positively energized, regardless of the situation.

T ___ F ___ 6. I like to push the limits of my ability.

T ___ F ___ 7. When a job is important, I am often able to perform to my full potential.

T ___ F ___ 8. Under pressure, I rarely feel helpless and fatigued.

T ___ F ___ 9. When necessary, I can enter a state characterized by calmness, alertness, and focus.

T ___ F ___ 10. I generally can do whatever I need to, emotionally, to get myself performing well.

T ___ F ___ 11. I thrive on pressure.

T ___ F ___ 12. When challenged, I am able to summon a wide range of positive emotions such as fun, joy, fighting spirit, and humor.

T ___ F ___ 13. I can become completely absorbed in what I'm doing.

T ___ F ___ 14. I find it easy to pay undivided attention to a task when I desire to do so.

T ___ F ___ 15. I often lose track of space and time when performing a challenging task.

T ___ F ___ 16. I can easily set negative feelings aside when called on to perform.

Totals: T _____ F _____

More than four *false* answers is a red alert.

4. Recognizing Emotions in Others.   This characteristic is *empathy*. People who are empathic are attuned to the subtle social signals that indicate what others want or need. This makes them better at teaching, sales, management, and professions where caring is important. Answer each of the following items true or false:

T ___ F ___ 1. I am sensitive to the needs of others.

T ___ F ___ 2. I am effective at listening to other people's problems.

T ___ F ___ 3. I am good at understanding the emotions of other people, even when the emotions are not directly expressed.

T ___ F ___ 4. I rarely get angry at people who come around and bother me with foolish questions.

T ___ F ___ 5. I am adept at reading people's feelings by their facial expressions.

T ___ F ___ 6. I am sensitive to the emotional needs of others.

T ___ F ___ 7. I am aware of the subtle social signals that indicate what others need.

T ___ F ___ 8. I am strongly attuned to others' feelings.

T ___ F ___ 9. I can easily "put myself into other people's shoes."

Totals: T _____ F _____

More than two *false* answers is a red alert.

5. Handling Relationships.   This involves managing emotions in others (e.g., helping others soothe their feelings). Included is the ability to know others' feelings and to act in a way that further shapes those feelings. The following statements are designed to assess your capacity to discern and respond appropriately to the moods, temperaments, motivations, and desires of other people. People who excel in these skills do well at anything that relies on interacting smoothly with others (e.g., leadership). Answer each of the following items true or false:

T ___ F ___   1. I find it easy to relax with other people.

T ___ F ___   2. Talking to strangers is not difficult for me.

T ___ F ___   3. I have a calming influence on other people.

T ___ F ___   4. I am often able to improve the moods of others.

T ___ F ___   5. I am a good person to come to for advice about handling emotional conflicts.

T ___ F ___   6. I respond appropriately to other people's moods, motivations, and desires.

T ___ F ___   7. I'm effective in motivating others to achieve their personal goals.

T ___ F ___   8. People view me as an effective coach for others' emotions.

Totals: T _____ F _____

More than two *false* answers is a red alert.

Overall totals, factors 1–5:   T _____ F _____

Scoring key:

Number of True Answers	Emotional Intelligence Rating
52–48	High
47–44	Good
43–40	Marginal
39–less	Red alert

More important than knowing your total score is knowing which of the five factors contributing to emotional intelligence is the most problematic for you. Any red alert category should be considered as a possible theme for your training log.

Tool 2. Toughness Training Profile[3]

With this tool, you rate yourself on each of the following 25 factors, using a 1 (lowest) to 10 (highest) scale. Each of the factors listed contributes to overall toughness in some specific way. Keep your self-rating within the context of *how you typically respond in high-pressure situations.* Be as honest and accurate with your answers as you can. There are no right or wrong answers. Fill in one circle in each horizontal row.

	1	2	3	4	5	6	7	8	9	10	
Rigid	○	○	○	○	○	○	○	○	○	○	Flexible
Nonresponsive	○	○	○	○	○	○	○	○	○	○	Responsive
Nonenergetic	○	○	○	○	○	○	○	○	○	○	Energetic
Nonresilient	○	○	○	○	○	○	○	○	○	○	Resilient
Fearful	○	○	○	○	○	○	○	○	○	○	Challenged
Moody	○	○	○	○	○	○	○	○	○	○	Even-tempered
Noncompetitive	○	○	○	○	○	○	○	○	○	○	Competitive
Dependent	○	○	○	○	○	○	○	○	○	○	Self-reliant
Uncommitted	○	○	○	○	○	○	○	○	○	○	Committed
Unfriendly	○	○	○	○	○	○	○	○	○	○	Friendly
Passive	○	○	○	○	○	○	○	○	○	○	Assertive
Insecure	○	○	○	○	○	○	○	○	○	○	Confident
Impatient	○	○	○	○	○	○	○	○	○	○	Patient
Undisciplined	○	○	○	○	○	○	○	○	○	○	Disciplined
Pessimistic	○	○	○	○	○	○	○	○	○	○	Optimistic
Not Open to Change	○	○	○	○	○	○	○	○	○	○	Open to Change
Unmotivated	○	○	○	○	○	○	○	○	○	○	Motivated
Poor Problem Solver	○	○	○	○	○	○	○	○	○	○	Good Problem Solver
Poor Team Player	○	○	○	○	○	○	○	○	○	○	Team Player
Unwilling to Take Risks	○	○	○	○	○	○	○	○	○	○	Risk Taker
Physically Unfit	○	○	○	○	○	○	○	○	○	○	Physically Fit
Negative Body Language	○	○	○	○	○	○	○	○	○	○	Positive Body Language
Not Playful at Work	○	○	○	○	○	○	○	○	○	○	Playful at Work
Defensive	○	○	○	○	○	○	○	○	○	○	Open
Poor Sense of Humor	○	○	○	○	○	○	○	○	○	○	Great Sense of Humor

After you have completed the Toughness Training Profile, go back and place an asterisk alongside what you consider to be your four areas of greatest weakness. Then ask a minimum of four people, who know well how you act under pressure, to fill out the Toughness Training Profile as they see you. Ask them for the truth, and have them complete the profile anonymously. (Copies of the

Toughness Training Profile can be made for distribution; see Appendix A.)

When all the profiles have been collected, add the scores for each item together and divide by the number of evaluations received. The results will provide you with a composite picture of how others see you. Place asterisks alongside what others perceive as your greatest weaknesses, and then compare their assessment to your own. This information is invaluable for helping you face the truth about the areas of your life that need special attention.

Tool 3. Team Building Perceptual Assessment[4]

The Team Building Perceptual Assessment is included in here for those who work on teams. Fill out the assessment on yourself, and have your team members do their own assessments of you. Ask each team member for the truth, and keep the evaluations anonymous. (The Team Building Perceptual Assessment is provided in Appendix A. Copy it for your team.)

As with the Toughness Training Profile, compare *your* perceived strengths and weaknesses with the *composite* created by all your team members (1 = lowest rating; 10 = highest rating).

	1	2	3	4	5	6	7	8	9	10	
Defensive	○	○	○	○	○	○	○	○	○	○	Open
Unfriendly	○	○	○	○	○	○	○	○	○	○	Friendly
Poor Sense of Humor	○	○	○	○	○	○	○	○	○	○	Good Sense of Humor
Critical of Others	○	○	○	○	○	○	○	○	○	○	Accepting of Others
Negative Attitude	○	○	○	○	○	○	○	○	○	○	Positive Attitude
Unmotivated	○	○	○	○	○	○	○	○	○	○	Motivated
Nonenergetic	○	○	○	○	○	○	○	○	○	○	Energetic
Thinks "Me"	○	○	○	○	○	○	○	○	○	○	Thinks "We"
Constantly Seeks Praise	○	○	○	○	○	○	○	○	○	○	Rarely Seeks Praise
Poor Communicator	○	○	○	○	○	○	○	○	○	○	Good Team Player
Moody	○	○	○	○	○	○	○	○	○	○	Even-tempered
Poor Team Player	○	○	○	○	○	○	○	○	○	○	Good Team Player
Distant	○	○	○	○	○	○	○	○	○	○	Caring
Uncooperative	○	○	○	○	○	○	○	○	○	○	Cooperative
Poor Listener	○	○	○	○	○	○	○	○	○	○	Good Listener
Suspicious	○	○	○	○	○	○	○	○	○	○	Trusting
Threatens Others	○	○	○	○	○	○	○	○	○	○	Challenges Others

Tool 4. The Mentally Tough Test[5]

This test is for your own self-knowledge and improvement. Be honest. Don't make yourself better than you are or less than you are. Face the truth. It's the first and most important tool for achieving mental, physical, and emotional toughening. Check (✔) T (true) or F (false) for each of the 60 items listed below:

T ___ F ___   1. If I'm in a bad mood or angry at work, I don't try to hide it. I tend to show on the outside whatever I feel on the inside.

T ___ F ___   2. I almost never skip breakfast.

T ___ F ___   3. I'm eating some low-fat, low-sugar snacks approximately every 1½ hours.

T ___ F ___   4. My largest meal of the day is typically dinner.

T ___ F ___   5. I know my body-fat percentage, and it is within 2 percent of ideal.

T ___ F ___   6. I exercise 3 times per week, at a minimum.

T ___ F ___   7. I can create the state of fun almost anytime at work.

T ___ F ___   8. People I work with would agree that I look confident, energized, relaxed, and positive most of the time.

T ___ F ___   9. I often find my job boring and unchallenging.

T ___ F ___ 10. I can perform at high levels on demand, regardless of circumstance.

T ___ F ___ 11. Fear is not an issue for me in the context of my job.

T ___ F ___ 12. My emotional state on the job is typically more negative than positive.

T ___ F ___ 13. I typically feel a great deal of pressure at work.

T ___ F ___ 14. I have a problem of low energy.

T ___ F ___ 15. I typically do not feel a sense of enjoyment in the context of my work.

T ___ F ___ 16. I'm quick to turn against myself during tough times.

T ___ F ___ 17. My job helps to fulfill many important needs for me.

T ___ F ___ 18. I generally give myself what I want.

T ___ F ___ 19. I feel I have a good balance among productivity, health, and happiness in my life.

T ___ F ___ 20. People I work with would say I'm overly defensive.

T ___ F ___ 21. People at work tend to see me as emotionally inflexible.

T ___ F ___ 22. When things get too bad at work, I tend to give up emotionally.

T ___ F ___ 23. I bounce back emotionally from bad news very quickly.

T ___ F ___ 24. People at work would say I am very strong emotionally.

T ___ F ___ 25. I can laugh easily at myself.

T ___ F ___ 26. People at work would say I have a great sense of humor.

T ___ F ___ 27. I have a tendency to make excuses.

T ___ F ___ 28. I can make myself change from a bad mood to a good one very quickly.

T ___ F ___ 29. I often wake up tired in the morning.

T ___ F ___ 30. My body doesn't come alive until after 10:00 in the morning.

T ___ F ___ 31. I typically get 7 to 8 hours of sleep at night.

T ___ F ___ 32. I generally go to bed and get up at the same time each day.

T ___ F ___ 33. I frequently wake up in the middle of the night and have trouble falling back to sleep.

T ___ F ___ 34. I can sleep anywhere, anytime, under any circumstances.

T ___ F ___ 35. I smoke cigarettes.

T ___ F ___ 36. I typically drink more than one alcoholic drink per day.

T ___ F ___ 37. I'm always dieting.

T ___ F ___ 38. I'm always craving the wrong foods.

T ___ F ___ 39. I get colds and flus often.

T ___ F ___ 40. I can leave the problems of work at the office. I don't take them home.

T ___ F ___ 41. I can take a nap easily and quickly without feeling groggy or tired.

T ___ F ___ 42. Most of my calories come from complex carbohydrates.

T ___ F ___ 43. I have a hard time relaxing after a tough day at the office.

T ___ F ___ 44. I drink a minimum of 6 to 8 glasses of water per day.

T ___ F ___ 45. I am very disciplined in the use of my time both on and off the job.

T ___ F ___ 46. Travel has become recovery time for me.

T ___ F ___ 47. I give high priority to close relationships.

T ___ F ___ 48. I make time for myself.

T ___ F ___ 49. I have a problem with anger and negative emotions on the job.

T ___ F ___ 50. I am not a risk taker in the context of my job.

T ___ F ___ 51. My coworkers would say that I'm open to the truth about myself.

T ___ F ___ 52. I've learned to trace negative emotions to their source.

T ___ F ___ 53. My coworkers would say that my tolerance for stress is pretty limited.

T ___ F ___ 54. How I see myself and how my coworkers see me are very much the same.

T ___ F ___ 55. I can summon and sustain the emotions that bring out the best in me during work.

T ___ F ___ 56. My coworkers typically see me as a person who thrives on stress.

T ___ F ___ 57. I'm very disciplined when it comes to meeting my needs: e.g., nutrition, sleep, time with my family, and so on.

T ___ F ___ 58. I work hard and play equally hard.

T ___ F ___ 59. My coworkers would say I'm a moody person.

T ___ F ___ 60. I tend to get into a rut with my life and work. I
have trouble keeping balance.

After you have answered all 60 items, use the scoring key below
to determine how many of the 60 items were answered correctly.
Scoring Key (Give yourself 1 point for each correct answer):

1. F	21. F	41. T
2. T	22. F	42. T
3. T	23. T	43. F
4. F	24. T	44. T
5. T	25. T	45. T
6. T	26. T	46. T
7. T	27. F	47. T
8. T	28. T	48. T
9. F	29. F	49. F
10. T	30. F	50. F
11. T	31. T	51. T
12. F	32. T	52. T
13. F	33. F	53. F
14. F	34. T	54. T
15. F	35. F	55. T
16. F	36. F	56. T
17. T	37. F	57. T
18. F	38. F	58. T
19. T	39. F	59. F
20. F	40. T	60. F

Scoring interpretation:

Number of Correct Answers	Mentally Tough Rating
53–60	World-class toughness
45–52	Certifiably tough
37–44	Passing but marginal

Number of Correct Answers	Mentally Tough Rating
29–36	Special attention
29–less	Red alert

After completing all four Toughness Training tools, you are informed to finally decide which weaknesses you are going to attack now.

Theme 1 _____ (your greatest weakness, converted into a strength).

Theme 2 _____ (your second greatest weakness, converted into a strength).

Theme 3 _____ (your third greatest weakness, converted into a strength).

Theme 4 _____ (your fourth greatest weakness, converted into a strength).

Enter your themes at the top of your training log, as shown on page 33, and you're ready to begin the program. The simple act of acknowledging your weaknesses and vowing daily to improve on them, accelerates personal growth in that area.

We are only as strong as our weakest links. Shoring up our weaknesses changes the odds dramatically for successful completion of our toughness mission.

"It's the Heart, Guts, and Determination"

EMOTIONS RUN THE SHOW

WHEN I FINALLY understood that emotions run the show, it was unquestionably the single greatest breakthrough in my career. It eventually came to be the central organizing principle for everything I was learning and doing with my clients. Whether I was training them mentally or physically, my goal was always the same: CHANGE THEM EMOTIONALLY. Years of searching taught me that the most important factor in performance is EMO-

CHAPTER 3

TIONAL. When you are right emotionally—when you can *perform emotionally*—you can go toe-to-toe with the devil himself, stand firm, bring to life all the talent and skill within you, and make big things happen. But when you are wrong emotionally—when you fail to *perform emotionally*—all the talent and skill in the world won't save you. Consumed by anger, fear, doubt, or hopelessness, you lock up inside and fall short of the mark again. What is possible for you remains tragically out of reach.

The truth is, emotions run the show in your personal life, in your corporate life, and even in your spiritual life. Emotion is actually running the show right now as you read this book. If you are emotionally challenged by what you're reading, you are flying through the pages. Your concentration and focus are dead on target. If, on the other hand, you are emotionally disconnected, bored, troubled about something else, or consumed with anger or frustration, the words on this page become blurred and meaningless. You may read the page three times and have no idea what was discussed.

Emotion drives everything. The most important component of customer service is emotion. Regardless of what you do to help a customer, how you make the customer feel *emotionally* is what counts. The stock market is not driven nearly as much by world events as by how people respond *emotionally* to those world events. Success comes not from how brilliant your product line is but from how *emotionally* connected your customers are to your product line. Your best salespeople are the ones who are most skilled in *emotionally* connecting with customers and getting customers to *emotionally* connect with your products. The most important element in communication is *emotion*. Your choice of words is less important than the feelings behind your words. The strength of your marriage, your effectiveness as a parent, your ability to lead your staff, and even your ability to conquer a threatening illness all depend on your ability to connect *emotionally*.

And as we will see, if you try to move others emotionally, your emotions cannot be fake, phony, or pretended. You must learn to genuinely stir the feelings and physiology within yourself. Your passion, beliefs, and convictions are contagious *if they are real*. Every cell in your body must drive toward the emotional target if you intend to lead others in the same emotional direction.

Ultimately, the most important dimension in toughness is emotional. Let's look closely at the four primary indicators of emotional toughness:

1. Emotional flexibility.
2. Emotional responsiveness.
3. Emotional strength.
4. Emotional resiliency.

1. Emotional Flexibility. Emotional flexibility is the ability to be open, expansive, and nondefensive in the face of crisis. Corporate athletes who have developed emotional flexibility as part of their toughness response can summon a wide range of positive emotions (humor, joy, a fighting spirit, and so on) without fear of the competitive outcome. Emotional flexibility adds depth of understanding and emotional balance to their arsenal of toughness; it helps to preserve their creativity and problem-solving ability in stressful situations.

Example

Theresa is a customer service representative for a large department store. An irate customer entered the store and began verbally attacking Theresa in a highly abusive way. The floor manager on duty in the area observed the incident and wrote the following comments on his daily report form:

"Theresa stood there and took the abuse without saying a word. When the customer let up for a minute, she clutched her chest as if she had been shot and fell back against the counter. As she fell back, she moaned, 'You got me—I think it's mortal.' Her action completely took the customer by surprise and she broke immediately into a big smile. The matter was quickly resolved and the customer left laughing almost hysterically. Theresa is the best we've ever had here."

A man is born gentle and weak.
At his death he is hard and stiff.
Green plants are tender and filled with sap.
At their death they are withered and dry.
Therefore the stiff and unbending is the disciple of death.
The gentle and yielding is the disciple of life.
Thus an army without flexibility never wins a battle.
A tree that is unbending is easily broken.

Lao Tzu
Chinese Philosopher

2. Emotional Responsiveness. During the heat and stress of corporate life, the emotionally responsive remain fully connected and in touch with the forces around them. They are not emotionally dull, withdrawn, distant, or callous. On the contrary, as the storms of life and business intensify, their emotional response to the world around them remains alive, spirited, and sensitive to whatever is happening.

Example

In the following comments, a shoe manufacturing department head was trying to help me understand the dynamics of his department:

"In the past six years, we've downsized once, rightsized once, and reengineered twice. The company leadership has changed three times, in efforts to get profitable. Every new president rolled out a new salvation plan for the whole company. People take bets on how long each new president will last. The attitude in my department is cynical, sarcastic, distant, and negative. Nobody believes, nobody cares anymore. It's like they're all dead emotionally. There's only one notable exception and that's Neil. He's amazing. He continues to hang in there. He listens and gets involved. And it's not for the politics. He really wants it to work. I don't know how or why he does it. He's my only glimmer of hope."

3. Emotional Strength. Under the greatest pressure, toughness is reflected in the ability to resist and exert great positive force emotionally. Perhaps the single hallmark of toughness in the corporate athlete is his or her ability to summon whatever levels of emotional strength are necessary to get the job done and be successful.

Billy Weisman started out as a vending machine route man. Afflicted with severe dyslexia, he struggled to finish school. According to Billy, he was a poor student who possessed no extraordinary scholastic abilities. Today, he is chairman and CEO of Weisman Enterprises, which has revenues of $500 million in managed vending sales, 220 employees, and 70,000 managed locations across North America. Billy explained his success: "In the early stages of growth, maybe I was fueled from feelings of inadequacy and fear of failure, but I was bound and determined to do a good job. I simply would not give up. My persistence led to success. I would creatively convert setbacks into opportunities. I always found a way to keep moving forward. Happiness for me was not so much about achieving a goal as it was connecting my passion with the world around me. The most important part of overcoming adversity is a positive attitude."

4. Emotional Resiliency.   A sure sign of a tough person is his or her ability to bounce back from setbacks, losses, and emotional hits quickly and easily, without being deterred from a goal. Maybe a deal didn't go through as planned after months of preparation; maybe the staff was cut in half, forcing everyone to double up on work assignments. The truly great leaders, in sports and in business, can take the serious emotional hits—the kind that can rock you back on your heels—and still come right back to the battle. They hammer away at new solutions and somehow find a way to win. This capacity to rebound emotionally from the cliff-edge of defeat is a critical part of toughness.

> Depending on the circumstances, you should be as hard as a diamond, flexible as a willow, smooth-flowing like water or as empty as space.
> Morikei Ueshiba

EMOTIONS AND PHYSIOLOGY

What you are feeling at this very moment is being driven by powerful physiological events. Every minute of every day, you are experiencing emotions that are either appropriate and adaptive or conflicted enough to block your path. For example, you're driving your car, and your physiology is filling you full of rage because of heavy traffic and gridlock. If you start pounding the steering wheel and screaming, that would be considered an inappropriate response to that situation. Real physiological events drive such an emotional response.

One of the most important functions of emotion is to mobilize the body to respond. The physiology behind emotion drives behavior. Anger mobilizes the body to attack, to use force, to strike out. Fear mobilizes the body to retreat, to move away, to withdraw. Challenge mobilizes the body to engage, to pursue, to go after. Love mobilizes the body to nourish, to care for, to protect. The

Ideal Performance State (IPS) similarly has a strong emotional component and mobilizes the body to express talent and skill and to perform to its maximum limits.

> I don't think it was my swing that made me the player I was or am. I actually think it's just the heart and guts and the determination. [1]
> Lee Trevino, one of golf's all-time great champions

Real emotion is deeply rooted in complex biomechanical and hormonal releases and has a powerful motivational component (to do or not do). To control emotion is to control physiology, which in turn enables us to control our body's response to the world. That is, in fact, what being "in control" really means.

NOT JUST IN YOUR HEAD

The word *emotion* actually is derived from a Latin word meaning *to set in motion.* People commonly make the mistake of thinking of emotion as an event occurring in their head. In reality, emotional experience and emotional expression involve the whole body. Emotion is both of the spirit and of the body. Many scientists now view emotion as the connecting link between mind and body. For example, simply focusing on a *mental image* of something very sad in your life can trigger a cascade of powerful changes in the *physical body.*

Every cell in your body, from your facial muscles to the interior lining of your intestines, contains receptor sites for the chemicals involved in emotions. Within the brain, these chemicals are called *neuropeptides.* In the body, they are simply called *peptides.* Even cells of the immune system, *lymphocytes,* contain receptor sites for emotion. In a real sense, when we fight emotionally, the battle extends through intricate biochemical channels all the way to the core of our immune system.

As the scientific world has become more precise in measuring biochemical and physiological changes in the body, it is becoming increasingly clear that every emotion has its own signature. Fear, anger, joy, sadness, and challenge share many common physiological rhythms but also have distinct brain and body markers. Our challenge is to learn methods of controlling or modifying these complex biochemical responses in order to promote improved performance, greater happiness, and better health.

A NEW WAY TO FIGHT

The brilliant 19th-century psychologist William James said: "Ancestral evolution has made us all warriors." He was referring to the fact that, to survive, our ancestors had to develop a powerful passion for living. They had to overcome enormous odds just to stay alive; they had to develop the fighting spirit of a great warrior. Those who didn't have it didn't make it; but those who did became our ancestors and passed on to us a certain depth and legacy of fighting spirit.

Unfortunately, however, the emotional tools our ancestors were given, although appropriate for their times, are not easily adaptable to modern life. Their tools were based on the primitive fight-or-flight response.[2] Ironically, the same instinctive tools our ancestors used to fight their battles so successfully in ancient times—powerful hormonal mechanisms designed to fuel anger and fear—are the very tools that are tearing us apart today. Modern corporate athletes have to learn a whole new way of fighting. In Toughness Training, we are teaching our clients to override anger and panic and to summon a different set of emotions. Today's warriors must be calmer and more in control; they must adopt a new paradigm in which stress and recovery are mixed in a healthy balance. We have to learn to subdue many of our instinctive mechanisms and replace them with productive, functional, and varied emotional responses that complement the lives we live today.[3] We can't wait for the slow process of evolution to change us; evolution will simply not get us there fast enough. Instead, we're going to have to revolutionize the way we respond emotionally to the forces of modern life. We must find shortcuts for learning how to fight successfully in the corridors and conference rooms of power.

Let's return for a moment to Dan Jansen. Like all of us, Dan had doubts and fears. He is human, and the mistakes he made along his journey impeded his progress. However, during his pursuit of

Olympic gold, he was a remarkable warrior because he refused to surrender his spirit. Many times, he could have packed it in; he could have given a psychological shrug and said, "It's not meant to be. I've been doing this for 10 years, and every single time I turn around something horrible happens in my life. It's not my fault—but the death of my sister and all the ridicule and doubt from the media—it's just too much." But he didn't do that. He never lost sight of his dream.[4]

It is true that the things Dan Jansen had to face were neither right nor fair, but he never wilted. Through his long ordeal, he grew stronger and became much more powerful in his ability to believe in himself and to fight in a positive way. That was how he was able to put it all on the line in his very last Olympic moment and emerge victorious. Dan's road to victory took remarkable courage.

Like Dan, we need to develop a powerful warrior spirit to follow our dreams, to not surrender our spirit, to continue to live a life that is consistent with our most enduring values and beliefs. The greatest battle is always against ourselves—our fears, our blind emotions, our retreat from personal truth.

To "tough it out" means:

1. To keep your spirit fully alive and engaged—100 percent vested emotionally.

2. To sustain whatever emotional response is necessary to drive answers that reflect your deepest values and beliefs.

This is the essence of courage and the core of what it means to be a great fighter.

As modern-day corporate warriors, we are constantly struggling to respond to the world in the most adaptive, most appropriate way possible, so that our genius comes to life and we can find real answers. Dan Jansen ultimately came to understand that it was not the death of his sister and all the painful memories that were holding him back. Instead, how his body was responding to those forces was the deciding factor. And, as he came to understand, the enormous difference between the two lies in what Dan had control over. His past experiences might have been difficult to endure, but they were out of his control. He was at their mercy. However, what Dan *could* control was his response to the traumatic events that marked the years leading up to the races at Lillehammer. Because he had yet to learn how to control his response to such situations, his response produced a physiology that was inconsistent with high-level sport performance.

IT'S THE RESPONSE—NOT THE STRESSOR!

The great historian, Arnold Toynbee, once said that all of history could be summarized in two words: *challenge* and *response*. The course of all history, he argues, is determined not so much by what actually happens as by how countries, alliances, and leaders respond to what happens. A crisis occurs and a response follows. From revenge to retreat and from challenge to surrender, the fate of nations hangs in the balance. In precisely the same way, how we respond as individuals to the stressors that are thrust upon us throughout our lives dictates our future, our character, and who and what we eventually become.

> Fury doesn't work in competition . . . it works even less well as the competition gets tougher. Anger is the real enemy in basketball. . . . You have to get into this warrior attitude where you do not lose control and erupt.[5]
> Phil Jackson
> Coach of the Chicago Bulls

The same restraint holds true for companies, for divisions within companies, and for your own department. Show me how these entities emotionally responded to whatever crisis they faced, and their situation today starts making historical sense. The critical factor is the emotional response. As Nick Faldo, winner of the 1996 Masters golf tournament, will tell you, it's not what happens to you on a golf course that determines your future but rather how you respond to what happens. The storms and challenges of business simply represent forces that require responses, and how you allow your body to respond to those forces can determine your future. But remember, you can gain control over those responses.

Steve Schwarzman is an excellent example. Steve is president of the Blackstone Group, a preeminent investment banking firm. Steve and his partners quickly established themselves in the private equity investment business by raising the largest amount of capital ever achieved by a first-time fund. Steve's goal was $1 billion—despite the fact that Blackstone did not have an established track record.

> We were turned down by 483 people, many of whom were friends. That's a lot of no's but we would not give up. I knew what we wanted to accomplish, and I simply would not be deterred. I'm just like an athlete in sport. I define an objective and then do whatever is necessary to achieve it. Most everyone I know would have given up long before 483 rejections. We actually never raised the full billion. We ended up at $950 million. My response to the no's was the key factor. I simply didn't accept that we would never reach our goal.

IMPORTANT! It's not what happens to you that determines your character and future. It is how you respond to what happens to you. The storms and challenges of life simply represent forces. How you allow your body to respond to those forces determines your future, your character, and the fabric of your life.

EMOTIONAL INTELLIGENCE— THE ULTIMATE WEAPON

The concept of emotional intelligence first appeared in 1990, in the work of two psychologists, John Mayer, of the University of New Hampshire, and Peter Salovey, of Yale University.[6] More recently, Daniel Goleman's excellent book, the 1996 best-seller *Emotional Intelligence,* goes right to the heart of the matter.[7] Evolutionary forces have honed two distinct adaptive capacities in all of us. One is of the heart or gut, which is emotional, and the other is of the head or brain, which is rational. Both capacities are critical to optimal adaptiveness. The traditional notions of intelligence have focused almost exclusively on cognitive and rational processes such as analytical skills, retention, logic, verbal reasoning, and so forth. Widely diverse intelligence tests have been devised over the years to assess what is generally accepted as one's innate intellectual capacity.

Until the work of Mayer and Salovey, little attention was paid to the notion of *emotional capacity*. They proposed that a high emotional IQ involves five factors:

1. The ability to recognize and be aware of various feelings as they come and go in our lives. Self-awareness is the foundation of emotional intelligence.

2. The ability to control emotion. Those unable to control the flow of emotions in their lives reflect little emotional intelligence and have considerable difficulty rebounding from the ups and downs of life.

3. The ability to self-motivate—in other words, one's capacity to mobilize sufficient energy and force to accomplish difficult tasks and meet important goals.

4. The ability to recognize emotions in others. The key issue here is one's ability to read emotions in others and to empathize.

5. The ability to adjust to and manage the emotions of others. At the core of this factor are the ability to get along with others, interpersonal effectiveness, and leadership capacity.

Whereas most traditional notions of IQ involve innate capacities, the emotional factors that Mayer and Salovey describe are clearly acquired through learning. Whatever your emotional IQ is now, it remains trainable.

 Although many of our day-to-day emotional responses are traceable to the autonomic nervous system, which is considered largely involuntary, it is entirely possible to replace inappropriate reflexive responses with adaptive and appropriate ones. As we will see, maximizing productivity, health, and happiness demands that we get control of many of our primitive emotional urges. To thrive in today's world, corporate athletes must train to become smarter emotionally. The most important and often most difficult battles we face—those that require the most intense warrior spirit—are the emotional battles. Responding in the right way at the right time emotionally, even when we are pushed to our absolute limits on playing fields that are brutal and unfair, can amount to nothing short of "the mother of all battles."

When a Powerful Stressor Hits

Immediately ask yourself: What is the most intelligent response that is consistent with my deepest values and beliefs? Then, with courage and a warrior spirit, fight to bring that response to life. Immediately start thinking and acting in ways that drive the targeted emotion called for in the battle plan. No excuses. No cursing the playing field. Just fight with everything you have; and keep fighting.

WHICH CAME FIRST?

Human emotional capacities developed first on the evolutionary scale. The human brain's evolution helps provide insight into our emotional versus our rational development. The most primitive brain structure, which preceded all other development, was the spinal cord and brain stem. The most essential life functions, such as breathing and instinctive movement, are regulated by this neurological component. Next to evolve were the limbic structures.[8] Included were the hypothalamus, which regulates the fight-or-flight response; the thalamus, which serves as a sensory relay station; the amygdala, essentially the brain's emotional computer, which enables us to respond in an appropriate way emotionally; and the septum, which serves to suppress aversive emotional states.

Our emotional response capacities have been honed for hundreds of thousands of years; our rational capacities are comparatively new. The emotional brain is the senior member of the team, and the rational brain is the apprentice. Logical processing, abstract thinking, strategizing, and conscious awareness were add-ons to the cortex of the brain, which gave humans a distinct survival advantage. The new dimension in intelligence, stemming from unprecedented growth in the neocortex of the brain, moved humans to a whole new level of adaptiveness. But as the neocortex evolved, so also did the conflict between humans' rational and emotional sides. Should I let my feelings or my head rule? Should I be rational or instinctive? A person of the head or of the heart?

As Daniel Goleman so aptly points out, emotional intelligence involves the whole brain. Being able to respond in an appropriate way with compassion, empathy, determination, love, fear, or assertiveness requires a merging of both limbic and neocortical structures. The solution for corporate athletes is to find a balance between the extremes of blind emotion and blind logic. Every human emotion has a time-tested survival value. Every emotion has its time and place. However, the complexity of modern life, particularly corporate life, dramatically exceeds any instinct or equipment nature has given us. For early humans, the emotional "software" they were given was adequate; for modern humans, it's catastrophically deficient. Major modifications in the present software system are required, and time is of the essence. We can't wait 1,000 years, 100 years, or even 10 years for the evolutionary forces to catch up. We've got to get the changes going now, today, this minute.

THE INTELLIGENT CORPORATE ATHLETE'S RESPONSE

The bottom-line issue in corporate America revolves around performance. Every ounce of your talent and skill must surface day after day, year after year. If it doesn't, in all likelihood, you simply will sink to the bottom of the pool. Too many competent competitors are waiting out there, more than eager to take your place. The critical questions then are: What do we know about performance? What factors drive the consistent expression of talent and skill in high-stress arenas year after year?

My first efforts to answer these questions began in 1976. I had just resigned from my position as chief psychologist and executive director of a large community mental health center serving the southern and central parts of Colorado. My resignation came as quite a shock to the 21-member board of directors, particularly when I told them I was moving to Denver to begin a practice in sport psychology. Most, I am sure, thought I had truly lost my mind. No one on that board had ever heard of sport psychology.

Suddenly, there I was at University Park Psychological Center. I was a private practitioner specializing in performance problems of athletes, and I nearly starved to death! My board of directors weren't the only ones who thought what I wanted to do was strange. Just about everybody did, including many athletes.

In spite of some resistance and cynicism, I persisted in my belief that the marriage of psychology and sport could be exciting and rewarding. But I needed answers. Existing research was woefully inadequate. I was certain, from my own experience as an athlete, that ongoing feelings and emotions played a critical role in performance. Nine years of baseball, 8 years of basketball, and 23 years of tournament tennis convinced me that performance level was directly linked to an athlete's emotional state. But where was the evidence, where was the research to confirm it? It simply hadn't been done yet. If I needed to know, I would have to break the ground myself.

For the next 6 years, I immersed myself in the search for what I eventually came to refer to as the Ideal Performance State (IPS). Over 400 interviews, representing 23 separate sports, produced compelling evidence that (1) feelings and emotions play a central role in high-level performance and (2) a highly specific state of mind–body interaction is invariably linked to performance at the highest level. That special state of mind–body balance was described over and over by the interviewees, using the same descriptors. Words like *relaxed, calm, energized, positive, automatic, effortless, confident,* and *focused* kept reappearing. When we began to analyze the data, one fact came as a complete shock. Regardless of the sport or the position they played within the sport, athletes chose to describe in the same way the internal conditions that existed when performing optimally.

The tougher it gets, the more I enjoy myself. I thrive on competition and pressure. My greatest enjoyment comes from seeing how I handle the situation. Can I execute? Can I perform under the circumstances?[9]

Corey Pavin
U.S. Open champion and Ryder
Cup superstar

We were so intrigued with the findings, we decided to go outside the boundaries of sport and explore high-pressure arenas in real life. Businesspeople, surgeons, musicians, law enforcement officers, teachers, and military personnel were interviewed in precisely the same way the athletes were. To our astonishment, many of the same descriptors were again used; in fact, it was impossible to determine, from reading the transcripts, whether the interviewees were describing an exceptional sport performance or an exceptional real-life performance. Some of the most important understandings from the research are detailed here:

1. The Ideal Performance State (IPS) is a highly unique and specific response to stress, and it has a strong and distinct emotional component. Like anger, which mobilizes the body to ward off an attacker, or fear, which mobilizes the body to escape an impending danger, IPS mobilizes the body to express talent and skill within a performance context. IPS is the most intelligent and adaptive response one can have to most of the demands of corporate life.

2. The most commonly used descriptors of IPS are: *physically relaxed, mentally calm, fearless, energized, positive, happy, effortless, automatic, confident, mentally focused and alert* and *feeling in control.* Although a wide diversity of descriptors are used to characterize IPS, it represents a single, generalized stress response. Each descriptor simply points to a specific mind/body dimension associated with that particular response.[10]

3. IPS is clearly a learned response, not an inherited or instinctive one. Those in corporate America who demonstrate a high degree of control over this response have simply learned it. A central component of the Toughness Training program is mastery of this response *on demand,* regardless of the circumstance.

4. Each of the IPS descriptors is linked to specific underlying physiological and neurochemical events. For example, feelings of relaxation reflect low levels of muscle arousal, as measured by an electromyograph (EMG; electromyographic impulses are a measure of muscle tension); feelings of calmness reflect specific patterns of neurological arousal, as measured by an electroencephalograph (EEG; electroencephalographic impulses are a measure of brain wave activity); and fearlessness reflects suppression of what is referred to as the adrenal cortical axis in the body, particularly the release of high concentrations of the adrenal hormone, cortisol. Feelings of high

positive energy correspond to specific levels of adrenaline and noradrenaline, two powerful hormones (called catecholamines) that are released by the sympathetic nervous system and increase energy. Even feelings of fun and enjoyment have distinct neurochemical anchors in the form of beta-endorphin releases (morphine-like brain hormones that produce a sense of well-being and mask pain). The real point here is that IPS is more than a constellation of feelings. It is deeply rooted in powerful physiological events. To summon an IPS response, therefore, we must activate the underlying physiological mechanisms, the "chemical soup" of IPS.

5. The one word that best captures the IPS response is *challenge*. Challenge connotes a very special kind of engagement of our spirit. It includes a willingness and an eagerness to do battle—but in a positive, nondistressful way. The response is a willingness to put oneself on the line without fear. The emotional feeling tones are not toxic, unpleasant, or distasteful. To the contrary, feelings of challenge, fun, enjoyment, and risk become intimately bound together.

6. Perhaps the most remarkable and distinct characteristic of an IPS response is that, as soon as it occurs, feelings of pressure and distress disappear. With IPS, a unique mind–body unity is formed wherein what we are doing and what we are thinking are one and the same. This merging of action and awareness creates an almost magical sense of spontaneity and freedom from stress.

7. One of the most important and critical battles we must wage as corporate warriors is to summon IPS on a daily basis, particularly as the storms of business intensify. *The new warrior spirit is the spirit of IPS.*

THE IMPORTANCE OF CONTROL

In an ingenious experiment conducted by Neil Miller at Yale University several years ago, two white albino rats, perfectly matched for their heredity and environment, were placed in cages with grid lines through which electrical current could be transmitted. There was a lever in the cage of rat number one; when the lever was depressed, it shut off the current for both rats simultaneously. When the lever in the cage of rat number two was depressed, nothing happened. The genius of this experiment was that both rats were exposed to exactly the same intensity and duration of stress. The only difference was that rat number one had control over when it stopped—but not, of course, over when it started. This is pretty much like your situation: you don't have a clue when the next disaster might descend.

When the electrical current in the cages was initially turned on, the rats displayed a powerful stress response, until rat number one bumped up against the lever accidentally and shut the power off. This rat soon learned to hit the lever the instant the current was turned on. Researchers then tracked the effects of the experiment by doing a multiyear study of the rats' lives. As time passed, rat number one, given his ability to manipulate the lever, suffered virtually no measurable adverse effects; reproductive functions continued normally, appetite mechanisms remained intact, and there was no evidence of suppressed immunity or increased susceptibility to disease. In fact, the rat with control over his environment continued to show surprising resiliency and responsiveness. He clearly seemed to absorb the stress in ways that did not compromise either health or longevity.

And what about rat number two, which had precisely the same stress exposure but did not have the ability to shut down the stressor? The picture was very different. Reproductive functions began to change almost immediately. Eventually, the rat's immune system became seriously compromised. Continued exposure to the stressors overwhelmed the rat's coping skills, leaving it vulnerable to a host of deadly pathogens. So what really was the culprit here? Was it the stress caused by the electrical current passing through the bottom of the cage? That doesn't make sense because both rats were exposed to the same intensity and duration of stress. Was it lack of control? But how can lack of control compromise immunity so severely? What could possibly be the mechanism?

What cut the rat's life short was the way in which the rat's body responded to the constant stress caused by lack of control. Early in the experiment, the researchers discovered that massive doses of stress hormones were released in both rats when the electrical current was turned on. But when rat number one began to realize that he could control the electric current, his stress level would rise but then quickly return to normal. Not so with rat number two. The electric jolts sent the rat's adrenal hormones sailing upward and they never returned to normal even when the current was turned off. His immune system was constantly bathed in toxic by-products associated with continued and protracted stress—stress became distress. The chemicals of his own body, triggered by the lack of control, literally overwhelmed rat number two. The real issue was helplessness, and what is true for the rats is true for us as well.

LEARNED HELPLESSNESS

As early as 1960, a number of researchers, most notably M. E. Seligman, S. F. Maier, and S. M. Miller, began connecting perceived helplessness with important changes in brain chemistry.[11] The perception of an event as being beyond control is associated with a high distress factor, a predisposition to depression, and a wide diversity of health risks. Important links have been made between giving up emotionally and being vulnerable to illness.[12]

> My most important stress buster is acknowledging that some things are under my control and others are simply not. I focus all my energy where I have control. The impact on my stress is dramatic.
>
> Ilene Lang
> President and CEO of Alta Vista
> Software, a subsidiary of Digital
> Equipment Corporation

Researchers have concluded that it is not the exposure to stress trauma itself that causes the undesirable changes in brain chemistry to occur.[13] The culprit is invariably the perception of helplessness.[14] And once the debilitating perception of "no control" has been acquired, *future* stressful situations are much more likely to be labeled unavoidable, inescapable, and beyond control.

Because corporate athletes are continually facing problems of enormous complexity, the tendency to perceive various situations as having no solution is very tempting. According to the research data, the two most critical factors in learned helplessness are:

(1) the expectation that there's nothing you can do to alter a situation, and (2) how you think about what caused the problem in the first place. If you attribute the causation of some lasting flaw within yourself ("I'm too stupid" or "I'm a loser"), the risk of illness is compounded. Overexaggerating a personal limitation also heightens negative risk factors. Using words like *never* or *always* intensifies feelings of helplessness and loss of control. Risk factors were lowest for those individuals who attributed the cause of their problems to their own behavior and believed they could do something to correct it. Poor adapters repeatedly were those who blamed forces outside themselves, particularly other people, for all their problems. Perceptions of helplessness and poor coping were also associated with the inability to attribute any real meaning or purpose to the conflict or problem situation.

Based on these and other research findings, corporate athletes should do the following when traumatic events occur:

1. Never give up or surrender your spirit emotionally.
2. Take some kind of corrective action. Do *something!* Do *anything!* Taking action prevents feelings of helplessness from consuming you.
3. Attribute causes for the problems to factors within yourself that are changeable. Resist blaming others and resist exaggerating the hopelessness of the situation.
4. Attribute some important purpose to the struggle and crisis. "I'll use this to correct personal weaknesses that have needed addressing for a long time."

I call it better performance through better chemistry. That's what I do with my people. I impact the chemistry of my whole office. I've learned how to get the chemistry going in empowering directions. That's really my job as a leader. My passion, my enthusiasm, my dedication get the juices flowing.

Rob Knapp
First Vice President, Mid-West
District Director for Merrill Lynch

PART II

PERFORMER SKILLS AND THE TOUGHENING PROCESS: TARGETING THE STRESS RESPONSE

"Keep Things Simple and in the Same Routine"

THE RITUALS OF SUCCESS

CHAPTER 4

RITUALS ARE ONE of the most important tools you can use to achieve toughness as a corporate athlete. A major objective of this book is to help you acquire the rituals of success. Repetition of the right physical, mental, and emotional habits eventually brings them under automatic control. Conscious awareness and targeted energy expenditure will gradually give way to automatic rituals of eating, sleeping, resting, stretching, exercising, thinking, planning, acting, recovering, and wave making—all of which will keep you in balance.

Without positive rituals, we cannot hope to succeed. Rituals signal *importance* in our lives. Where there is ritual, there is value and meaning.[1] Rituals are disciplined patterns of thinking and acting that enhance our ability to respond to the forces of life in the most appropriate and meaningful way. Once you learn how to anchor these rituals, your health, happiness, and performance quotients will rise to new levels. If you were to read only one chapter in

Stress for Success, I would consider this one as most indispensable. Every day of Toughness Training will move you closer to acquiring your own rituals of success. Here is a partial list of ways in which rituals empower and enrich our lives:

1. Rituals help us to shift gears, to oscillate between stress and recovery, and to alter the rhythm of our days.

2. Rituals help us to access the underlying physiology of stress and recovery.

3. Through the employment of prayer, song, bells, weddings, birthdays, anniversaries, funerals, and holidays, rituals mobilize such emotions as joy, sadness, remembrance, love, loyalty, and bravery.

4. Rituals increase personal control and facilitate living a life that is consistent with our deepest values and beliefs.

5. Rituals bring order and structure to chaos and change.

6. Rituals are familiar and comforting during unpredictable storms of stress.

7. Rituals magnify and focus attention like a zoom lens.

8. Rituals signal what to do and when to do it to successfully complete a mission.

9. Rituals help us to execute complex tasks with perfection—mentally, physically, and emotionally.

10. Rituals can powerfully stimulate past emotional states by activating sensory memory.

Rituals can become powerful triggers for mobilizing the physiological mechanisms that underlie specific emotions. Many involuntary processes associated with the autonomic nervous system are affected in a positive way through the use of rituals. Blood pressure, heart rate, muscle tension, and brain wave activity can be powerfully influenced by ritualistic breathing, meditation, prayer, concentration, visualization sequences, and affirmations.

SOME RITUAL SUCCESS STORIES

Jimmy Johnson, the Miami Dolphins' and former Dallas Cowboys' coach, is a perfect example of someone who is intuitively and deeply in touch with his IPS through his understanding of the power of ritual. When asked about his preparation for the 1993 Super Bowl game against the San Francisco 49ers, he had this to say:

> Our approach to the week of preparation for the 49ers has been exactly the same as what we've done for the past seventeen games. I believe that one of the keys to developing a team that performs with consistency on the field under pressure is to maintain consistency and continuity in everything you do off the field. As a result, we have followed the exact same daily routine this week that we would for any other Sunday game. We have made no special allowances for extra meeting time. Our practices are exactly the same length. We have not limited or extended the amount of access everybody has had to many of the media people who have been at our headquarters. We will go through the same walk-through practice at the stadium that we would for any other road game. We always like to visit a road game stadium prior to the game; it's part of our pregame ritual. We go through the lockers, examine the playing surface and the overall atmosphere.

Jimmy Johnson concludes his comments by saying:

> Keeping things simple and in the same routine has been a proven practice for not allowing distractions to arise and for performing at optimal levels under pressure.[2]

"Keeping things simple and in the same routine . . . ." yes, Jimmy Johnson had it right. He knew that proper rituals would protect his players and help them to triumph. He understood that by not deviating from the normal routines, his players would be better prepared to perform at their very best. Next time you go to a basketball game, watch the top free-throw shooters. Invariably, they are the players with the best, most elaborate rituals. Some will rotate the ball in their hands, first one rotation toward them, then one rotation away. The same is true for the best hitters and pitchers on a baseball team—and the same is also true with the most successful corporate athletes. They don't use rituals only when they need them, at the moment of the crucial board meeting, or the key presentation to 500 stockholders; they use their rituals on a routine basis, day by day.

Following are two dramatic examples of people who, through the use of ritual, mobilized remarkable strength and courage under extremely trying circumstances. One story came from my work with elite FBI SWAT teams; the other was narrated during an interview I conducted with a heroic firefighter. They can serve as role models for what you can achieve in your ever-more-challenging business environment.

Agent John

In his early forties, living in Oregon with his wife and daughter, "John," an FBI undercover agent, was asked to infiltrate a very powerful organized-crime drug operation in New York City. The operation specialized in drug trafficking between Europe and the United States. John was fully aware that this group was connected to Mafia activity; the FBI had been trying to penetrate its inner core for more than a year. John had distinctly Italian features, and he radiated the kind of toughness and stability that convinced his superiors he was the man for the job.

With gradual, carefully planned steps, John skillfully worked his way into the drug operation. He rented a small apartment in New York. Every Friday night, he would fly home to his family in Oregon; every Sunday afternoon he would fly back and reenter the world of drugs, crime, and violence. Whenever he had to wear a "wire" under his shirt to record his conversations, he knew full well that, if detected, he would be murdered in an instant.

The FBI had warned him about the stress involved on this assignment. He would be evaluated constantly to determine how he was standing up under the strain, and at the first sign of trouble, either physically or psychologically, he would be relieved. Ordinary burnout time in this type of work, he was told, is six months. That was the outer limit of what most agents could handle, given the constant life-and-death pressure.

At the end of his first six months, John underwent a complete physical and psychological examination, and the doctors were surprised at how well he was handling the stress. His marriage was as solid as ever, he was sleeping well, his appetite was good, and when asked if he wanted to be transferred, he said, "No, I'm OK. I'd like to stick around till we take these guys."

His daily work wasn't nearly as easy as John portrayed. Every time he put on the wire, he broke into a cold sweat. "In a strange way," he told me, "I became the man I was supposed to be Monday through Friday. Then on the weekends I was my normal self again with my wife and daughter." He mowed the lawn, went to his daughter's dance class, barbecued out by the swimming pool, performed all the usual family and neighborly functions. Then, on the flight back to New York, he would gradually but systematically take on his Mafia role. When the plane finally touched down at Kennedy Airport, he had fully engaged what I call his Performer Self and had become the person of his disguise. He wasn't faking it. In a bizarre kind of way, he said, it was real. His underworld hours were typically from 11:00 at night until 4:00 in the morning. That's when the dealing was done. He was like a shift worker—weird hours during the week and normal hours on the weekends.

After John had completed one full year as a mob impersonator, he was tested a second time—and *again* the doctors could find no adverse effects of stress. He willingly signed up for another six months and then for one more term after that. He was on that assignment for a full two years! He told me that he was accused of being a cop three times. With his life hanging in the balance, he managed to think on his feet, say the right things, and send out believable body language to keep his accusers from checking for a wire. Never a day passed without his keen awareness of the high-stakes, life-and-death role he was playing.

I questioned John closely on his feelings. Did he ever come close to cracking under the strain? He smiled and said that he didn't like the hours (he was an early-morning person), but the assignment gave him a lot of satisfaction because he was doing something worthwhile. "What I was doing, I felt, was very important work," he told me, "I felt I was making a real contribution." The more we talked, the more I could see that he possessed a deep reservoir of emotional balance. He was profoundly connected to the people and the principles that were most important in his life. He was also a fierce competitor. "I wasn't about to let those guys find me out," he said. "I figured I could do it and I did." He was obviously a superior performer who had great confidence in himself.

How could he live in that brutal environment for two years and not become brutalized himself? How could he keep from becoming morally calloused? How could he go on, for two whole years, being a brutal tough guy during the week and a considerate and sensitive family man on the weekends?

The answer, as I suspected, lay in his use of rituals. Thoughtfully, he explained:

> I think the whole thing was my routine. I figured out a routine that completely kept me protected. When I finished work at 4:00 in the morning, I'd go back to my apartment and sleep for exactly three and a half hours. No more, no less—I felt that any variation would screw up my head. Then I'd get up, go to the gym, and work out for two and a half hours. All the stuff inside me—the bad stuff building up during the night, all the fear and rage—I'd get rid of it. By the time I left the gym, I was OK. Then I'd go back for a nap.

John was just as precise about his eating routine. He ate as strategically as any Olympic athlete preparing for competition. He knew exactly what he had to do to keep on top of his situation. He was careful not to drink or take drugs. He ate a low-fat diet and grazed during the day—many small meals consisting of lots of fruit and vegetables and complex carbohydrates.

John knew that success with his mission meant he had to be a world-class pretender. He actually saw himself as being very much like a Hollywood actor, and he took great pride in his ability to fool clever and hardened criminals. With the help of rituals that were firmly in place, he *became* the person he needed to be in that world, and because he *was* that person, his level of distress was minimal. He wasn't afraid. In spite of the time-bomb-ticking environment he had to face daily, his internal climate was the Ideal Performance State, and the plane ride home each weekend was his decompression time. He turned the plane ride into a three-step ritual: (1) his head would hit the backrest and his mind would see colors and slowly rid itself of thought; (2) he would fall asleep; (3) he would wake up reenergized and would walk off the plane with his *real self* intact, anxious to see his family and be back home.

He told me:

> If you took my routines away, I would've come apart completely. They kept me sane and on top of things. No question about it—the work was tough. It was definitely dangerous, but you know—you can accomplish just about anything if you set your mind to it and prepare for it properly. It's the preparation you've got to take care of.

Firefighter Tom

"Captain Tom" was assigned to a firefighting team that was called in moments after a massive boiler explosion tore apart a six-story apartment house, killing and injuring a large number of people, many of whom were children.

Tom, in his early fifties, was a powerfully built man with a full beard. He reminded me of a rock—big, strong, tough. He told me that this assignment was emotionally the most difficult one he had ever performed in his life. He had to lead his team through smoking rubble and flame flareups, looking for survivors and subduing the fire. He said there is no way to describe the emotions that crowded in. Overwhelming sadness, compassion, sorrow, helplessness, fear, grief—all were part of the experience. All Tom knew for sure was that he was witnessing a horror of massive proportions.

I'll let him tell the story in his own words:

> You go in there and you have to remove the body of a child. The confusion, the danger, the horror of it all. You can't begin to understand—the sadness, the grieving—it's beyond all understanding. You look over to your right and your left, you see the rescue workers and the team you're leading in with terror and disbelief on their faces.
>
> The bodies—you've got to go right up and pick them up, go back out with them, and then come right back again, and everybody's got to see that you're OK. I knew I couldn't lose it emotionally. Somebody had to do the job. Somehow I had to mobilize myself and my team to get through it emotionally. The emotional pressure was the most intense of my entire life. Nothing comes close.

I asked him how he did it. How could he possibly stay in control emotionally under such extreme conditions? He told me that he didn't really know. But as he talked, the importance of ritual became more and more apparent in his fight to stand up under the awful and unrelenting kind of stress he endured.

> It was my first hour there. I was searching through the debris and smoke, and pulled out this soot-covered terry-cloth bunny rabbit. It obviously belonged to one of the children caught in the blast. Right then and there, I started to come apart. I have children of my own, and all of a sudden I began to realize that that was the reason I was there—for the children, for their families, for all the people who suffered

indescribable losses. Somebody had to do it; I was that somebody. I had to be strong. I couldn't let myself come apart.

As a sort of ritualistic gesture to affirm to myself how important this horrific job was, I instinctively reached down and put that furry little creature into my pocket. No matter where I was throughout the entire ordeal, it came with me. Whenever I would face a particularly dangerous situation or confront an unthinkable horror, I would simply think of that little bunny. I thought about the child it had belonged to, and instantly I'd get this sense of deep calm and conviction that no matter how long or dangerous this job, I would handle it.

I interviewed Tom sixty days after this traumatic ordeal. His words and his look are still etched in my memory:

I've been carrying this little guy with me every minute. Somehow it has helped me deal with the whole thing. I'm not a bitter or a cynical person. I'm not callous. What I saw and experienced in that blast scene was the hardest experience of my life, and having that little guy somehow helped me through it.

Suddenly, Captain Tom stopped, paused for a moment, and then very gently began wrapping the little bunny in a soft terry-cloth towel. When finished, he turned toward me with tears welling in his eyes and handed the bundle to me with the following words:

I need to finish this. I need to move on. I'm ready now. I want you to take this so that this can be finished for me. I can now move forward and leave the past behind.

It's clear how powerful and important ritual was in Tom's getting through the horror and danger and the subsequent recovery and healing process. The most important element in Tom's ritual was that it anchored his struggle to his most important values and beliefs. The ritual helped mobilize his strength and focus, so he could fight to do whatever was necessary to complete the job. The core of our emotional strength is always the same—our deepest values. Given the right rituals, you will not become callous and cold and insensitive to the world—beaten to death by the brutality of your playing field. Instead, you will *deal* with the problems as they arise.

You will maintain your strength and your hope, and you will be able to summon whatever courage is demanded of you.

A Corporate Performer

The final example of a person who uses the power and value of ritual comes from the corporate arena. Troy Shaver strongly believes ritual has been an important key to his success as well as his ability to manage high stress.

Troy is Executive Vice President of State Street Research and Management, one of the largest institutional money management and mutual fund companies in the United States. He holds the distinction of starting more mutual funds (and growing them to more than $1 billion) than anyone in the United States. This mega performer explained:

> The key to the whole thing for me is my rituals. When I finally understood their value and place in my life, everything changed—the quality of my personal life, my health, and my productivity. Here's what a typical day looks like for me.
>
> I'm up at 4:10 A.M. every day. I need no alarm and I wake super-energized. I drive into Boston and am at the office by 5:30 A.M. The first thing I do is make a priority list for the day. This is one of my most important rituals for getting started with my day. Then I do one thing that I don't particularly like to do—something that I need to do but don't really want to. This gives me the feeling of accomplishment and reinforces the expectation that today will be highly productive. At 6 A.M., I either go to our fitness club or go for a run along the Charles River. I finish my workout by 7:10 A.M. and then I shower and have breakfast. I'm back in my office by 7:30. I literally feel like I can conquer the world at this point in my day. I've missed all the traffic, I've got all my priorities straight, and I'm in control.
>
> My typical day of work is 14 hours. I usually get home about 7:30 P.M. I'm not beat up and I'm not tired when I walk in the door. Family time is very important to me. My wife and two boys and I make dinner an important time together. It's really an important family ritual. I retire at 10 P.M. Six hours of sleep is all I need. I fall asleep almost immediately when my head hits the pillow.

Two of my most important rituals are regular snacking and fly fishing. I'm literally eating all the time. It completely stabilizes my energy and, surprisingly, it was the secret of my losing weight. My favorite snack is roasted soybeans! I've learned to avoid foods high in sugar. Fly fishing is my recovery passion. Fishing is best with a full moon, and I mark off one day each month, on my calendar, whenever the full moon happens to occur. Everyone knows I'm gone fishing when the full moon hits. It's such an important recovery time for me. I always take my sons, my wife, or someone important to me. It's a sacred ritual.

"THE GOOD, THE BAD, AND THE UGLY"

Even if only unconsciously, you have certain rituals that are repeated each day, to prepare for that day's performance. It's possible they can be traced all the way back to the first time you had to stand up and talk to your grade-school class. And you have been adding to your preperformance routine ever since. The rituals tell you that it is time for a performance, that you are ready to perform, and that you *can* perform. Your preperformance rituals, if they are valid, put you in a state of high positive energy.[3]

When we explain preperformance rituals at our workshops, most people catch on immediately. Others insist that they have no rituals of any kind. But, more likely, they are simply not aware of their rituals. If you find that you can't think of a single ritual you go through before attending a meeting, giving a speech, or having a strategy planning session with your boss, ask the people you work with and the people you live with. You may not have noticed all the little ways in which you ready yourself for your day, but those around you have. You may learn surprising things about yourself. For instance, perhaps you always check your hem or your fly (even when you're sure no adjustment is necessary) before entering the board room. Or, you always rummage through your top desk drawer before you settle down to work on a new project. Or, you can't properly address a question without first leaning back in your chair and then rocking forward.

The value of ritual is clearly evidenced in these comments by Tony Schwartz (coauthor with Donald Trump of *The Art of the Deal*):

You CAN have it all!

Discover how a personal coach can help you:

- Clarify Your Priorities
- Develop a Strategy to Achieve Your Goals
- Provide the Support and Guidance You Need to Stay on Course

The program is free of charge and you may bring a guest. Please call to see when the next seminar will be!

Participants will identify common stressors, learn how coaches can help you manage them so you can improve performance, life enjoyment, and enhance health. A live demonstration will show some methods he uses and will enable you to leave with tools that will work immediately. You will also learn about upcoming monthly stress management workshops.

Michael H. Kahn, Ph.D., A personal coach and health psychologist specializing in stress management, will explain and demonstrate what coaching is and how it works.

- *Optimum Work Productivity*
- *Satisfying Personal & Family Relationships*
- *Spiritual Fulfillment*
- *Healthy Lifestyle*

Big Vanilla
ATHLETIC CLUB
Where fun meets fitness!

1209 Ritchie Hwy., Arnold, 410.544.2525 • www.bigvanilla.com

I am a freelance writer, forever struggling with the issue of how to keep focused and productive, but also to have time for myself. To find out, I decided to really investigate my own chemistry. At what time of the day was I most alert and focused? How long was it reasonably possible for me to concentrate? Were there breaks I could take that actually allowed me to be more productive? How might I fit in physical activity and some time for myself?

What I discovered was utterly fascinating. For two decades, I had spent the first couple of hours every workday finding all kinds of excuses to avoid writing. I would read the paper, eat a leisurely breakfast, shuffle papers at my desk, make a few phone calls, and finally get to work sometime around 9:30 or 10:00. Some days, the distractions simply overwhelmed me, and I never got any writing done at all.

When I really started listening to my body, I discovered that I was actually most alert first thing in the morning. I was far less able to concentrate as the day wore on—most especially, in midafternoon. I also discovered that if I tried to get up before 6:30 A.M., I wasn't really fully awake and rested.

With a lot of experimentation, I evolved a set of rituals that I have now stuck by for more than a year, with remarkable success. During that period, I have written more productively and consistently than at any time in my life, and I have also been more resilient in the face of various stresses, and happier in my life generally.

I now get up every morning by 6:45 A.M. I begin the day by meditating for 20 minutes. That helps me get centered and focused. Then I go downstairs and make myself a protein drink. Now I spend just a few minutes having my drink, glance at the newspaper headlines (I'm too addicted to postpone looking till later, which I *should* do) and head straight to my desk. I make no phone calls, and permit myself no excuses to avoid writing.

I get to work about 7:30, and I now find that I can work with almost complete focus for three hours—up from 90 minutes, when I first started the routine. At 10:30 or so, I take a three-mile run. By this point, I am feeling burned out mentally, and I welcome the shift to a physical activity. I also find that, in the course of a run, I often have spontaneous ideas about my work that don't tend to occur when I am consciously looking for them. At 11:00 A.M., I come back home and have a bagel or a piece of fruit, and spend a half-hour relaxing and reading the newspaper.

By 11:30, I am feeling refreshed and I go back and write for somewhere between 90 minutes and 2 hours. At 1:00 or 1:30 P.M., I stop for lunch—generally low-fat, although I don't starve myself. I have the luxury of taking some time off if I want to during this period, and so I might go play tennis for an hour, or work out with weights, or make personal phone calls, or read for pleasure—or some blend of the above. Much like the run at 11:00, I think of this as a recovery period.

I return to work around 3:00, but I am under a lot of pressure. I no longer try to write new pages. I find that my concentration is far less sharp at this point, so I turn to activities that require less of it: interviewing, reading, researching, or rewriting. I usually work for a couple of hours, take a brief break to have something to eat and see my kids when they return home from school, and then go back for another couple of hours. I finish around 7:00 P.M., when we eat together. I rarely work in the evenings, except to read.

Under this schedule, I find that I still put in at least five solid hours for writing, and that my total workday is approximately eight to nine hours. Where there was once a struggle, I now find my days very relaxing, and vastly more pleasant and balanced than they ever were before. I have two opportunities during the day to do something physical, and I eat frequently enough that I never feel hungry, but I never stuff myself either. It helps to have given up sugar.

My life has a wonderful wavy rhythm to it—made more possible, of course, by the fact that I set my own schedule. In any case, I have found a blend of structure and freedom that seems to work for me exceptionally well.

Good rituals, bad rituals, and superstitions all affect our performance and our emotional state. Reaching our highest potential in high-stress arenas means systematically replacing bad rituals and superstitions with activities that really work. For better or worse, they represent an attempt, usually unconscious, to reach the relaxed energy state of IPS.[4]

I want to make it clear, though, that some rituals work to your disadvantage. If the rituals turn into superstitions, then you're asking for trouble.

Let me explain the difference between a ritual and a superstition. A ritual is a controllable sequence of thinking and acting that enhances your ability to perform at your best; effective rituals rely on factors within your voluntary reach, and they ensure that all signals are go for the countdown to your performance. Superstitions, on the other hand, depend on factors beyond your control, and they are negative. You know that you'll do better if you follow your rituals, but you're scared that something terrible might happen if you don't abide by a superstition.

THE PROBLEM WITH SUPERSTITION

Let's say that you are about to receive a very important overseas call that will have a major impact on your business. You must be prepared to think on your feet, articulate your position with absolute clarity, and, equally important, sound convincing and in control. The moment your secretary announces that Director So-and-So is on the line, your voice and hands are trembling and you devoutly wish that, at that very moment, you could be fly fishing in Maine. The person on the other end of the line is going to want good answers; he is a very busy, very powerful man who doesn't suffer fools gladly. You sense deep down that you're not prepared for this call, that you don't have good answers, and that you're about to fumble the ball for your firm.

This is when superstition kicks in. Although you make a half-hearted attempt to wing it, you believe you're in trouble because your assistant laid a book on your desk opened to page 13! Every time the number 13 shows up in your life, something bad happens. You think to yourself, as you stare down at the open book, "How could my assistant be so stupid! Why was the damned thing open to page 13? She knows things like this affect me." How or where this superstition got started you're not sure. The point is, it hurts you. It turns your chemistry in a negative, almost helpless direction.

This happens all the time in sport. National Hockey League Hall of Famer Phil Esposito would go crazy when he would walk into the dressing room before a game and see two hockey sticks crossed. For him, it was an omen that bad things would happen during the game. Goalie Jim Carey, of the Washington Capitals, barred his sister from attending games because he became convinced she brought him bad luck. When the Detroit Red Wings were on the road, coach Scotty Bowman refused to stay on the thirteenth floor of any hotel, or in any room where the numbers totaled 13. He had somehow come to believe that it might hurt the team's chances of winning. Such superstitions abound in professional sport because playing well or badly is so delicately balanced, and people are always searching for reasons why. In the absence of accurate observations, troublesome superstitions can creep in.

Maladaptive Rituals

When the going was tough, the great movie star, Humphrey Bogart, always lit a cigarette and took a deep drag. The cigarette seemed to put him on top of the situation; it added toughness to his makeup and put him in charge. How many of us grew up watching Bogart, and other manly men, light the cigarettes that enhanced their image as extra-tough and resolute under trying circumstances? These images on the silver screen taught many of us our first bad ritual; smoking is hazardous to health, and is clearly *not* performance-enhancing. It may make us feel tough on some subliminal level, but, in fact, smoking generally impairs performance. The drug nicotine is a central nervous system stimulant, and a cigarette actually increases nervous tension while ultimately decreasing physical energy. Despite the seductive imagery surrounding smoking, reaching for a cigarette eventually becomes addictive and undermines personal control.

Similarly, using alcohol as a ritual for relaxation can become tragic. The volume of stress in the lives of corporate athletes requires powerful doses of recovery if overtraining is to be avoided. Overtraining occurs when the volume of recovery is no longer adequate to balance the volume of stress. It's important to understand that recovery is *healing.* When too little sleep, poor nutrition, no exercise, and little or no personal time are combined with high stress, overtraining problems are virtually ensured. And when cycles of rest and recovery are consistently paired with the consumption of alcohol, corporate athletes find that relaxing and recovering *without alcohol* become increasingly more difficult. As stress levels intensify, the importance of alcohol also intensifies.

Using alcohol to take the edge off *before* pressure-filled performances—before that critical board meeting, or the third-quarter sales presentation, or the termination of a long-standing employee—can become equally dangerous. Eventually, you begin to feel that, without that quick drink, you won't be able to perform well under pressure. Over time, because performance pressure is repeatedly paired with alcohol consumption, your ability to perform well without alcohol is gradually eroded. Feelings of self-control and self-direction are diminished by this ritual rather than enhanced by it. As you may already know, alcohol also can be very disruptive to sleep cycles, is potentially addictive in itself, undermines appetite, and can interfere with motor and memory function.

Using drugs and chemical agents to psych-up for performances or get relief from competitive pressure can be very seductive. It's a major problem in professional sport. These rituals, in addition to posing great health risks, viciously tear away at feelings of self-control. With constant use, the user becomes helpless without them.

Another negative ritual involves using food to ease feelings of nervousness or depression. By repeatedly pairing the ingestion of food with the easing of painful feelings, food consumption can become compulsive under conditions of high stress. Eating disorders, unrelenting guilt, low self-esteem, and obesity are among the possible results.

When rituals involving drugs, alcohol, and food are used to relieve tension, the negative consequences are often easy to see. Many other forms of maladaptive rituals, however, are less obvious but extremely important in the overall picture. Examples include: a minimum of five cups of coffee in the morning and four in the early afternoon, to stay alert; routinely driving at very high speeds, to keep from falling asleep at the wheel; watching late-night TV or midnight movies, to unwind from the stresses of the day (negative because of the impact on sleep cycles); taking sleep medication, to sleep at night; eating only one or two meals each day (negative because of the impact on blood sugar levels and metabolic rate); pouting and whining when you are frustrated; throwing temper tantrums when you are angry, and refusing to talk when your feelings are hurt. Inflexible rituals, those that do not allow for change or variation, often become problematic as well. Even rituals around holidays, birthdays, anniversaries, and so on, are considered maladaptive if they don't serve to powerfully mobilize the appropriate feelings around the event. If, for instance, your Christmas rituals leave you feeling emotionally unconnected and disengaged, they need to be changed. Rituals that don't properly ignite our minds and bodies to achieve IPS when performing on the job must also be changed. The right rituals bring balance, poise, rhythm, and harmony to our lives, both corporately and personally. The wrong rituals take away much more than they give back and, most importantly, they rob us of personal control.

Rituals in the Best of Times

Take a few minutes and reflect on your life during a time when you were on a roll, when you could handle almost anything on your plate, and when your health, happiness, and productivity were at their highest level. What was going on then? Like a zoom lens, zero in on the rituals you had in place at that time. What were the rituals you had with your family, your friends, your work? What routines were in place for sleeping, exercising, eating, time alone, hobbies, resting, pets, children, music, travel time, sports? Consider each of the following:

- Family.
- Friends.
- Work.
- Sleep.
- Exercise/sports.
- Health.
- Hobbies.
- Rest.
- Children.
- Pets.
- Travel.
- Music.

Now go back and check off any of those rituals that are in your life now.

Your checklist may shock you. The rituals that provided great balance, rhythm, harmony, and healing in your life during exceptional times are often no longer there. The daily exercise, the time with your family, the patterns of eating and sleeping, and so forth, were abandoned for a variety of possible reasons—you moved to a new city, you have no time now, or you got divorced.

THE TWELVE MOST IMPORTANT RITUALS

Our work with Olympic and corporate athletes over many years has confirmed the importance of the following rituals in the overall Toughness Training process:

1. Sleep.
2. Exercise.
3. Nutrition.
4. Family.
5. Spirituality.
6. Preperformance.
7. Travel.
8. Telephone.
9. Office.
10. Creative time.
11. Home.
12. Time alone.

Each type of ritual is described below.

I. Sleep Rituals

Consistent patterns for getting up and going to bed protect the sleep cycle. Going to bed early and getting up early works best for most people.

Sample Sleep Ritual

1. Go to bed and get up at the same time as often as possible.
2. Get up at the same time regardless of the length of sleep.
3. Exercise daily but not too close to bedtime.
4. Start a specific pattern of presleep activities 30 minutes before you intend to be asleep.
5. Consume no caffeine or alcohol.
6. Follow a very disciplined pattern of thinking, once you start your sleep countdown. Clear from your mind all arousing thoughts, either positive or negative—no arguments, no deep discussions; only the same soothing and relaxing progression of thoughts and images.

---

2. Exercise Rituals

Daily exposure to exercise stress of some kind is critical to overall balance. Walking your dog in the morning, taking stairs instead of elevators, or walking around the block between meetings can add significantly to the wellness ledger.

Morning Rituals of the Dalai Lama (Age 61)

4:00 A.M. After cleaning/washing, he recites the sacred mantras, takes his medication, and bows repetitiously for 30 minutes in order to express his humility.

5:00 A.M. A 30-minute walk in the garden of his ashram in Dharansala (India), where he has been in exile since 1959. Then a 30-minute ride on a stationary bike. He wants to stay fit.

6:00 A.M. Breakfast. Takes about half an hour and includes sliced bread and jam and sweet tea. Afterward, he listens to the morning news, then meditates until 8:00 A.M.

8:00 A.M. Reads the old scriptures, followed by meditation again, then takes private audiences until lunch at noon.

---

3. Nutritional Rituals

The timing, frequency, and content of your meals are extremely important. Without highly specific nutritional rituals to guide you, successfully navigating through troubled high-stress waters, particularly for a long term, becomes an impossible nightmare.

4. Family Time Rituals

Time with family grounds you, connects you, affirms real value and meaning in your life. The right family rituals help to ensure that those who mean the most to you get that message. From eating dinner together to playing together on the weekends; from how you spend your holidays to the ceremonies you have for family birthdays and anniversaries; the various rituals that protect family time are essential to optimal health, happiness, and productivity.

5. Spiritual Rituals

Like family time, spiritual time heals your soul and brings you home to the deeper, more essential truths of life. The question of why you are here, the meaning of life, and where you are going must be continuously explored and expanded on a deeply personal level. Failure to make time for spiritual growth erodes the very foundation of all other personal growth.

6. Preperformance Rituals

Like tennis players before serving and golfers before putting, corporate athletes need precise preparation routines before stepping into the batter's box at the office. Some specific examples include: creating a priority list of things to do before you start your day, clearing your desk and putting files away before you take your first appointment, and visualizing how you want your day to unfold.

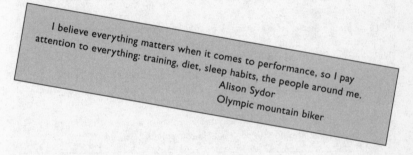

I believe everything matters when it comes to performance, so I pay attention to everything: training, diet, sleep habits, the people around me.
Alison Sydor
Olympic mountain biker

7. Travel Rituals

If you want to get control of your emotional response to traffic on your commute to work, build a ritual around it. An example would be to leave fifteen minutes earlier so traffic won't make you late, play motivational or music tapes that get you feeling positive, make a sign for your dashboard that reads, "Caught in traffic gives me more precious time alone," or "Is this great traffic or what!" or "I love traffic!"

If you want to get control of jet lag, build a ritual around airline travel.

Sample Flying Ritual
to Prevent Jet Lag

1. Drink lots of water and juice during the flight. The humidity on planes is very low, which contributes to dehydration.

2. Be well recovered before you depart. If your biological clock is out of sync before you start, the effects of jet lag will be even more profound.

3. Begin shifting your sleep/wake cycle to the new time zone before you leave.

4. Set your watch to the new zone as soon as you depart.

5. Attempt to follow the sleep/wake cycle of your intended destination during flight.

6. Eat high-protein meals when you are trying to stay awake, and high-carbohydrate meals when you are trying to sleep.

7. Avoid alcoholic beverages.

8. Adapt local eating and sleeping schedules the moment you arrive.

9. During flight, get up and move around every 1 1/2 hours unless you are sleeping. Periodically, do stretching and isometric exercises to relieve muscle stress.

10. Exercise moderately as soon as possible when you arrive, to help reduce the stress of flying. If exercise is not possible due to late arrival times, exercise first thing the next day.

11. Make a conscious effort to enjoy the flight, and don't let petty things bother you. Set a goal to reduce jet lag to a minimum by following your anti-jet-lag plan.

12. Keep a log tracking the severity and intensity of jet lag each time you fly. Your rituals should lead to steady improvement.

8. Telephone Rituals

Telephone stress is a major problem for many corporate athletes. They are tied to the phone all day. Adopting a ritual such as spending 50 percent of your time on the phone moving (i.e., walking, bending, stretching) can significantly reduce telephone stress. Hands-free (speaker) phones make it possible to actually do exercises with things like rubber tubing while you talk. A preperformance telephone ritual might include putting a smile on your face, throwing your shoulders back and assuming a powerful presence, and locking on like a laser to your best IPS image *before making or receiving a call.* Even having the words "I love telephone stress" taped across your phone can begin to trigger changes in how you think and act on the phone, and, ultimately, change your stress chemistry.

9. Office Recovery Rituals

Just as sport scientists have confirmed that the between-point time in tennis and the between-shot time in golf are critical to success, so also is your time between phone calls, between appointments, between meetings. This is not wasted time. It's time for recovery and then for preparation. Traditional coffee breaks don't qualify. Taking a small carbohydrate snack, such as an apple; stepping outside momentarily into the fresh air and sunlight; walking up and down five flights of stairs; leaving a few minutes early to get mentally prepared for your next meeting—all of these do qualify. This is *trained recovery.*

10. Creative Time Rituals

Playing a musical instrument, photography, creative writing, gardening, and artistic pursuits of all kinds play a critical role in balancing stress. Because they are viewed as relatively unimportant in our lives, creative time rituals are often the first to go when the time crunch of modern life starts beating us up.

11. Home Recovery Rituals

Establishing clear-cut routines for shifting gears, from pushing hard at the office to letting go at home, is what I call *oscillating.* Learning how to shut down, turn off, and reenergize is as important to success as firing up, getting psyched, and turning on the juices. One without the other eventually breaks you in half. Health, happiness, and high productivity require both.

12. Time Alone Rituals

We have found that many corporate athletes have virtually no time alone during the day; they are always surrounded by people. There

In the list below, circle Yes for any of the ritual areas in which you feel you need improvement.

The 12 Most Important Rituals	Needs Improvement
1. Sleep Rituals	Yes/No
2. Exercise Rituals	Yes/No
3. Nutritional Rituals	Yes/No
4. Family Time Rituals	Yes/No
5. Spiritual Rituals	Yes/No
6. Preperformance Rituals	Yes/No
7. Travel Rituals	Yes/No
8. Telephone Rituals	Yes/No
9. Office Recovery Rituals	Yes/No
10. Creative Time Rituals	Yes/No
11. Home Recovery Rituals	Yes/No
12. Time Alone Rituals	Yes/No

is something very healing and balancing in time spent alone. Just a little time alone, once or twice daily, can make a substantial difference in your ability to stay in control and remain emotionally on track.

BREAKTHROUGH RITUALS

Invariably, great breakthroughs in life are associated with the incorporation of rituals that powerfully impact thinking and behavior. Some examples are described below.

"How Fortunate I Am" Ritual

Bob is a superstar in the investment business. His performance record for nearly 30 years is incomparable. He is simply the best of the best. Clients and competitors are in awe of his achievements. In an interview with Bob, I asked him to explain how he produced such brilliant consistency for so many years. He paused for a moment and then described an important turning point:

In my twenties and thirties, I wasn't such a good performer. My attitude and view of the world were decidedly negative at that time. I had big ideas but I was always emotionally off balance when things didn't go as I wanted them to. I always saw the dark side of things. One of the greatest turning points in my life was when I got into the habit of starting a new sentence—immediately after something bad would happen—with the words "How fortunate I am!" For example, if I were in an automobile accident, rather than go nuts, I'd simply say, "How fortunate I am that I was not hurt!" This simple routine completely changed my internal psychology. It substantially changed my view of the world. That's when good things started to happen for me. Something so simple had a profound impact.

"Is This an Intelligent Response?" Ritual

Whenever you find yourself experiencing a powerful emotional response, get into the habit of simply asking yourself the following questions:

- Is this emotion appropriate?
- Is it likely to lead to positive and constructive answers?
- Does it reflect high emotional intelligence?

If your answers are "No," immediately take steps to change the response. This ritual increases self-awareness, which is essential to accelerated personal control.

"Dive into the Present" Ritual

In his excellent book, *Time Shifting,* Dr. Stephen Rechtschaffen states that "in the present moment, there is no stress."[5] The simple act of turning one's attention to the here and now changes chemistry. By focusing on your breathing as you breathe, on your walking as you walk, on the texture of the grass in front of you, on the sunlight's warmth against your face, a deep sense of quiet and internal peace begins to form immediately. The ability to live "in the present moment" is life-transforming from a stress perspective.

Here is one corporate athlete's regimen:

As President of Melrose Management Company, I manage 6,500 acres of prime real estate for a London-based group. I deal with stressful situations every minute of the day. I have to oversee projects in different states. I have to handle delicate negotiations in Park City, Utah, for acquiring a public golf course, Park Meadows, with the plan of taking it private. That means dealing with the egos of existing property owners as well as prospective property owners and club members. But that is only part of my stress quotient. There are, at times, as many as 100 to 125 employees reporting to me. It is OK now, though, because I am learning to handle stress so much better.

Each day, I say to myself, "If I can't get this piece of work done today, I'll do as much as I can and finish it tomorrow." I also say to myself, "Enjoy what you're doing right here and now. There isn't a better job in the world and you're lucky to have it and that you can handle it so well." Day by day, I felt myself growing stronger and tougher. I began to relish the tough assignments. I wanted to be the pitcher out there with the bases loaded and the game on the line. The greater the dollar volume, the more at stake, the better. I found that this new confidence—new toughness—spilled over into my personal life. I enjoyed my friends and my family more than I had in years. In my head, I was a young striver again, not a harried executive burned out before his time.

My newfound toughness has also had an effect on my great passion—golf. For years, I played tense and fearful; I would fret over the last shot. I was always living in the past. But no longer. Now when the shot it done—good or bad—it's history. I recover and go on to the next shot. I have learned that you can't correct past mistakes through anger. It only tenses you up and paves the way for further mistakes so that you can get angrier and make even *more* mistakes. It's a vicious cycle. If there is a secret to toughness, for me, it's the ability to look forward to what comes next with serenity and confidence but, most importantly, to stay in the present.

"Yes, I Can" Ritual

When you are pushed to your absolute limits, affirm to yourself, "I *can* deal with this. I *can* make this day work for me." Tough thinkers are "I can" thinkers. The I can affirmative ritual is a silent one. Repeat it over and over whenever you feel the need for it.

Paul is an advocate of the I can principle of toughness. His company makes boxes for commercial shipping and is one of the biggest of its kind in the country. At the start, however, his career path was rocky. He says:

I started out without a dime until my father, with whom I had a poor relationship in my teens and early twenties, said, "OK, Paul, I'll loan you ten thousand dollars to start a business. That's it. Don't come asking for more." He was even more blunt with me when he said, "Frankly, I don't think you can pull it off. Business is cutthroat and you have to be result-oriented. You're kind of a soft guy." Then he told me something I'll never forget. "Life is like those old cowboy movies where the bad guys are drinking and a fight breaks out in the saloon and the piano player goes on playing right through the mayhem. You have to learn to be like the piano player. No matter what happens, you keep on playing."

I used that ten thousand to start this business on a shoestring and now we're worth many millions. But there were plenty of rough stretches along the way. I couldn't always meet the payroll. I had to jolly people into working harder than they thought they were capable of, and I had to fire the lazy ones. When we merged with another company, I had to fight to keep control, but I kept saying, "You *can* do it, Paul." Now we're in the process of downsizing and that's another big load of stress to deal with. But when things get really tough, I imagine that I'm the piano player in that saloon out west, just playing along and enjoying the music while the tough guys slug it out. Funnily enough, the image helps me, keeps me calm. And by the way, I paid my father back the first year.

A Preparation Ritual in Six Parts

Repeat with conviction before important performances:

1. I will put myself totally on the line emotionally.
2. I will support myself during tough times.
3. I will come totally prepared to perform.
4. I will not show weakness on the outside.
5. I will love it even more, the crazier it gets.
6. I will love performing just as much as winning.

Rituals and Biological Clocks

Hundreds of body rhythms appear to be controlled by a cluster of brain cells called the suprachiasmatic nucleus (SCN). The biological rhythms are synchronized, or entrained, by environmental cues such as light and darkness, regular meals, and timing of exercise and rest periods. These external cues are called *zeitgebers*.

According to chronobiologists, your rituals should take into consideration the following natural rhythms:

- Peak alertness occurs around noon.
- Peak physical output occurs around 5:00 P.M. (best time to exercise).
- Lowest period of sleepiness is 6:00 to 9:00 P.M.
- Peak capacity for mental precision and detail work is early morning.
- Peak period for repetitive tasks is late afternoon.
- Peak capacity for logical, analytical thinking is midday.
- Peak period for napping is between 2:00 and 4:00 P.M.
- Period of least sensitivity to pain is early morning.

A Mistake Ritual

If you fear mistakes, you're bound to make them. It's not unlike playing defensive tennis or basketball. Instead of playing to *win,* you're playing *not to lose.* Conducting yourself so that you won't lose or make mistakes is a sure recipe for coming up short. How you think about mistakes has a major impact on the emotional state you carry into your business. A winning way to think about mistakes is to make them into affirmative rituals:

- Mistakes are a necessary step in my moving forward.
- No mistakes, no progress.
- I will make my mistakes intelligently, fearlessly, and aggressively.
- I will never play it safe, hold back, or look for excuses.
- I will go for it, accept whatever happens, and move on.

A Spontaneous Ritual

Some people can become overly obsessed with the use of controlling rituals in their lives. They lose any sense of spontaneity and freedom in what they do. It is important to understand that some rituals are controlling and others are freeing. If more spontaneity is what is needed to balance your life, simply incorporate rituals that free your spirit and facilitate letting go. Examples could include a spontaneous day ritual where you set aside time in which nothing is planned—you just go with the flow. Whatever you feel like doing, you do.

Two important keys to toughness are enjoyment and humor. I learned that focusing on enjoyment of the work process itself invariably produces the best outcome and completely reduces my stress. Humor has become like a ritual for us. At our meetings, we are upbeat, laugh and joke. We are far more productive and efficient than when we approached the same tasks grimly.

Margaret Pyles,
Vice President of Training and
Development, Bristol-Myers Squibb

DESIGN YOUR OWN PLAN

Design a specific plan for reworking your deficient rituals. Eventually, your goal is to organize new patterns of thinking and acting on a daily basis that put you in control and moving forward to new, exciting frontiers in personal strength and balance. The model on page 94 can get you started.

Appendix B provides reminders and suggestions regarding the kinds of things you should consider in your life plan. Specific suggestions such as eliminating caffeine are optional and would be included in your plan only if you chose to do so.

Stress for Success Training Log							
Daily Rituals	Mon	Tue	Wed	Thu	Fri	Sat	Sun
5. Up same time—early							
6. A.M. exercise							
7. Small breakfast							
8. Every 2 hours A.M. snack							
9. 10 minute mental preparation (++)							
10. Completed priority list							
11. Followed A.M. rituals							
12. Office preparation ritual							
13. Every 2 hours A.M. oscillation							
14. Small lunch							

"It's Showtime Every Day"

LEARNING TO CREATE
EMOTION ON DEMAND

CHAPTER 5

AS A CORPORATE athlete, how and what you are thinking in a stressful, high-pressure situation, the look on your face, your posture and physical presence—all impact your body's physiological stress response in powerful ways. The objective is to get your body to mobilize the most adaptive and appropriate possible responses to whatever stressors are encountered. Fear on airplanes is inappropriate and nonadaptive. So is anger in traffic, fear and panic when speaking in front of a group, defensiveness and insecurity when criticized, and frustration and hostility toward bosses or coworkers. Even such things as sleepiness while driving, alertness and high energy when trying to sleep, and sadness while trying to concentrate on an important project are clearly inappropriate. Collectively over time, these nonadaptive responses form a powerful mosaic of *distress* that rips away at happiness, health, and productivity.

Here are just a few examples of times when acting skills can be used to control physiology:

- Snapping out of the bad mood you're in, so you can deliver an inspirational talk to your sales staff.

- Not allowing the bad news about third-quarter profits to affect your enthusiasm for the company's new initiatives.

- Overcoming feelings of fatigue and sleepiness in the midafternoon.

- Getting yourself excited and challenged about a project you've been dreading.

- Not allowing yourself to get defensive or upset in a meeting.

- Remaining positive and enthusiastic with a customer who is obnoxious and illtempered.

- Not allowing your personal feelings about a coworker to negatively affect your ability to work together.

For years, I fought the use of the word *acting* to explain a vital component in the Toughness Training program. Acting, to me, connoted phoniness—something that's not real, done on a stage. But once the physiology involved in acting was better understood, it was the only word that could effectively convey the concept I was trying to explain.

Each of us spends as much as 90 percent of our day modifying, filtering, and adjusting our emotions and behavior to fit what are considered to be the most appropriate scripts for particular moments—in other words, we are acting. Think for a minute about the span of time in a typical day when you can allow your feelings on the inside to be freely and openly expressed on the outside. For most people, being completely transparent rarely occurs, particularly in the context of work. A very small percentage of your time is spent being the basic, unfiltered, uncensored "you." But don't rush to judgment and proclaim yourself a phony who puts on a personality like a suit of clothes for any occasion. Instead, consider yourself a success for being able to summon whatever emotions and physiology are required to drive real answers and to live a life that is consistent with your deepest values and beliefs. That is, by the way, your script.

THE PERFORMER SELF AND THE REAL SELF

We need to define these terms. The Real Self is the way you actually feel and the accompanying physiology that drives those feelings. The Performer Self is how you need to feel to respond in the most appropriate and adaptive way possible, given unique conditions. Anytime you intentionally attempt to move your feelings and physiology from where you are to another, more adaptive place, you engage what I call *performer skills*. Once performer skills are engaged and feelings and physiology have actually moved in a new targeted direction, the Real Self and the Performer Self merge and become one again. How you feel and how you need to feel are now the same. Initially, however, the disparity between Real Self and Performer Self can set the stage for a difficult struggle, as illustrated in the following story, told to me by Richard W., a former client:

> I came home one night after a long day at the office. It was one of the very worst, most brutal weeks I'd ever been through. We were in the throes of downsizing and reengineering, and I'd had one late-night meeting after another. I'd negotiated with my wife that on this one night I'd break away, come home, pop open a beer, and veg in front of the TV. She'd take the kids out for pizza and a movie. I'd have the house to myself for a few hours—blessed silence, regroup, try to get myself together.
>
> Driving home, I was practically salivating for this recovery time. I was so beat up I just didn't know how much longer I could handle it. I mean, it's not as though I don't love my family, but I just had to have this time alone. Doesn't everybody feel like that once in a while? You don't want to *desert* the family, run away, but you've got this craving for a few quality hours alone.
>
> So anyway, I came cruising into the driveway, thinking, "*Yes,* order that pizza, sit down, put the feet up, check the movies and games on tonight." I put my key in the door and all of a sudden the door opened. "Oh, hi, honey," my wife said. "I'm sorry I couldn't make arrangements for the kids, a PTA meeting came up, eight o'clock; there's some meatloaf in the oven." And my two boys yelled, "C'mon, Dad, let's go play ball!"

What was this man's Real Self saying right then? It was screaming, "*No! Don't do this to me! Go away! Leave me alone!*" He came within a hair of taking out his frustrations and pent-up anger on his wife and children. Here he had been working day and night on a plan to reorganize his division, a plan that demanded his last ounce of energy and patience. Even though he hadn't seen his children in three days, he was clearly in no frame of mind to interact with them in a way that would be beneficial for either himself or them.

Although his Real Self feelings and emotions are completely logical and understandable, given the situation, what would be the likely consequence for his children if he did in fact fully express and act out the underlying physiology? They would think he didn't love them. They would figure that he loved his pizza, beer, and TV more than he loved them, and that time for himself was more important than they were.

However, because he had worked hard to acquire keenly honed performer skills, he was able to alter his chemistry and respond in a more appropriate way. Literally within seconds, a broad smile appeared on his face and a remarkable response took form. "OK, here's what we'll do, guys. We'll play ball for thirty minutes, then I get an hour for myself. How does that sound?" That sounded just fine to them. "So we're going out now," he said, "and have some fun, and then I get my hour."

He sounded enthusiastic at the prospect of playing ball, and by now his sons were smiling and he was already feeling better inside. His Performer Self was changing his physiology and slowing his pulse and heart rate. The smile on his face had worked its way into his system. What began as acting was quickly becoming real.

Richard went outside with his sons and had a good, fast, three-way catch and a great time. He went on to tell me:

> The thirty minutes flew by and we went another fifteen. Then I packed it in and they were cool about it. I loved them, I showed them I loved them, and then I was out of there, I was gone. They were completely OK about it.

Because of Richard's ability to access his Performer Self, he managed to exert control over both his physiology and the potentially damaging family situation that arose. At the beginning of his career, he used to think it was "spontaneous" and "honest" to follow wherever his Real Self emotions took him. As long as the right emotions surfaced at the right times, he was OK. But when emotions of the moment were inappropriate and counterproductive, Richard was in real trouble. When he felt angry, frustrated, insecure, tired, bored, nervous, or depressed, that's exactly what other people got. He was the embodiment of the let-it-all-hang-out 1960s, "I've got to be me" personality. In sport, coaches refer to such individuals as "head cases" or "wimps." They simply can't follow the emotional script and, as a consequence, their performance output is unpredictable. They literally are at the mercy of their emotions. Head cases don't last very long in sport, regardless of their level of talent. The ability to use Performer Self skills is even more urgent for corporate athletes.

THE AMAZING AMYGDALA

How did Richard improve his emotional control skills so dramatically? How did he go from wimp to tough? The answer is, he trained every day to make it happen. And one of the most important components to his training was learning to use acting skills to turn on and off various structures in his brain that control the flow of emotion. The "emotional brain" is sometimes referred to as the limbic system (a group of cell structures in the center of the brain that, among other things, regulates emotion). Although a variety of structures within the brain are involved in an emotional response, one of the most critical is the amygdala—literally, the brain's emotional computer and the last relay point in an emotional response.[1] One of the principal roles of the amygdala is to place an emotional valence or value on various life experiences. The most powerful emotional events in our lives are granted the strongest neurological imprints and potentially have the most profound effect on behavior. This is particularly true if the valence is highly negative, as it would be for a traumatic automobile accident, an incident of abuse, or a personal failure. Once a signal is received by the amygdala and a specific emotion is turned on, response time can be as little as twelve one-thousandths ($^{12}/_{1,000}$) of a second! Because it is connected to nearly every area of the brain via an extensive network of neural pathways, when the amygdala sends a "go" signal, it can turn on any and all physiological and hormonal systems involved in that emotion.

One of the most important features of this central brain structure is that it works either in concert with or completely independent of the rational, logical human brain. As we'll see in this chapter, the ON switch for an emotion can be fully activated regardless of whether it fits reality as judged by the rational brain. And once the switch is pulled and the emotion takes hold, the *feelings* we experience simply confirm that the underlying physiological mechanisms have been activated. What we feel when we are nervous, anxious, angry, or joyous are the mental and physical consequences of highly specific hormonal surges. Once the targeted neurons in the amygdala are turned on, the corresponding physiology rolls out. This sequence occurs for positive and empowering responses as well as negative and disempowering ones.

EMOTION ON DEMAND

The key to mobilizing a particular emotion is to somehow turn on, in the amygdala, the memory cells that hold the physiological signature. Of considerable importance is the fact that the memory cells of the amygdala are surprisingly accessible. Let's look at fear. One way to turn on the physiology is through sensory stimulation. You see a dark figure at the door of your car as you walk toward it in a dimly lit parking lot; or you hear a rumor that 30 percent of your department will be eliminated and you're sure you'll be one of them; or you feel a hand reaching into your purse on a crowded bus. Even a faint smell of smoke or fire can trigger a full-blown fear response for someone who has had a terrifying experience associated with these odors. Physiology follows sensory perception; when a real threat is perceived, fear materializes.

But what happens in the case of movies such as *Jurassic Park?* Millions of people became petrified with fear as they sat in movie theaters. Every person in the film's audiences knew full well there was no chance of being hurt or even being in danger. But their bodies were mobilized in precisely the way they would be if they were in a real-life Jurassic Park and real dinosaurs were on the hunt. The amygdala, fooled by the screen images, signaled the fear alarm. Even though the rational brain says this is just a movie and no true danger is present, the fear memory cells get turned on. The same thing can happen when you watch a TV show in the comfort of your own home or attend a live on-stage theatrical production. Even reading a book, listening to a good storyteller, or hearing certain kinds of music can trigger the amygdala fear alarm.

And that's not all! You can also turn on the fear cells by simply creating in your mind an image of something that is very frightening. You can go either backward or forward in time—back to something that was truly frightening in your life, or forward to something that could happen in the future.

Again, rationally and logically, you know these are just images in your head. These events are not really happening. You are not in any danger. But the amygdala turns on anyway. The physiology comes racing forward to protect you, to mobilize you to flee from something that is life-threatening.

There's one more "cells on" switch in the amygdala. In 1983, researcher Paul Ekman made an important discovery.[2] He confirmed that simply moving facial muscles in the direction of fear, anger, disgust, sadness, surprise, or happiness actually caused autonomic nervous system reactors to move in the direction of the respective emotion. Changes in such things as heart rate, blood pressure, and skin temperature moved in targeted directions that were consistent with the facially acted-out emotion. Since 1983, a number of researchers, most notably R. W. Levenson, have confirmed the connection between movement of the physical body, via posture and facial expression, and activation of emotion-specific physiology.

In summary, we basically have four emotion-ON triggers:

1. Real-life occurrences.
2. Make-believe experiences in the context of movies, TV, live theater, reading, and storytelling.
3. Visualization of past or future events that are loaded with the emotions you are trying to summon.
4. Movement of the physical body (posture, facial expression, and so on) in the targeted emotional direction.

Now let's go back to the issue of emotional control. Our goal in Toughness Training is to summon the most appropriate and adaptive emotional response to whatever stressors we face in business and in life in general. To bring to life the chemistry of IPS for a high-stakes sales performance, to respond with empathy and love to your children when you are tired and beat up, to find the motivation to exercise at the end of a long and hard day, you must flip the right switches so the amygdala can turn on the mobilizing physiology. The question is: Of the four triggers on the list above, which can you use on a moment-by-moment basis to access emotion? Waiting for real-life experiences to match how we want to feel isn't practical, and trying to find movies, TV programs, books, songs, or storytelling isn't going to work either. As you'll see in this and later chapters, precision thinking and imaging, and precision acting with the physical body represent core factors in controlling emotion ON DEMAND. Ironically, these two strategies form the basis of what is referred to as method acting.

METHOD ACTING

I was shocked when I finally realized that what I had been for all these years of work with thousands of athletes was an acting coach! Most participants in our workshops are taken aback when I make the statement that the best performers in the room are invariably the best actors and actresses. I even suggest that the most accomplished among them could rival the best Hollywood has to offer. The immediate question is then: What does acting have to do with performing at one's peak? What possible connection is there between issues of IPS, productivity, emotional intelligence, and the notion of acting? The answer is: EVERYTHING!

To make the connection, let's review an experiment in which highly trained professional actors are instructed to portray anger.[3] Their assignment is to artificially summon (that is, fake) anger as they would in front of a live audience. Once the portrayal is achieved, comprehensive physiological and biochemical profiles are made of the faked anger response. An autonomic nervous system reactor profile is recorded that includes heart rate, blood pressure, core temperature, hand temperature, galvanic skin response, muscle tension, and many other measurements. Blood is drawn so that levels of a number of hormones in the blood (catecholamines, cortisol, and assorted immune markers) can be recorded.

The next step in the experiment is to record the same measurements when the actors have become genuinely angry, when their emotion is real, not faked. The final step is to compare the two profiles.

What do you think the difference would be? For someone who has acquired considerable skill in artificially summoning a targeted emotion, what is the difference between the real and faked emotion from a biochemical perspective?

The answer is, NOTHING! They are indistinguishable because once the amygdala is turned on, the physiology follows. And when the physiology is activated, the emotion becomes real. This phenomenon has profound implications. Without question, the tools professional actors are using to summon emotions called for in their scripts could have powerful applications in the real world. Highly skilled actors clearly understand that to bring a script to life they must genuinely stir their own emotions; they must move their own physiology in the targeted direction. Successful actors have learned to control *on demand* many physiological functions thought to be beyond the reaches of voluntary control. To replicate the physiological signature of a particular emotion, actors have to move blood pressure, heart rate, blood flow, cortisol levels, EEG patterns, and neuroendocrine circuits in specific directions.[4] The issue is: How do they learn to do it?

The legendary Konstantin Stanislavski, "the father of method acting," asked precisely this question in 1918. During the next 20 years, until his death in 1938, he perfected a systemic method for accessing emotions. In 1962, R. V. Simorrov, a prominent physiologist and member of the Academy of Science of the USSR, published a summary of his work and aptly titled it *The Method of K.S. Stanislavski and The Physiology of Emotions*. Referred to as the great teacher of "affective memory," Stanislavski worked toward an ultimate goal of giving an actor control over the phenomenon of inspiration.[5] He realized that, to be effective, actors could not simply pretend to feel various emotions. They had to intentionally "turn on" the underlying physiological mechanisms. Stanislavski's entire method was directed toward harnessing voluntary control of these mechanisms.

What surprises readers of Stanislavski's works is his understanding of physiology. Remember, he was formulating most of his ideas in the early 1900s! Stanislavski's thinking was heavily influenced by Ivan Pavlov (1849–1936), the most brilliant physiologist of that era.

Even modern-day scientists are astounded by Stanislavski's insights and discoveries.

For Stanislavski, the most important understanding an actor can achieve is that the emotion must be true, not fake; given the way the human brain is wired, emotions cannot be stirred directly. For him, the actor's senses, imagination, intuition, and, particularly, muscles must all participate to produce true emotion. A concrete thought or image and a bodily expression combine to form the core of his system. When an actor fully focuses, so that imagination and physical body completely merge with the role, true emotion follows. The more experience Stanislavski had over the years with actors, the more importance he placed on physical actions to stimulate emotional memory. He came to believe that somehow emotions are stored in the muscles of the body. Eventually, he argued that there are as many varied nuances of emotions as there are different physical actions.

SUMMON SADNESS FOR $10,000

To illustrate the role of thought and actions in the production of emotion, suppose I told you that if you could summon real, genuine sadness for me in two minutes, you'd get $10,000. Sounds like a new game show, doesn't it? To get the $10,000, you have to move your physiology toward sadness in a measurable way. Visible tears will be the criterion. Remember, they have to be tears of sadness, not some other emotion such as joy or pain. When participants in our workshops are asked for a show of hands from those who would be able to summon sadness in two minutes and win $10,000, as many as 30 percent of the audience believe they can do it.

The next question we ask is: Of those who raised their hands, how many almost never cry? We respond to this group by saying they have virtually no chance of getting the $10,000. Emotions and the accompanying physiology are very much like muscles. Those that are stimulated the most become the strongest and the most available. The volunteers in the audience who have been crying most recently would have the best chance of pocketing the $10,000. To reinforce this point, the audience is asked how many think they could summon the physiology of anger for $10,000. Virtually every hand goes up. And why is anger so available to us? Because we are practicing it all the time!

To find out how much actual control participants have, the dynamics of pressure are added to the challenge. "Ten thousand dollars to you if you can summon measurable tears of sadness in two minutes—no excuses—and $10,000 *to me* if you don't!"

Now there is a major downside if the targeted physiology can't be summoned. The hands drop like flies. We've just elevated this challenge to the level of professional sport. Can you summon IPS and sink the overtime free throws, knowing that, if you don't, your team will surely lose the game and be eliminated from the playoffs? And if you don't come through, you may well lose your position on the team for next year. Precisely the same pressures exist for the corporate athlete. Failure to summon IPS can have profoundly tragic consequences. The downside for choking in the boardroom, for panic in a critical negotiation, for fumbling the ball on an important sales call can be enormous. But if you can bring to life—under pressure—the emotions called for in the performance script, you have acquired what we define as a *professional* level of skill.

In a class of fifty, invariably one or two people will believe they have enough control over the physiology of sadness that they will risk $10,000 to prove it. They are asked to come to the front of the room and to face the audience. A stopwatch is readied.

Suddenly, the rules of the game are changed. The volunteers are told that they won't have to pay if they can't summon the tears. They are greatly relieved. Instead, they are instructed to move their facial muscles upward in the direction of a smile, to look like they are having a good time. Then—*summon sadness for $10,000!*

To date, we have never had to pay the $10,000. No one has even come close. Why?

We have volunteers who've acquired such control over a targeted emotion—sadness—they will risk $10,000 to prove it. Simply having them move their facial muscles in the direction of a smile completely short-circuits their ability to summon the physiology. What's happening here? Why can't they perform on demand?

The answer: *Emotions are so deeply rooted in the physical body that they can't be separated*. Stanislavski was right! As we learned in Chapter 3, emotions are not just in the brain. Every cell in the body carries receptors for the messengers of emotion, and the pathways are bidirectional. The muscles in your face can be used to express current emotions, or they can be used to send signals back to the brain that will substantially change your current emotional state.

> Posture is not solely the manifestation of physical balance. It's also an expression of mental balance. Think about the way you stand when you are depressed or tired: you stand with your shoulders rounded and dropping. Your body represents your emotions by giving up the fight against gravity, sagging just as low as you feel.[6]
>
> David Imrie, MD
> Specialist in Occupational Medicine

Trying to summon sadness with a smile on your face sends conflicting messages that block the targeted physiology from taking hold. The effort is not unlike trying to summon IPS while simultaneously projecting an outward look of nervousness, disappointment, defeat, or fatigue.

To help our workshop audiences gain insight into the exact method of how targeted emotions can be summoned, we always ask the participants who were willing to risk $10,000 to explain how they would do it. Their descriptions are always the same. A two-step process is involved, a process that mirrors precisely what Stanislavski ultimately came to embrace in his work: (1) thinking and imaging, and (2) acting with the physical body.

Step 1. Targeted Thinking and Imaging

The first step, invariably, is to begin focusing on some very sad real-life event that either has happened or potentially could happen. The key is to have a thought or image available that is powerfully loaded with the emotion that is to be summoned (sadness), and then to focus on it like a laser beam. No gut-wrenchingly sad thought and/or image to focus on, no $10,000! And if participants have a thought or image available but are unable to focus on it because of all the pressure, no $10,000. We've had subjects report that, to trigger the targeted emotion, they used images of events that occurred as far back as 50 years. Others ventured several years forward in time to jump-start the physiology. Choosing from anything that did happen (past) to anything that could happen (future) gives quite a range of images to work with.

What do you think would be the outcome if you had the $10,000 at risk and, about a minute into the test, you felt tears start to well up in your eyes, and then thought to yourself, "Yes, I'm going to get the $10,000."

Finished! History! Over! You just choked and lost $10,000. The nonadaptive neurochemical change occurred in fractions of a second. Focusing on thoughts or images that make you happy, even for a split second, can begin to block the physiology of sadness. This is exactly what happens when athletes choke. A free-throw shooter thinks about how the game will be lost if the free throws are missed; a golfer, just before impact of the club head, flashes an image of the ball splashing into the water. A tennis player breaks concentration for a split second with the thought of how great it will be when he or she wins. Corporate athletes are just as vulnerable.

In this first step, cells of the amygdala turn off and on in response to changing thoughts and images. Controlling the physiology of emotion requires precision thinking and imaging.

Step 2. Targeted Acting with the Physical Body

The second thing the "sadness experts" would do is immediately take on the physical look they would have if they actually felt deep sadness and were, in fact, crying.[7] The more the body, particularly the face, conforms to the way they look when tears of sadness are flowing freely, the greater the chance of winning the $10,000.[8]

In this second step, cells of the amygdala also turn off and on in response to changing patterns of muscle movement. Controlling the physiology of emotion also requires precision acting with the physical body.

The fact that acting skills can bring many physiological mechanisms within reach should be quite clear now. Ilene Lang, President and CEO of Alta Vista Software, puts it this way: "I get up early and deliberately put a smile on my face. I know for sure it affects my chemistry. I do it because it genuinely impacts how I feel."

THE CORPORATE ATHLETE'S CHALLENGE: IPS ON DEMAND

Now try this. Ten thousand dollars to you if you can summon the physiology of IPS in two minutes. You donate $10,000 to your favorite charity if you don't succeed! How would you do on this one? Would you be $10,000 richer or poorer? In most performance situations you face, IPS is your script. Any chance you have of getting the $10,000 will depend on essentially two things: (1) how familiar the IPS experience is to you—specifically, how much recent practice you've had bringing it to life; and (2) how disciplined and precise you will be in your thinking and acting during the stressful two-minute test.

CHOKE AND YOU DIE!

So maybe you lost $10,000 or blew a big-time sales deal or fell flat on your face speaking in front of a large audience because you choked. The consequences for failing to control your physiology were clearly painful. But what if the stakes had been life and death? How much more difficult would it be to keep from choking if you knew failure to sustain an IPS response meant death for yourself or someone else? The answer is much more difficult. There are many such arenas in real life. A surgeon pioneering a new, high-risk surgical procedure; a pilot fighting to gain control of her plane in a thunderstorm; a law enforcement officer trying to convince an armed suspect to drop his gun; and a soldier engaged in hand-to-hand combat are just a few examples. Corporate athletes can gain valuable insights into the control of nonempowering emotions by studying such powerful arenas. Gerry Griffin, the Apollo 13 Flight Director, provides a powerful example:

> I was a performer on stage: the cameras rolling all the time; photographers, press conferences, interviews. We operated in a fish bowl. I was on stage for the flight team and the world. I had to project absolute confidence, calmness, and courage. The slightest look of indecisiveness

or fear would immediately hurt the team. I was there to lead. My most important function was to lead my team in confidence and clear thinking. I was like the conductor of an orchestra. I had to know everyone's piece but I didn't play an instrument. My job was to get everyone working together to make music. Making music was solving the problems and getting everyone back home safely.

Exploring how the military prepares soldiers for combat provides penetrating insights into controlling fear. Training soldiers to be fearless, courageous, clear-thinking, and calm under fire is a major component of military training. The emotional transformation that occurs in young recruits during basic training is quite remarkable. The journey from fearful to fearless in the making of a soldier parallels precisely what we have learned in sport science research. Military toughening essentially involves a two-step process: (1) indoctrination in a strict code and (2) exposure to high levels of stress.

Step 1. Indoctrination in a Strict Code of Acting and Behavior Under Stress

As soon as new recruits arrive, they are required to look and act in a highly specific way. No visible sign of weakness or fear of any kind is allowed, no matter what they are really feeling. A major component of basic training for soldiers is disciplined acting. The look of a soldier at attention is the epitome of confidence, control, focus, and positive energy. Literally thousands of years of training soldiers to control choking have affirmed the powerful role physical presence plays in overcoming nonempowering emotions. And remember, this is a life-and-death arena!

Step 2. Exposure to High Levels of Mental, Physical, and Emotional Stress

Drill instructors are trained to deliberately apply doses of stress and then to rigidly enforce precise adherence to military acting and behavioral protocols. No whining, no complaining, no panic, nothing negative. Gradually, the emotionally undisciplined recruits begin responding with fearlessness and precision. If courage in the face of life-and-death stressors can be acquired through disciplined acting, there is little doubt that corporate athletes could use similar strategies to gain control of nonempowering emotional responses in their world. If acting skills can be used by the military to transform wimpy recruits into fearless warriors, they certainly can be used by corporate athletes to help conquer their fears and emotional weaknesses. Here are some remedies for typical stressors:

Stressor	*Precision Thinking and Imaging*
The world has turned against you and all your luck has gone sour.	Sustain powerful breakthrough images throughout the day. Think: *This is temporary. I can hang in there. I can turn this around. Is this great stress or what!*
Fear has a stranglehold.	Sustain powerful images of fun and challenge. Think: *I want to be here. I want to do this. I love the pressure. I love it all.*
Your back is against the wall and it looks as though your entire division may go down.	Sustain an image of anything that stimulates hope, optimism, and positive fight. Think: *Let's face reality and, with passion and conviction, find real answers.*
You feel burned out and negative before the week has even begun, and it takes all your willpower to drag yourself to the office.	Sustain images of effortlessness, of freedom, of gliding through the day. Think: *Today is an important test for me—a test of my toughness. If I can do it here, I can do it anywhere, anytime. I can do this. I will do this.*
You know you're the best qualified candidate for a promotion, but the company doesn't seem to agree.	Sustain an image of quiet confidence and strong self-belief. Think: *I will never surrender. I know my worth and they'll come to see it. I'll keep performing at my best and my worth will be evident.*

Stressor	Precision Behavior
You feel your energy and sizzle waning.	Close your office door and jump up and down on your toes. Start looking energetic and alive. Look on the outside the way you want to feel on the inside.
Everything and everyone seems lined up against you.	Look and act like a brave soldier preparing for a great battle. Act poised, in control, positive, and nondefensive.
Fear has you by the throat in an important situation.	Take a deep breath, slow down, and look calm, relaxed, and fearless on the outside.
The pressure is at a peak and you must perform at your maximum potential.	Signal loud and clear, with your body and your facial expression, that you love being right where you are. Square your shoulders, hold your head high, physically radiate fun and fight, passion and poise—no matter what!

BETWEEN-POINT TIME IN TENNIS

In my work with professional tennis players over many years, I eventually came to realize that the between-point time during a match was really acting. I began to see that what appeared to be unimportant, nonplaying time actually represented a very special opportunity for summoning targeted emotions. Tough, highly successful competitors acted out the IPS script with remarkable precision and consistency between points; poor competitors (those labeled as "head cases") acted out whatever emotions happened to be flowing at the time. I came to understand that top competitors were instinctively using acting skills to reinvigorate themselves and optimally prepare for the next point. For them, acting confident, relaxed, and positive immediately following a disappointing or frustrating point—even for just a few seconds—helped prevent negative emotions from taking hold and undermining their ability to perform.

Former tennis champion Chris Evert was a superb actress and could summon IPS almost at will. Anyone who hopes to be a star in the corporate arena can benefit from studying her career. She dominated women's tennis as only a handful of people ever have, and she did it with fewer natural talents than many of her less successful contemporaries. Compared to her peers, she had neither great foot speed nor genius athletic ability. So how did she come to dominate women's tennis so completely for so many years? She learned a unique response to the same conditions that were destroying her competitors: *she thrived on the conditions of competition.* If a call went against her or she hit a bad shot at a crucial moment, she went about her business in her controlled, cool way, letting nothing ruffle her. As a skilled actress, her every action on the court evidenced remarkable emotional intelligence. She responded to the stresses of competition in ways that brought her talent and skill to life without compromising her personal health or happiness. Chris Evert was always driving the IPS script, and it is important to see just what IPS accomplished for her:

1. She went to the absolute limits of her potential. Chris Evert became the best that she could be.

2. In spite of all the mental, physical, and emotional stress of the tour, she remained remarkably free of sickness and injury.

3. She sustained a love affair with the game of tennis that, to this day, is as intense as it ever was.

We have studied hundreds of hours of footage of Evert's matches. We could stop the videotape anywhere and never find a place where she didn't have a flawless grasp of her Performer Self. Her shoulders were always square, her head was held high, her gaze was steady and fearless. She always showed absolute, supreme confidence, whether she was winning or losing. She never slumped, never muttered angrily, never appeared beaten, never spent futile effort berating the umpire or her opponent. Chris Evert's real genius was her exceptional acting skill. She controlled the way in which the forces of the professional tour impacted her physiology.

And she wasn't born with it! She acquired it just like everyone else who has it. Once you understand that skill, you will find it much easier to master.

IS IT REAL OR FAKED?

As you're walking through the doors of your office building, you suddenly become aware of how grouchy, negative, and tired you feel. And you've got a very important meeting with your sales team in one hour. Your Real Self is a far distance from the IPS target.

Recognizing how important it is for you to change how you feel before your meeting begins, you intentionally engage your performer skills and, within 30 minutes, have completely changed how you feel. Your Real Self is now IPS. But is it real? Are the feelings of energy, calmness, enjoyment, challenge, and confidence real, or are they phony?

The answer depends on what actually happened in your physiology. If by engaging your Performer Skills you truly moved your physiology and chemistry toward IPS, there's nothing phony about it. Your feelings are real.

On the other hand, if you were unable to move your chemistry toward IPS but keep trying to project IPS on the outside during your sales meeting, that's faking it. Your Real Self and Performer Self are still a long way apart. Faking is much better than simply going with whatever non-IPS emotions might be stirring at the time, but you won't genuinely empower yourself or others until your chemistry actually moves to the target. And you can expect the negative feelings you had when you walked into the building to come back after the meeting. Negative feelings often reflect unmet needs, a stress–recovery imbalance, overtraining issues, and so forth. If the negative feelings stemmed from such imbalances and are not tended to, count on it—they'll be back. And if the imbalances become too extreme, as we'll see in later chapters, even world-class acting skills won't be enough to truly move your chemistry in empowering directions. Faking it is the best you can do, but your Real Self will be unmoved.

In Hollywood, on-screen performers who appear to be faking it are simply called bad actors. The emotion portrayed must be perceived as real by the audience. In most cases, that means the actors must be genuinely experiencing the emotions themselves. Bad actors don't last—in Hollywood or in corporate life. In business, success demands that you follow the script and make it real, regardless of how you might feel at the outset. To achieve toughness in business, corporate athletes must work hard every day to perfect world-class acting skills.

AN EXAMPLE FROM MY OWN LIFE

In my work, I travel constantly. Within a single week, I'll be in Belgium, Hawaii, and Sydney, Australia, and the next week may find me in Mexico City, Washington, DC, and Boston. On one occasion, I had given a seminar to a group of corporate leaders in Portland, Oregon, and was flying out on a red-eye to Cincinnati, Ohio. During many years of travel, I've often flown in very bad weather, but it quickly became evident that this was going to be an unusually rough trip. About half an hour after takeoff, just as dinner was being served, the pilot announced that rough weather was ahead and that we should keep our seatbelts on. And then came the words that chilled me. "We're going to get through this," he said. "No problem." In all my years of flying, I had never had to be reassured that we would make it to our destination; it had always been an absolute given of the situation.

Fighting to control a rising tide of apprehension, I fastened my seatbelt, put my head back, closed my eyes, and told myself that everything was going to be fine. Planes almost never crash. It is the safest way to travel. That's why flight insurance costs only pennies. Just get some sleep and the whole thing will blow over. Then, suddenly, we hit a magnitude of turbulence like nothing I had ever experienced before; it was awesome in its violence. It seemed as though the plane suddenly dropped hundreds of feet like a stone, nearly flipped over on its back, and then righted itself. I had been in pretty wild turbulence in my life, but nothing that remotely compared to this. I could hear the plane give out metallic groans, and I wondered how long it could withstand this kind of force.

By now, everyone on the plane was screaming—even the flight attendants. The plane was flipping, dropping, rolling, and rising like some new and vicious amusement-park ride. Boxes and suitcases were falling out of the overhead bins. Drinks and food were spilling everywhere. It was chaos. People were throwing up into paper bags and all over themselves. The smell of vomit soon permeated the cabin. The pilot came on again, and fear could be heard in his voice. He said that this new weather pattern had taken ground control completely by surprise, and all he could do was fly us through it.

The buffeting was simply brutal. We had been in the turbulence not more than five minutes, but it seemed like hours. The woman next to me was wailing and leaning toward me as though I might afford some protection; the people behind me were sobbing; the panic was almost tangible. Someone was chanting the Lord's Prayer. I was petrified.

I sat back, closed my eyes, and tried to think things through. I knew I was terrified and my body was in a state close to panic. I affirmed that, and then I thought to myself:

Wait a minute. Is this an intelligent response—this all-consuming fear? Is this going to help me if the plane crashes? If there is any chance at all of escaping, am I going to be able to get to the exit faster when I'm carrying this heavy weight of anxiety? *Is this response serving my purpose?* All it means is that I'm going to die miserable and unhappy. Then I told myself that it wasn't the turbulence that was causing my physiology to self-destruct, *it was my body's response to the turbulence.*

I told myself I had to change it right then. I rested my head against the back of my seat, closed my eyes, and intentionally moved the muscles of my face in the direction of a smile. I knew that to turn the fear cells off in the amygdala, I would have to use a powerful image. I tried success images, power images, sexual images; suddenly, out of nowhere, came an image that I had not thought of since I was a young boy. I was born and raised in a suburb of Denver called Wheatridge. During the summer months, my buddies and I would ride our bikes to a nearby amusement park called Elitches. My absolutely favorite ride was the bumper cars. We would get behind the wheel of a car and go nuts bumping anybody and everybody who got in our way. I suddenly saw myself laughing and having the time of my life as I sideswiped and collided with other cars. I could even hear the carousel music. The screaming on the plane became the screaming of people having fun. Within seconds, my entire physiology changed. The fear cells turned off. The amygdala was completely fooled into believing that I was actually riding the bumper cars at Elitches—not being transported on a plane that was struggling to remain airborne.

I was told later that the plane was caught in the wild eye of that turbulence for over 40 minutes. I had no sense that so much time had passed; I knew that the plane was in a great fight and might not make it; I knew there was a real chance of being hurt; I even was aware that we were about to land and that the airstrip was engulfed in high winds all the way to touchdown. But I remained deep inside my images. I was having a wonderful time in the Denver summer of my youth. After touchdown, I opened my eyes and almost wanted to say, "Was that a great flight or what!" I'm sure the people around me must have thought I had gone completely mad when they looked over and saw the big smile on my face during the flight.

A number of passengers had to be carried off the plane. As I walked by the pilot, I noticed that he looked sick. His skin had a kind of jaundiced pallor, he was glistening with sweat, and his shirt was open to his belt. I heard him tell one of the flight attendants that it was the worst turbulence he had experienced in his 23 years of flying. I hung around, watching people disembark. Most of them looked as though they had been through a war.

I could tell, from the shocked state they were in, that many would have a hard time recovering from the flight, and that the adjustment process would be slow. Some would never fly again. I knew that if I asked any of those people why they felt the way they did, they would look at me as though I was crazy. "It's the turbulence, stupid," they would answer, as though it were the most obvious thing in the world. But the turbulence did *not* cause their distress. I was in the turbulence too, and it didn't defeat me. What happened to them was independent of the turbulence; it was a physiological state they allowed themselves to be trapped in. They didn't have to be trapped that way. I was saved enormous grief and anguish. If the plane had crashed, we would have all died. Their grief and anguish would neither have saved them nor killed them. They had allowed a negative state to invade inside themselves. I refused to go through all that needless misery; it wasn't necessary *and it wouldn't have protected me from anything*.

CONCLUSION

In the context of Toughness Training, acting means intentionally moving feelings and physiology in targeted directions. Good actors are those who can follow their script and make their emotions real, not phony. Acting involves a two-step process: (1) precision thinking and imaging and (2) precision behavior (emotion-specific gestures and posturing of the physical body).

Daily Training Log	Mon	Tue	Wed	Thu	Fri	Sat	Sun
1. Theme 1:							
2. Theme 2:							
3 Theme 3:							
4. Theme 4:							
IPS Acting Skills							
1. Disciplined Thinking							
2. Disciplined Acting							

"It's About Being Right Upstairs"

Getting a "Head" Start on Your Day

> **Whether I finish** first or tenth in the Atlanta Olympics, I want to be able to walk off the track saying that I was the toughest bastard out there. I was definitely more prepared mentally than anyone else.

These are the words of Bob Kennedy, one of the best 5,000-meter runners in the world. According to his coach, Sam Bell, "He's not the most physically talented, but he's definitely the toughest in the head I've ever coached."[1]

What does it mean to be the toughest in the head? And why does Bob Kennedy have it and not somebody else? What forged this capacity? How does it happen? Can almost everyone get there? For over two decades, questions like these have bounced around inside my head. Here are my answers as they have evolved over time.

Toughness of the mind and toughness of the body are part of the same continuum and share many of the same markers. Adaptations in the ability to exert and resist force, and in

CHAPTER 6

flexibility, responsiveness, and resiliency form the basis of toughness in both arenas. And, like others who have it, Bob Kennedy has it because he acquired it. Those who don't have it, whether Olympic or corporate athletes, simply haven't acquired the underlying mechanisms. What Bob has is neither a gift nor a genetically coded factor. Like physical toughness, mental toughness reflects a deep capacity for tolerating stress and is rooted in complex biochemical and physiological adaptations. This mental capacity is forged in the same way physical capacity is forged—by exposure to the forces of energy expenditure and energy recovery. Muscles become stronger when they are challenged by energy expenditure and then allowed to recover and heal. The strongest persons, physically, have typically been exposed to the most activity, physically. Mental toughening adaptations follow the same principles. Mental strength, like physical strength, is a consequence of targeted energy expenditure. Physical toughness involves biochemical and structural changes that are concentrated primarily *in the muscles and in the heart and lungs*. Mental toughness involves adaptations and structural changes that are concentrated primarily *in the brain and central nervous system*. And both connect on the common turf of *emotions*. Feelings of strength, confidence, energy, spirit, fight, control, and determination reflect toughness both physically and mentally. As mentioned in Chapter 3, emotion represents the connecting link between mind and body. Ultimately, all toughness is emotional. Every cell in the body is affected by toughening adaptations. Toughness is of the heart, of the lungs, of muscles, of how and what you think, of the images you hold and, ultimately, how you *feel*.

This mental toughness synopsis is important here because we are now going to zero in on the area of mental training, particularly the importance of mental preparation in the toughening process.

MENTAL TRAINING

Mental training leads to mental toughness, which in turn leads to increased feelings of personal control, confidence, strength, and positive energy in high-stress arenas. Mental training is simply targeted thinking and imaging (energy expenditure) that lead to the desired neurological adaptations. In a real sense, mental training "rewires" the brain. Some neurological connections are strengthened, others are replaced with completely new ones, and still others are simply reconditioned. But make no mistake—mental training changes brain structure.

Most corporate athletes are shocked when they learn that every thought or image they entertain creates a measurable neurological impulse and has both short-term and long-term consequences. Novel thoughts and images can literally stimulate new pathways in the brain (called dendritic growth). Thoughts and images that are constantly repeated become stronger, become more readily available, and have the greatest impact on behavior. For example, constantly thinking "I hate that jerk of a boss," or repeatedly thinking about all the things the boss does that are unfair to you, strengthens those neurological connections. The thoughts and images you repeat about your boss eventually become a strong belief system that powerfully affects your mood, your behavior, and your ability to perform on the job. In a real sense, you are unknowingly using mental training principles to strengthen the response of hating your boss. You are expending mental energy and modifying brain structure so that a specific emotional response will occur. If hating your boss is your objective, your mental training is perfect. But if you're trying to achieve an Ideal Performance State (IPS) and hope to enjoy your work, your pattern of expending mental energy will have potentially catastrophic effects.

Tremendous neurological advances are currently being made by researchers through the use of a new generation of brain scanners—positron emission tomography (PET), computed tomography (CT), and magnetic resonance imaging (MRI).[2] It is now possible to detect a single neuron firing in the brain and to pinpoint its location. As an example of such research, subjects were asked to move each of four designated fingers in a prescribed pattern while brain scans tracked the precise patterns and areas of neurological activity. Subjects were then asked to *visualize* moving their fingers in the same pattern without making any conscious movement; in other words, they mentally practiced the motor sequence. Brain scans revealed that when subjects visualized the finger pattern, the neurological circuits that were activated were similar to those observed when subjects practiced the sequence physically. Researchers have known for years that physical practice of motor skills, when combined with mental practice, is far superior to physical practice alone.[3] Now, researchers can explain why and how. They can graphically record how various forms of mental training help to wire and rewire neurological circuits.

MENTAL TRAINING FOR CORPORATE ATHLETES

I sometimes refer to mental training as inside-out training. It starts inside the brain and moves outward to the body. Physical training starts with the muscles and moves inward to the brain. This section lists what I have found to be the most useful and effective mental training strategies for accelerating the toughening process. Remember, mental training consists of targeted energy expenditure that modifies or stimulates neurological adaptations. Here are the seven best approaches for corporate athletes:

1. Changing beliefs through affirmations.
2. Controlling negative thinking.
3. Desensitizing fears.
4. Writing.
5. Preparing with mental rehearsal.
6. Practicing mental focus.
7. Practicing positive thinking.

1. Changing Beliefs Through Affirmations

Dan Jansen didn't believe he would ever triumph as an Olympian in the 1,000-meter event.[4] He had a laundry list of reasons why it could never happen. He had the mentality of a sprinter, not a distance skater; he possessed too much fast-twitch muscle fiber; he was lacking in both physical and mental endurance; and on and on. According to Dan, the only reason he competed in the 1,000-meter event was for training purposes. Competing in the 500-meter race was fun and exhilarating; competing in the 1,000-meter race was entirely different. He publicly stated that he really didn't enjoy "the 1,000." I was convinced that Dan's beliefs about the 1,000 blocked him from uncovering his genius. For six months preceding the Lillehammer Olympics, Dan wrote "I love the 1,000, I love the 1,000" across the top of his daily training log. Each day, he

I LOVE THE 1,000

Daily (Diary)	World Cup–Hamar, Norway
Thoughts	1st **500**–35-92!! I did it! 1st person
	ever under 36! 1st place
	2nd **500**–35-96 Did it again! with
	a last inner turn! Even with 1 slip!
	Remember this feeling!
	1000–1:13-01 1st place
	Very good race, Great weekend
	Keep it up!

Daily Training Log
for Dan Jansen

Physical Stress (Training)	1 Low	2	3	4	⑤	6	7	8	9	10 High
Emotional Stress (Training)	1 Low	2	3	4	⑤	6	7	8	9	10 High
Emotional Stress (Life)	1 Low	②	3	4	5	6	7	8	9	10 High
Overall Stress	1 Low	2	③	4	5	6	7	8	9	10 High
	1 Low	2	3	4	5	6	7	⑧	9	10 High

A Page from Dan Jansen's Training Log

expended energy thinking and writing in ways that were completely the opposite of how he actually felt. As silly as it sounded to Dan, I knew that repetition of the simple affirmation would eventually alter his emotional response. Roughly three months later, Dan peevishly remarked that he didn't know how it was happening but he was actually starting to like the 1,000-meter race. And six weeks before Lillehammer, he made the statement, "It's really strange but I think I like the 1,000-meter race as much as the 500."

How ironic that Dan went on to win his gold medal and break a world record in an event he didn't believe he was suited for and didn't enjoy. Only two years earlier, at Albertville, he came in 26th in the same Olympic event. Now he was the best in the world. That's the power of belief! The repetitive self-talk created neurological impulses that modified his brain structure, his belief system, and, eventually, his emotional response. In a real sense, Dan was actively rewiring his circuitry.

As I have done with hundreds of clients over the years, I'll now help you to take your first step. To get started, you must identify any of your current beliefs that are blocking your path. Here are some examples:

I hate giving (speeches) _____

I hate doing (budgets) _____

I'll never get comfortable with (computers) _____

I hate my (boss) _____

I cannot work with (person) _____

I hate (traffic) _____

I'm not smart enough to _____

I'll never make it to _____

Things never work out to _____

I always get the short end of the stick when _____

The second step is to reverse your thinking process. From "I hate giving speeches" to "I want to give speeches"; from "I fear speaking in front of groups" to "Speaking in front of groups is great fun for me." The more often you repeat the words and the more you repeat the words with feeling, the greater the neurological impact.

Get-You-Moving Sayings

If you're not in front of the pack, the scenery never changes.

If you're not making dust, you're eating dust.

Think of this premeditated self-talk as positive brainwashing. It's precisely how most of your current beliefs were formed. How many times did your mother tell you to wash your hands before eating? Eventually, a strong hand-washing belief was formed, and now you don't *feel* right if you don't wash before eating. You may even find yourself repeating it over and over to your children. Religious doctrine, personal ethics and values, and beliefs about family, work, and so on are often formed in this same way.

> **Affirmations for Golfers Who Hate Putting**
>
> As you approach the green, put a smile on your face and start saying to yourself, "Yes! I get to putt again! I love to putt. Get me the putter. I'm a putting genius!" And if you miss the putt, say, "Yes! Another opportunity to putt again. I love putting."

2. Controlling Negative Thinking

Once you realize that, over time, negative thinking can modify brain structure, you're not as likely to accept it in your life. Because everything from mood state to belief systems and from productivity levels to personal happiness can be adversely affected by habitual negative thinking, it's important for corporate athletes to find ways to control it. The forces of life and business can beat you up to the point where negativity seems perfectly natural and normal. The following three-step mental training sequence has proven effective in controlling the occurrence of negative thinking:

Step 1. Increase personal awareness to the point that, as soon as your thinking turns negative and nonproductive, an alarm goes off inside your head.

Step 2. Say "Stop," either silently or aloud, the moment you become aware of your negativity. Saying "Stop" invariably gives you a brief window of opportunity, and you can break the negative pattern.

Step 3. Immediately replace any negative thoughts with realistic positive ones. Rephrase a negative thought or completely replace it with something new.

Most corporate performers are quite surprised to learn that they can exercise considerable control and direction of their thoughts with this simple three-step procedure.

3. Desensitizing Fears

Consider the following scenarios and evaluate whether any of these situations are at least partially relevant to you:

- Just thinking about speaking publicly in front of her peers made Suzanne break into a nervous sweat. The origin of the fear was unknown; she had never experienced any particularly memorable failures in front of groups. Her refusal to make presentations and speak in front of groups was clearly a stumbling block to her career advancement.

- Darrel failed his CPA exam for the second time. On both tries, he experienced such intense levels of anxiety that he was unable to think clearly or recall past learning. His problem was not failure to know the material but failure to retrieve it under nearly blinding exam pressure.

- Tom's fear of flying suddenly became a nightmarish problem when he was promoted to district sales manager. The opportunities, the recognition, and the money were great but one week out of every month he would have to fly constantly. Turning down the promotion would be a career catastrophe.

One of the most valuable applications of mental training is in the prevention and control of choking—failing to perform because of interfering and troublesome emotional responses; the emotional culprit is invariably fear. Examples of choking in sport are legion. Greg Norman's collapse in the final round of the 1996 Masters Championship, and Todd Martin's failure to win his semifinal Wimbledon match, when he had a 5–1 lead in the fifth set and was serving, are representative. Desensitization can be an effective tool for controlling and reconditioning nonadaptive fear responses.

Here is the procedure:

Step 1. Achieve a deep state of mental and physical relaxation. Use music, meditation, deep breathing, or any other relaxation technique that works for you. One of the most basic techniques is called progressive relaxation. It involves successively tensing and relaxing each of the major muscle groups of your body, beginning with your head and neck and ending with your feet.

Step 2. When you have become deeply relaxed, begin to create nonthreatening images that are associated with the troublesome response. Picture an airplane off in the distance, a brief glimpse of your CPA exam room, a snapshot of you talking to a few friends. If you start to feel any tightness or fear, simply return to your relaxation. When relaxation is again achieved, begin to introduce the problematic images again. Over time, a reconditioning process occurs. Eventually, you will be able to visualize yourself feeling relaxed and calm in the traumatic situation. A typical desensitizing session lasts 15 to 20 minutes, and 20 to 30 practice sessions are required.

4. Writing

Writing releases negative emotions and creates new scripts. One of the most powerful forms of mental training for many people is writing. In a classic study conducted by James Pennebaker and Janice and Ronald Glaser, subjects who wrote about traumatic events for 20 minutes a day, during 4 consecutive days, had significantly more robust immune systems and reported far less distress than subjects who did no writing.[5] Writing about one's conflicts also resulted in less illness and fewer visits to the doctor.

Daily Journal

Thoughts	Impact
I hate snow!	I was angry and upset during drive to work
The deadline pressure is exciting	I was pumped during the recent production deadline

Negative Thoughts	Positive Thinking Rewrite
I'm not up for this discussion	I have studied the issue and I'm ready

Mood	Cause of Mood	Positive Rewrite
Frustrated	Too many meetings didn't get anything done	Made great progress in understanding and controlling my moods

A Sample Rewriting Exercise

Writing is cathartic and can eventually lead to lower physiological arousal levels. The actual writing itself may be somewhat painful and uncomfortable, but the long-term results will invariably be less distress and improved health.

One of my favorite exercises for corporate athletes is to have them write down their negative thoughts as they occur throughout the day, at the moment they become aware of them. After 4 days, the most frequent and most disruptive thoughts are targeted for mental training. Here is a former client's partial list of negative thoughts he selected to write about:

> I'm the first one here and the last one to leave, and nobody appreciates it.
>
> I'll be stuck in this stupid department forever.
>
> There is no leadership here. They have no clue what they're doing.
>
> I hate this place. The best thing that could happen to me is that I would be downsized right out.
>
> I really blew it. I was the center of things and let it all get away from me.

A sampling of his rewrite went like this:

> It's unimportant whether people appreciate my long hours. I'm doing it because I choose to, not because I have to or because I want to be appreciated. It simply confirms to me that I'm committed and will do whatever it takes to get the job done right. I'm proud of what I've done here and the quality of my work will eventually be recognized. I'm in this department because that's my choice. If I want to leave, I can. Because of my skills, I will always find challenging work. This company suffers from a lack of strong leadership. I am part of that leadership and I can do a better job of holding up my end. I need to communicate better and be more enthusiastic with my people. I don't really hate this place. I hate all the confusion, back stabbing, and politics, but I really love my work. I will not let these tough times destroy my attitude. If the company downsizes even more and I get released, I'll be OK. It's not what I really want, but if it happens, it happens. I'll handle it and so will Betty [his wife]. I've made some political mistakes that were very costly but I've learned a valuable lesson. It won't happen again.

What is really being created here is a new, more effective script for keeping the positive juices flowing. Once completed, it is to be read on a daily basis—*with emotion*—before the start of the day. The results can be very powerful.

5. *Preparing with Mental Rehearsal*

In Chapter 4, we learned that the cells of the amygdala can be turned on or off by conjuring up various images in the mind. Once activated, the amygdala floods the neurocircuits with electrochemical impulses the produce emotion. The brain uses the same pathways to *trigger* an emotion as it does to *respond* to one. The more pathways that are utilized, the more powerful and available they become. In keeping with this, one of the most important forms of mental training is that of mental and emotional rehearsal.

Just as visualizing moving your fingers in a specific sequence strengthens the neuromotor circuits that are involved in real physical practice, visualizing how you want to respond mentally and emotionally to the day's events at the office strengthens the probability of those responses' occurrence. Seeing images of yourself staying calm and relaxed under fire, previewing the speech you are to make at tomorrow's meeting, and visualizing a successful sale to your toughest customer are truly dress rehearsals and can impact neurophysiology. The more options the amygdala has to choose from, and the more those options are reinforced with mental and emotional practice, the greater is the likelihood that your response will be adaptive and appropriate. When you're surprised, the amygdala is likely to short-circuit the thinking brain (neocortex) and react instinctively and spontaneously. The chance that you will respond adaptively to unfamiliar and unrehearsed stressors is significantly reduced. On the other hand, the more you have rehearsed positive behaviors, emotions, and outcomes, the more likely those pathways will be activated.

Also, the more your rehearsal involves your senses (visual, kinesthetic, and auditory) and the more you can stimulate real emotion, the more likely your rehearsal will lead to positive outcomes in reality.[6]

Gerry Griffin, the Apollo 13 Flight Director, said,

> The most important factor in my ability to successfully manage the
> Apollo 13 catastrophe was preparation. We were constantly rehearsing
> catastrophic failure. We built layers of options. One of our mission
> rules was: *No surprises!* Failure was simply not an option. I never once
> considered we might not get them back. Our motto was "Shining Ex-
> ample of Perfection." We rehearsed finding answers to impossible sit-
> uations so many times before, we absolutely believed we could solve
> the Apollo 13 crisis. We just knew we could. Without the preparation,
> however, we had no chance. Preparation is knowing what to do and
> rehearsing it over and over.

6. Practicing Mental Focus

Performing well in anything requires a calm mind and a clear
focus. Both calmness and focus reflect specific patterns of neurological arousal. Anything that strengthens the capacity for calmness and focus could be considered a form of mental training.
Various kinds of meditation are examples. Most forms of meditation involve relaxation of the muscles, calmness of the mind, and
precise concentration. The mental and physical effects of meditation are generally achieved by turning one's attention to the present moment. Performing well in almost any task also requires a
predominantly present focus. In a real sense, meditation is "present focus" practice. Learning how to become completely absorbed
in the present moment is life-changing for many people. Distress
simply vanishes.

A common meditation technique is the repetition of a particular
word, called a mantra, in coordination with exhalation. The word
one is often used. Others include focusing on the process of breathing, for example, by counting one's breaths from 1 to 10 and then
starting over. The goal is a "here-and-now" focus that becomes completely absorbing. When you become aware that your mind is wan-
dering, you gently return it to the present focus.

The same results can be achieved when you focus your attention
on walking as you walk, or when you become completely absorbed
in eating as you eat, or when you step outside your office and become totally engrossed by the beauty of a tree or a passing cloud.

Learning to direct one's attention to the present moment is also fundamental to IPS control. Meditators refer to this state of present focus as "mindfulness." The opposite is "mindlessness," which essentially means one's attention is completely lost in the past or future and there is virtually no awareness of the present. Stephen Rechtschaffen, founder of the Omega Institute for Holistic Studies, in Rhinebeck, New York, put it this way:

> Mindfulness is about embracing all of our life, every moment, the 89 percent that's mundane along with the extraordinary remainder. The answer is that, each time we push away the present moment and resist being aware, we cease to be alive.[7]

Virtually any focusing activity that redirects our attention away from past or future toward the present moment has potential mental training value. Long-time meditators insist that the present moment is the fundamental pathway to spirituality, lasting peace and harmony, and personal enlightenment (see Appendix D for meditation resources).

7. Practicing Positive Thinking

High-achieving corporate athletes fully understand that a positive and optimistic view of things is essential to continued success, but it can never distort the real truth about what's happening. If it does, you end up playing in a fantasy world. As Shane Murphy put it, in his book *The Achievement Zone,* "One of the greatest myths of our time is that we can achieve greatness simply via the power of positive thinking."[8] It's clear from my work in corporate America over the past ten years that successful achievers invariably possess the ability to *think critically* without becoming *negative.* They're able to see the naked truth and critically analyze a situation, but they do so within a positive context. That's the essence of what I mean by the notion of productive positive thinking.

Richard Davidson's research on the neurophysiology of positive and negative emotions is very relevant here. In 1992, he discovered that positive and negative emotions originate in different areas of the brain.[9] The left prefrontal lobe is more involved in positive emotions, and the right prefrontal lobe is more involved with negative emotions. Davidson found that activation of the left prefrontal lobe was associated with euphoria, happiness, and positive mood. Activation of the right prefrontal lobe was associated with depression, disgust, and negative mood. Right and left hemispheres of the brain can be selectively anesthetized by injecting sodium amobarbital into the left or right carotid artery. Positive emotionality—laughter and elation—occurs from right-hemisphere anesthesia, and negative emotionality—crying and anger—occurs from left hemisphere anesthesia. The discovery that increases in positive emotionality occurred spontaneously when negativity was inhibited was important. The notion that inhibiting negative thinking and behavior will automatically increase positivity has real practical value. Most would agree that this conclusion is entirely consistent with human experience. Equally important was the finding that hemispheric specialization regarding emotion begins very early in life. Evidence of specialization has been found in infants as young as 10 months.

Hemispheric specialization of positive and negative emotions helps explain why habits of positive and negative thinking can have such profound effects in people's lives. Negative thoughts stimulate right prefrontal lobe activation. The more you excite the right side, the more negative, disgusted, pessimistic, and depressed you become. Positive thinking stirs a completely different neurological pot so to speak. Stir the left prefrontal lobe by placing a positive valence on whatever happens (positive thinking), and positive emotions keep rolling out—even during challenging and difficult

> I learned to focus on solutions, not problems. It's one of the most important factors in my leadership. Everyone is seeing problems everywhere. I'm 100 percent focused on solutions. Problems are negative and solutions are positive. Growing Prince requires solutions. I want solution-minded people leading the way.
>
> Charles L. Peifer
> President and CEO, Prince Sports Group

times. This may well be what's happening when you have the powerfully positive experience of "getting on a roll." It may simply be intense activation of the left prefrontal lobe as opposed to the right. Excessive stimulation of the right side has exactly the opposite effect. And that's what negative thinking does—it stirs the negative pot. But again, the critical component to being productively positive is the ability to clearly confront the negative within a positive and optimistic framework.

The words of National Hockey League superstar goalie Mike Richter make total sense, given this neurological understanding:

> The 1995–1996 season started out great for me, but it didn't last long. I was taken out with one of the worst injuries I have ever had. I never knew a groin pull could be so painful and serious. The whole inside of my leg turned black and blue for weeks. The doctors felt there was a good chance I would be out for the entire season, but I was bound and determined to be back before the playoffs. I was actually playing again in six weeks. For sure the difference was my attitude. I called it proactive positive. No matter what the doctors would say, no matter how much pain I was in, I put a positive spin on everything. In a way, I became obsessively positive. Whenever anyone asked me about my injury, I'd always say something optimistic and hopeful. It was a full-time job staying on the positive track. I even spent a lot of time writing positive stuff to keep the momentum going. I can honestly say I never got negative about the whole thing. It was like I was still performing on the ice. I know my emotional state had an incredible impact. The doctors were shocked at how fast I was healing and rehabilitating. If I had gotten depressed and negative about the whole thing, I'm sure I wouldn't have played the rest of the season. And normally, if I had been out for six weeks, it would have taken quite a long time to get my confidence and timing back to play well. My first game back I was shaky, but, by only the second game, I played tremendously. Everyone—except me—was shocked. The rest of the year was super. I think my stats this season were the best since I turned pro.

Another good example is the Atlanta Braves' Cy Young Award right-hander, pitcher John Smoltz. After pitching the longest winning streak in major league history (13 in a row), he explained how it happened:

> My success this season doesn't lie in what kind of pitches I'm throwing, whether or not I'm getting ahead in the count. It's not

about fastballs or sliders. It's about being right upstairs. I don't let people or things bother me the way they used to. I have a deeper understanding and faith. I'm more positive and happy with myself.[10]

A former client, who is CEO of a Fortune 100 manufacturing company, came to us to get physically fitter. He explained:

> I'm here for physical toughness. The mental side I acquired over many years. The first 35 years of my life, I wasn't mentally tough. I finally got it, and it continues to be my single greatest asset. It's hard to describe what it is but it is somehow learning to use my brain differently. Gradually, I learned to control more and more of my negativism. It's like I have a light and a dark side . . . . Positive thinking is part of it but it's much more than that. The way I feel about things is the difference. I can see the real world, with all the negatives, but I don't become negative. My emotional state remains constructive and positive. I've learned to keep the dark side quiet. It sounds a little ridiculous when I try to talk about it, but I really believe it's the most important part of my leadership.

> What Olympic-caliber athletes do that most of us don't is learn what they need to from a bad experience, then dump it.
> Bob Rotella, PhD
> Sport psychologist

THE CORPORATE ATHLETE'S DAILY PREPARATION PLAN

Of all the mental training strategies I've used over the years, one of the most valuable and effective is that of *daily mental preparation*. It requires no more than ten minutes each day, and it incorporates several important elements of the mental training strategies previously discussed in this chapter. Our experience over the years has repeatedly shown that this simple daily mental training routine is both powerful and effective for enhancing performance and productivity. This section tells you how it works.

Set Aside a Minimum of Ten Minutes Daily

Your mental preparation time should become a daily ritual, like brushing your teeth or having breakfast. It should also be completed in the early morning, before your day becomes officially launched. Whenever possible, complete the training sequence at the same time every day and give it a HIGH PRIORITY.

Quiet and Alone

To maximize the positive benefits, find a reasonably quiet environment where you can be alone and are not likely to be disturbed by phones, family, or TV. You can play carefully selected background music to enhance the effects of the training. Music from the soundtracks of movies tends to work best because it is specifically composed to move audiences in targeted directions called for in the director's script. Music without lyrics is also preferred; it has proven to be less distracting. If you elect to use music, it should first help to relax you and should then gradually begin to ignite feelings of inspiration, confidence, high positive energy, and hope. Some of the most popular recently released soundtracks for this purpose are *The Last of the Mohicans, Crimson Tide, Dances with Wolves, Forrest Gump,* and *Lonesome Dove.*

Either Moving or Sitting

Your preparation ritual can be completed while you are either moving or sitting. Best results are usually obtained while sitting, but some corporate athletes prefer to complete the sequence while walking. Some prefer to do the mental preparation on their subway or train commute. Even though they are not alone, they can achieve a relatively deep state of concentration without disruption by closing their eyes.

Shift to a Present Focus

Your first mental goal is to shift to a moment-to-moment present focus. You can focus on your breathing as you breathe, your walking as you walk, or your thoughts and feelings today as they come and go. The goal is a merging of action and awareness that effortlessly leads to a highly distinctive state of inner calm and quiet. The more you practice this shifting of attention to the present, the easier and faster the positive effects are achieved. Eventually, in only two to three minutes, a peaceful sense of calm and quiet will prevail.

Fully Connect with the Importance of Today's Battle

When calmness has been achieved with your present-centered focus, answer this simple question: Why is it important to fight today? Try to connect today's challenges with your deepest values and beliefs. Why should you follow the Mentally Tough program on this day? What's really at stake here? Why try to improve your IPS control, show more emotional intelligence, or confront your weakness today? One thing is certain. If you can't come up with a reason that really connects with you emotionally, you won't meet any of your challenges. Without compelling emotion behind you, you won't exercise, won't eat right, and won't continue to search for new ways to deal with your nightmare CEO. Why? Because you don't feel like it. When the going gets tough, and it will, your fighting spirit will simply evaporate.

Connecting today's battle with your deepest values and beliefs changes the odds dramatically. Where there is meaning, you'll find passion and force. The problem is, we don't let the importance of today's struggle really sink in. So what if I drink too much or surrender my spirit today? What's the big deal?

Remember Captain Tom's fight to endure the horror of the apartment blast? Not until he connected, in a deeply compelling way, with why he was there was he able to find the strength to go forward. The terry-cloth bunny anchored the meaning. Merely the thought of that child's furry friend reignited his resolve and courage. We can endure almost anything as long as we can attribute some important meaning to our struggle. Something as simple as placing a picture of your loved ones on your office desk can help anchor the meaning behind your struggle.

A concentration camp survivor, Victor Frankl, believes his ability to endure the greatest horror and torture imaginable was a function of one thing—his ability to attribute meaning to his pain and suffering. Essentially, two things drove him to survive. He intensely wanted to see his loved ones again, and he wanted to tell the world what happened at the camp. Reflecting on the pain and suffering that he and others endured, Frankl concluded that the single most important thing in life is the search for meaning. Unquestionably, where there is meaning, there is also great strength.

Rob Knapp, First Vice President and Mid-West District Director for Merrill Lynch, put it this way:

> Going against my basic beliefs and values translates into great distress for me. When I follow my sacred principles, the stress is much more manageable and I'm more at peace with myself.
>
> One of my most important credos goes like this:
>
> > Do what's right.
> > Treat others like you want to be treated.
> > Do your very best.
> > Do what you say.

Create Your Vision of the Future

What vision do you have of yourself for the future? Where are you heading personally and professionally? For just a few minutes each day, affirm your commitment to reach beyond your current limits by creating an image of what you want to become and of the goals you want to attain in your life during the next few years. See your personal and professional goals take form.

Several months before Dan Jansen's last drive for Olympic glory at Lillehammer, I asked him to write 35.99 at the top of his training log and to visualize daily breaking the 36-second barrier. He wanted to achieve that distinction almost as much as he coveted the Olympic medal. But Dan was reluctant to fully embrace his sub-36-second dream because, first, no human being had ever achieved it, and, more importantly, he had failed as an Olympian in two previous Winter Games. "What if I fail again?" he asked me. "I can't set another goal and fail again." My response to Dan was that if he didn't make a conscious commitment to achieve a goal, he wouldn't have a chance of securing his place in history as the first speed skater to break the 36-second barrier for the 500-meter event. He had to consciously get every cell in his body to embrace it. He had to see it happen, feel it happen—he had to taste it.

Dan took the risk and did exactly that. Every day, he saw the impossible happen. His dreams of being an Olympic gold medal holder and of breaking the 36-second barrier became part of his daily preparation.

In the last two months before his final day as an Olympian, Dan broke the 36-second barrier three times, twice at exactly 35.99 and once at a remarkable 35.76!

Every day that Dan saw himself break the barrier, he created a neurological impulse that deepened his expectancy for success. By expending mental energy in a targeted direction, he literally altered the architecture of his own brain. As we've already learned, neurons cannot distinguish between something vividly imagined and something real. They are *both* real from a neurological perspective.

Take the risk and create images of your own personal breakthroughs. For just a few minutes each day, bring to life your vision of the kind of person you want to become and what you hope to achieve. See it. Feel it. Taste it.

Confront the Truth

The next item on your mental preparation agenda is to openly and honestly confront the weaknesses you are targeting for change. Facing the truth about your insecurities, fears, defensiveness, negativism, or lack of discipline anchors you to the real world and sets the record straight: "Here's the truth about where I am. No fluff. No smoke. No hiding." Then immediately contrast where you are now with where you want to be—the vision you have for yourself in the future.

Confronting your weaknesses is not negative. It is simply an acknowledgment that work must be done and energy must be expended if the vision you have for yourself is to truly take form and become real.

Convert Weaknesses into Strengths with Affirmations

After you've confronted your most important deficiencies, it's time to consciously repeat affirmations that positively address those deficiencies. If the problem is defensiveness and extreme self-criticism, your affirmations could be, "I am open and accepting." If the problem is fear and insecurity, your affirmation could be, "I feel safe and secure." If the problem is anger and frustration with a coworker, your affirmation could be, "I'll remain calm and positive with John." Remember, you are deliberately expending mental energy to build new response capacities in targeted areas. You are reconstructing new belief systems that eventually will lead to more adaptive emotional responses.

As you might expect, the more emotion you can summon with your affirmations, the more accelerated is the adaptation process. Even so, the change process does take time. Genuine emotional changes start to take form after 20 to 30 days of practice.

Rob Knapp starts his day with the same affirmation: "Today I want to go where no man has gone before!" Rob explained his affirmation this way:

> I always had to push harder than everyone else. I didn't have the talent. I was the worker. I had to be. As I look back, having to work so hard to get what I wanted was the best thing that ever happened to me . . . . Every time I say my daily affirmation, it triggers a memory of a special time when I was a kid. Every so often, I'd wait until I was all alone, and I would climb the tallest tree in our neighborhood. I would go all the way to the top, bend the top of the tree over and touch the very tip of the tree with my finger. I'd get a huge rush and then climb down. I loved it. When I say I want to go where no man has gone before, it gets the juices flowing again, just like touching the top of that tree did.

Rehearse with Images

The last step in your mental preparation plan is to simply visualize how you want your day to go. Particularly important are mental and emotional rehearsals of any scheduled performances you are to give on that particular day. Do a practice run-through, anticipate potential trouble spots, and see yourself responding with precision and poise. One of your objectives with this final step is to eliminate surprises. Anticipate the traffic—tough questions from your audience, or your staff's troubled reaction to the directive dealing with reorganization. Confront the problem and emotionally solve it as though it were happening right then and there. Remember, cells in your amygdala can't distinguish something vividly imagined from something actually happening. Recruit as many senses as possible to vivify and enhance the power of your images.

Once they become familiar with the mental preparation sequence, most of our clients report that only 7 to 10 minutes are required to complete all the steps and achieve positive results. Without question, this is one of the most powerful tools we have discovered for accelerating the toughening process.

MENTAL TRAINING AS A PLACEBO

In medicine, a patient may improve following treatment with a placebo, but the positive change is not in fact effected by the treatment itself. Positive changes often result from patients' beliefs and expectation about the treatment. I'm always surprised by the response I get when I ask physicians in the groups that I'm teaching to estimate what percentage of the positive treatment effects they achieve with their patients can be attributed to the placebo effect. I restate the question by asking them to estimate how much of the successful medicine they practice involves moving the belief systems of their patients in positive directions—in other words, how much of the medicine they practice as physicians would they attribute to placebo? The lowest figure I have received thus far, from literally thousands of physicians both in the United States and Europe, is 40 percent! Some estimated that as much as 80 percent of the treatment benefit could be attributed to the placebo effect. General practitioners acknowledge a strong link between the emotions and beliefs of their patients and successful treatment.

Pharmaceutical companies spend billions of dollars each year trying to factor out the effects of patients' belief systems on treatment outcome. Single-blind, double-blind and triple-blind studies have to be ingeniously designed to keep patients' beliefs from contaminating research findings. The placebo effect is bad news, a costly nuisance, to the pharmaceutical industry. For us, however, it is simply confirmation that our emotions and beliefs play profoundly important roles in healing and health.

Patients who are diagnosed as having a psychosomatic illness are often led to believe that the illness is not real—it's all in their head. Those who are told that their illness is simply a figment of their imagination typically get worse. When an illness is "in your head," the connotation is that it is not real or physical. Patients are led to believe that because their illness has no physical manifestations, it isn't real.

> Beliefs can bring on severe reactions . . . our brains are wired for beliefs and expectancies. When activated, the body can respond as it would if the belief were a reality, producing deafness or thirst, health or illness.[11]
>
> Dr. Herbert Benson
> *Timeless Healing*

This phenomenon in medicine also occurs in sports and business. Athletes who are labeled as "head cases" or "mental cases" are struggling with problems that are somehow not as real as problems with mechanics or strategy or fitness. The fact is: psychosomatic illnesses are just as real and physical as somatic ones, and "head" or "mental" problems, in sports or in life, are just as real as "nonmental" ones. *Psychological* should never be interpreted as meaning *nonphysical*. Mental training for corporate athletes is just as physical as any physical training you could point to.

PART III

LIFE SKILLS AND THE TOUGHENING PROCESS: TARGETING STRESS EXPOSURE

"The Things That Pushed Me the Most Were the Things That Helped Me the Most"

BECOMING A STRESS SEEKER

YOU SHOULD GET comfortable with the notion that, for as many years as you have remaining on this planet, you'll be working to expand your functional capacity for stress of all kinds. Just as you build a diversified financial portfolio to protect against financial calamity, you should likewise invest daily in a diversified portfolio for tolerating future stress when calamity strikes.

And if you want to be elite in your industry, if you intend to lead the troops into the 21st century, you will need a deep capacity for stress. Leadership and stress tolerance are nearly synonymous. Great leaders are constantly teaching those around them how to respond to the forces of life. If there is any hint that they can't handle the heat themselves, their leadership is over.

Over the past several decades, evidence has been steadily accumulating that the brain, in fact, works like a muscle. The more you stress it, the more it grows.

Father Hahn. Nearly 35 years have passed and I can still hear his voice. "Come on, Loehr, push yourself. Expand those brain cells. The mind is like a muscle. Use that brain of yours or you're going to lose it. Work it. Work it hard and it opens up. The harder you work it, the more you get back. Put the effort in and you'll have a brain that really works. Dumbhead or smart—it's your choice, Loehr!" Father Hahn was my Latin teacher in an all-boys Jesuit high school. He was tough. Real tough. And so were most of the other priests who taught there. Even though I heard their message for eight years—four at the Jesuit high school and four at a Jesuit college—I never really got it until well into my career with athletes. Over the years, I've come to deeply appreciate their insight into the role stress plays in the growth cycle.

Father Hahn was right. I still marvel at his wisdom. If the good father were to deliver his favorite stress speech to an esteemed audience of neuroscientists today, he would in fact get their blessing. For years, neuroscientists believed that brain circuitry was hardwired by the time early adolescence was reached, and that adulthood simply meant a progressive decline of brain function and output. A number of researchers, such as David Snowdon of the Sanders-Brown Center on the Aging, at the University of Kentucky, and Arnold Scheibel of UCLA's Brain Research Institute, have confirmed that, although the brain's sending and receiving mechanisms (called axons and dendrites, respectively) tend to shrink with age, intellectual stimulation can cause neurons to proliferate like the roots of a tree. The brain's capacity is limited by genetics, but the brain is far more expandable and modifiable than had been previously thought. Scientists are discovering that, even in old age, our brains have a remarkable ability to grow and expand. Performing challenging mental exercises—like learning Latin—can cause neurons to branch wildly. And the master key to neurological growth is always the same: *stress.*

SPORT SCIENCE AND STRESS

Ask successful coaches about the role of stress in elite athletes' lives and you'll get the same answer over and over, loud and clear:

exposure to stress is a necessary and essential component for expanding functional capacity and increasing performance potential. In a real sense, coaches are stress doctors. Their role is to continuously hand out stress prescriptions that stimulate targeted growth and development. To coaches, stress and personal growth are nearly synonymous.

For decades, sport science researchers have been diligently investigating the relationships between stress and growth. The optimal frequency, duration, and intensity of stress exposure for improving strength, speed, agility, endurance, stamina, and toughness of all kinds have been vigorously pursued. The most important confirmation in all the research is simple and direct: STRESS IS THE STIMULUS FOR ALL GROWTH. To an athlete, stress is not to be feared, avoided, or eliminated. On the contrary, stress is the vehicle through which dreams of great achievements and personal breakthrough become reality. For an athlete, the very idea of training is intimately bound to the concept of stress exposure. Notions of freedom from stress or protection from stress make no sense in the context of expanding personal growth or performance capacity. Hans Selye, the famous stress physiologist, made the point clear when he said, "Complete freedom from stress is death."[1]

Neither Olympic nor corporate athletes take themselves to the next level by being protected. Expansion of functional capacity occurs only when we are pushed beyond our normal limits but not to

I have spent a lot of time talking with other company heads, and we realize that we're all in pretty much the same boat. We've learned that managers—especially those who run relatively small, entrepreneurial companies—have to forget talking about stress reduction. In a world characterized by global competition, technologies that change almost by the day, and 24-hour accessibility via cellular phones/pagers/e-mail/laptops, the amount of stress that successful managers encounter will probably not decrease, at least as long as they continue to grow their businesses. Instead, we talk about facing stress head-on, dealing with it, and moving ahead to the next challenge.

John Hawks
Vice President, Hawks Communication

the point of overtraining. Stress that leads to new strength lies between normal stress, which simply maintains current capacity, and excessive stress, which causes real damage.

Here is what we have learned about stress during the past two decades.

1. *Protection from stress will not make you tougher, stronger, smarter, healthier, happier, or a better performer in any arena.* Have you ever broken an arm or leg and had it casted? Do you remember the day you took the cast off? What was the capacity of those muscles to exert or resist force after just a few weeks of complete protection? What happens to muscles happens to us mentally and emotionally as well. Look at what happens to children who are overprotected. How happy, healthy, or stress-resistant are they when forced to enter the real world? And what happens to retirees when they buy into the "freedom from stress" myth? When stress shuts down, everything shuts down. The growth process comes to a screeching halt—mentally, physically, and emotionally. The six-month period following retirement is one of the potentially most lethal periods in an entire lifetime. Eventually, even going to the grocery store for food becomes too stressful emotionally. Tragically, sustained protection from stress simply leads to an erosion of functional capacity. It is the antithesis of Toughness Training.

2. *Exposure to stress is the basis of all growth, mentally, physically, and emotionally.* World-class stress simply provides the foundation for world-class growth and world-class toughness. To be fully alive and fully functional in today's often brutal business world, we've got to keep growing in strength and resiliency every year.

To maximize health, happiness, and productivity, corporate athletes must become *seekers of stress* for a lifetime. Researchers now confirm that the most powerful anti-aging agent we know of is—ironically—stress. Use it or lose it is a reality of life. If we want to retain functional capacity for a lifetime, we must seek stress for a lifetime. And the older we get, the more we must seek.

3. *Tough times make us tougher.* Take away all the storms of life and business, all the tough times, and what strength of character, fighting spirit, and belief in yourself would you have? Take away all the tough times in Dan Jansen's life—all the struggling, the grinding, the failures, the gut-wrenching battles—and who would he be? How

> I want to be thoroughly used up when I die. For the harder I work the more I live. I rejoice in life for its own sake. Life is no brief candle to me. It's a sort of splendid torch which I've got to hold up for the moment and I want it to burn as bright as possible before handing it on to future generations.
>
> George Bernard Shaw

much growth in his character and belief in himself stem directly from the stress? And how meaningful would his triumph in the 1,000-meter race be if all the tough times had been removed?

In many ways, the storms of life nourish us and provide a foundation of personal strength for future battles. They also bring us face-to-face with our weaknesses and literally force us to get moving.

For just a moment, stop and reflect on your own toughness, your own capacity for handling stress. Each of us has a breaking point where we simply can't take it anymore. An inner voice starts screaming, "That's it! I'm cooked, fried, toasted! I'm out of here! I quit!" How would you rate your capacity? High, medium, or low? And whatever your capacity, how did you get it? Where did it come from? Was it principally from the good times, the joyous times, the wonderful sunsets, the intense pleasures, the happy moments? Or did it come more directly from the great struggles of your life, from the crises that pushed you, from the gut-wrenching stresses over which you somehow triumphed? Which of these two influences have most powerfully formed your character, fighting spirit, and belief in yourself? When you look closely at your life, you'll see that from your greatest trials generally came your greatest growth.

I recently was conducting one of our public seminars. Just after I had completed an explanation of how stress toughens, a participant raised his hand and stated he was also in the toughening business. He was in the business of toughening plants! His explanation was fascinating:

Every spring before we sell our plants, we take them out of the greenhouse and put them in cold frames. There they are subjected to extreme temperatures—not enough to freeze them but just enough to toughen them up. We also deprive them of water so they get thicker stems and thereby the plant becomes tougher. Sometimes we even deprive them of nutrients for a period of time, and through the process of depriving them of heat, water, and, to some extent, nutrients, they become stronger. Then when the homeowner plants them in the garden, the frost doesn't kill them. The plant goes through the same process that human beings do when exposed to stress. As a result of the crisis, plants get bigger and stronger and the root structure deepens and expands. If you don't do the toughening, the chance that the plant will fulfill its complete potential when it's put out in the real world is diminished considerably.

The Apollo 13 performance of Gerry Griffin and his team of flight controllers ranks among the greatest moments in all of aviation history. Thanks to Gerry and his team, what began as NASA's worst hour became one of shining brilliance.

In my interview with Director Griffin, now 61, I asked him to comment on how he learned to perform so precisely and to remain so focused and relaxed under such extreme life-and-death pressure. At the time of the Apollo 13 mission, he was 34 years old. Here's his response:

The thing that helped me the most was being exposed to intense pressure and stress in my training. The things that pushed me the most were the things that helped me the most. NASA's Simulator Supervisors played a major role. We called them Sim Supers. They would nearly drive us crazy. Their job was the create problems for us. They were like DIs [drill instructors] in our lives. They were constantly throwing catastrophic failure situations at us, which forced us to think under pressure and cope with the impossible. How many times we thought, "This is so stupid. This is never going to happen. Why do you do this to us?" The crisis of Apollo 13 was as bizarre as any Sim Super's nightmare . . . . And my physiology would respond in the simulator as if the events were actually happening. We were constantly practicing under great pressure so when the real thing came along, it was nothing new. The most intense pressure in the simulator was peer pressure—not to screw up in front of your peers. When I walked into the control room, I would have 100 percent total focus. Fear of dying was not nearly as intense as fear of making mistakes in front of my peers . . . . The other thing that helped me deal with stress was my very first year at Texas A&M's School of Aeronautical Engineering. I was in the service and the hazing in that first year was unbelievable. We were called "fishes." To put it mildly, this was intense high stress. It really toughened me. All the discipline and harassment taught me how to keep my cool, and not panic. When I finally started learning the lessons, that first year actually started to become fun for me.

4. *Stress is biochemistry.* DuPont's motto, "Better life through better chemistry," is right on target. Getting control of our personal chemistry, getting control of emotion, and getting control of stress are all one and the same. The hand that's dealt to you daily at the office, and the number and kind of stressors that flow in and out of your corporate life are not the determinants of your stress level. Plain and simple, your body's internal response dictates everything. Your unique biochemical response to the stressors you face day in and day out at the office will ultimately dictate the way in which stress will impact your happiness, health, and productivity.

As we have learned, stress is simply the body's response to a demand of some kind. And although the stress response always involves some form of energy expenditure, not all stress responses are the same. Each has its own highly specific biochemical component, which mobilizes the body to respond to the demand in a particular way. We can be mobilized in challenge, or we may cower in fear and impotency. The good news is that the stress response is highly modifiable.

5. *Perception dictates chemistry.* Change perception and the chemistry changes. Change your perception of your DI, boss, or coworker from a maddening psycho to a positive toughening force, and the distress goes away. Change your perception of traffic to positive time alone, and the distress of traffic goes away. Change your perception of your job so that your IPS flows, and your job distress vanishes like magic. Remember, IPS is a *nondistressful* response. The perception of threat, real or imagined, immediately triggers the release of the toxic chemicals of distress. When the amygdala places a negative valence on an experience and is presented with few or no response options, what you see is what you get. As we learned earlier in this book, rituals, acting skills, and mental preparation can be effectively used to change perception and emotional response.

The following example of how a trained perceptual shift completely alters a stress response was sent to me by a fast-lane, highly driven financial adviser:

It's amazing, but New York has truly become much more enjoyable for me. Things that used to drive me crazy *don't* anymore. Friday evening was a good example. A business associate and I were being driven by taxi from New York to Greenwich after a late dinner. The dinner was a big disappointment; it was supposed to be a superb event. Normally I would have been irritable as hell after such a big let-down. Both of us dozed off on the ride back and when we awoke we realized that the driver had either gotten lost or completely misunderstood our instructions. In any event, the guy with me, who is generally very calm and mellow, really lit into the driver and completely lost it. I surprisingly found myself relaxing and soothing him—what a switch. Normally, *I* would have gone ballistic. I just relaxed and rolled

---

Perception Drives Emotion

Your emotional state-of-the-moment stems not so much from what's actually happening as from your *perception* of what's happening, and that in turn reflects the kind of information you've been exposed to. As an example, pay attention to your emotional response to Terry as I unfold information about his situation.

FACT: Terry failed to appear at the hospital for his wife's delivery of their first child. Terry's wife was devastated. What are your feelings about Terry?

FACT: Terry was involved in a serious automobile accident on his way to the hospital. What do you feel about Terry now?

FACT: Terry's accident was the result of a drug overdose. Now how do you feel toward Terry?

FACT: Terry has suffered from attacks of debilitating arthritis. He took the drugs to reduce the pain so he could drive to the hospital. How do you feel about Terry now?

FACT: Terry had chosen to go away for a weekend to spend time with a friend, knowing full well his wife could deliver at any time. When he left to be with his friend, he had no arthritis pain. Check your feelings again.

FACT: Terry's closest friend in all the world recently lost his business and had entered a state of deep depression. Terry feared that his friend would take his life and he had gone literally to save his life. Now how do you feel about Terry?

Your emotional response flows from your perception, which takes form from the information you receive. To respond emotionally in the most appropriate way, get the whole picture and get the facts straight.

with the punches, even after being let out several blocks from my destination and having to carry two very heavy bags! I don't feel any loss of my intensity, desire, or fighting spirit, however. I just feel calmer and more in control. And the level of stress in my life has completely changed.

6. *Once you've exceeded your capacity for stress, perception turns negative.* Even if you're armed with world-class performance skills, once your tolerance for stress has been exceeded, your warrior spirit and IPS control start coming apart. If your business life demands that you sustain a metaphorical 7-minute-mile pace and, on your best day, all you can do is an 8-minute-mile pace, no matter how good your rituals, acting skills, and mental preparation are, you're going to be consumed in negative stress and emotion. You're going to start whining and complaining about everything. "Why do we have to do this? This is a joke! We never had to do this before. I hate this place. This is making me sick. Who in the hell do they think they are, making demands on me like this!"

But how different would your voice be if you had the capacity to maintain a 6:30-minute-mile pace with ease? What would you likely be saying? "No problem. This is OK. Let's get it done." Remember, all the same obstacles are present in both cases—same hills, same humidity, same opponents, and so on—but your response to them is completely different. Your perception of what's fair, right, and doable has dramatically shifted.

How did you increase your capacity from an 8-minute-mile pace to a 6:30-minute-mile pace? Not by protecting yourself or reducing stress in your life. The only way you got there was to expose yourself to progressively greater episodes of stress, followed by full recovery. The message is straightforward—world-class toughness demands world-class capacity, which demands world-class stress exposure. No hiding. No looking for cover. No retirement from life.

7. *Feelings of discomfort typically accompany stress that expands capacity.* If you didn't experience any discomfort today, chances are that you didn't grow any. Teaching athletes to know the difference between the discomfort associated with growth and the pain associated with overtraining is critical to the toughening process. Real pain is a physiological signal that you have dangerously exceeded

your limits. Please hear this—once and for all, loud and clear—PAIN IS A SIGNAL TO STOP! Most of us understand what pain means physically, but how about pain emotionally? How are we to recognize pain in this area? An alarm should sound when *intense* feelings of sadness, depression, anger, fearfulness, moodiness, helplessness, insecurity, and doubt break through. Not unlike pushing beyond the red line on a high-performance race car, pushing yourself beyond discomfort and into pain runs a high risk of completely undermining the toughening process and causing real damage. Feelings of discomfort signal that your normal mind–body limits have been exceeded, but the damage is still reparable with normal rest and recovery cycles. Whatever damage has been done can be repaired. This process, called adaptation, is, in fact, how growth occurs. The critical learning for corporate athletes is to be able to distinguish pain from discomfort. Teaching athletes to recognize and to properly interpret the body's stress signals has been the only successful way we've found to lower the risk of serious breakdown or injury. Expanding functional capacity carries a real risk. Emotion and feelings are the internal eyes and ears of the body. Negative feelings exist for a purpose: they are one of the only ways your body has of getting your attention. Negative feelings signal imbalance, and intensive negative feelings signal EMERGENCY!

Burying negative feelings is analogous to putting masking tape over the instrument panel of a race car. No Formula I driver would ever be so foolish. By removing the masking tape and opening up to the messages sent via feelings and emotions, the language of stress will eventually become understandable. Only then can the distinction be made between the discomfort of toughening and the pain of overtraining.

8. *Levels of personal health, happiness, and productivity provide great insight into stress tolerance levels.* One of the best ways to determine whether you have enough capacity for stress is to take a hard and close look at how the stresses of life have impacted your health, your happiness, and your ability to perform to your full potential. If your stress capacity is insufficient, you are *undertrained* (the sport term). When you are undertrained, the forces you must face consistently exceed what you can handle, and you are therefore always in a state of overtraining. Injuries, sickness, and negative emotions of all kinds—intense anger, choking, resentment, insecurity, and

poor performance—start showing up everywhere. If you don't have the capacity, the signs and signals will be there. A former client described it this way:

Every day was the same. I would wake up exhausted and go to bed exhausted. It would take six hits on the snooze alarm and four to five cups of coffee before I even knew what day it was. And the more I would come to life, the more my bad attitude would take hold. I was critical of and angry with everything and everyone. I was miserable, and I made everyone around me at the office miserable. At the time, I thought my emotional state was completely normal. I really believed that the people around me deserved what they got from me. I wasn't interested in stress management or help of any kind. If I hadn't gotten sick—very sick—and then been taken forcibly by my wife to your center, you wouldn't have got to me in a thousand years. Now, people at work can't believe I'm the same guy. It's like I'm on some mind-altering drug. My health, happiness, and work performance are off the chart. I wake feeling rested and don't even need an alarm anymore!

9. *Increasing your capacity for tolerating physical stress deepens your capacity for tolerating all stress.* Exercise is really stress practice. Remember that stress is energy expenditure. Anything that causes energy to be expended mentally, physically, or emotionally becomes a stressful event. And every time a stress response is triggered and energy is expended, a powerful biochemical and physiological set of events occurs with it. One's capacity for stress is inexorably linked to the chemistry involved in energy expenditure.

Physical exercise is literally energy expenditure practice! The same biochemical mechanisms that are involved in a challenge response at the office (i.e., catecholamine production) are stimulated during exercise. Learning to tolerate increasing levels of physical stress literally trains the body to make more energy available and to better adapt to energy demands of all stress.[2]

We become cowards and wimps when our energy resources are depleted and deep fatigue sets in. If you quickly experience physical fatigue, you'll quickly tire mentally and emotionally as well. Your warrior spirit will melt like an ice cream cone in the sun.

10. *The best way to DEEPEN capacity is to expose yourself intermittently.* Researcher J. M. Weiss discovered that low levels of a brain hormone called norepinephrine are associated with helplessness and a low tolerance for stress.[3] Depletion of this brain neurotransmitter clearly impacts helplessness and what might be called nontough behavior. According to Weiss, the real culprit in depleting norepinephrine is not ordinary stress but chronic and persistent stress that permits little or no recovery for rebuilding lost reserves. Weiss found that cycles of intermittent stress exposure that allowed ample time for restoration actually led to an increased tolerance for stress and resistance to norepinephrine depletion.

What does this mean to you as a corporate athlete? Two things:

1. Actively seeking exposure to stress through exercise can deepen your stress capacity and help reduce feelings of helplessness during periods of high stress (active toughening).

Exercise, Stress, and Mortality Rates

Exposure to physical stress is inversely related to all causes of mortality in both men and women—the greater the exposure, the lower the mortality rates from all causes. Increasing evidence points to a dose–response relationship—the fitter you are and the more vigorous and intense the exercise exposure, the greater the protection.[4]

---

2. The storms of life and business can be converted into opportunities for expanding stress capacity, as long as you build in adequate periods of recovery and restoration. For example, grieve in waves, never continuously; worry and then cease to worry; push, charge forward, and then completely shut down.

Seeker of Stress

Get moving. Go. Get after it. Fight on. Hang in. Pump up. Keep smiling. Engage and connect. Be there. Then disconnect. Shut down. Refuel and heal for the next battle.

As we will see in later chapters, *making waves* is the key to the entire toughening process. Intermittent stress exposure is at stage center.

11. *High stress cannot be equated with high risk of illness.* Chronic, protracted levels of anger, hostility, and fear undermine immune function. The real culprit is sustained high levels of the adrenal hormone cortisol, which can be extremely toxic to immune cells. Periodic or intermittent exposure to toxic chemicals is not a problem; prolonged exposure is.

Richard Rehe, the codeveloper of the Holmes and Rehe Readjustment Rating Scale, which assesses stress levels caused by the occurrence of traumatic life events, such as the death of a loved one, divorce, or loss of a job, eventually concluded that neither the magnitude nor the number of stressful events could account for whether someone will become ill.[5] You may remember filling out a stress test in the 1970s and 1980s that presumably would predict who would get sick because of stress. The test was a checklist of 43 items such as the death of a spouse, job loss, mortgages, and so forth. The thesis was that the more items you checked, the higher your stress score and the more likely you were to get sick. Tragically, from what we know now, those who had high scores and bought the interpretation probably were at a much higher risk. Feelings of helplessness and of resignation that little can be done can powerfully impact immune function. Researchers found that some individuals with extremely high stress suffered no stress-related health problems. They actually seemed to be thriving in the midst of all the stress. Researchers' eventual conclusion was that it is not the stress itself that compromises our health, but how we respond to it.

It is more important to know what sort of person has a disease than to know what sort of disease a person has.

Hippocrates

Widely diverse studies have been done on soldiers who were battle veterans and on survivors of prisoner-of-war camps.[6] Exposure to the brutality of war clearly ranks among the severest of stressors. Research conducted on Vietnam prisoners of war and on survivors of Nazi concentration camps, by Margaret Singer, of the University of California, and Joel Dimsdale, of Stanford University School of Medicine, as well as many others, point in the same direction:[7]

1. Severe trauma and high stress affect different people's health in vastly different ways.

2. Those who handled the stressors best from a health perspective possessed highly similar coping strategies:

   - They did not surrender or give up their spirit.
   - They maintained a sense of control—no matter how bad things got, they could still control their own thoughts.
   - They attributed some important meaning to their suffering and pain.
   - They focused on good or positive things throughout each day: "I got some food today" or "I didn't get beaten today."
   - They maintained a strong sense of purpose and they resolved to make it through the ordeal.

Researchers Suzanne Kobasa and Salvatore Maddi, of the University of Chicago, concluded, after several years of investigation into illness-prone coping styles, that people high in *psychological hardiness* are more resistant to life stressors and therefore less susceptible to stress-related illness.[8] According to their research findings, hardy personalities face life stressors with a sense of commitment, chal-

---

General Formula for Protecting Health in High Stress

1. Harbor less pessimism and more optimism.
2. Summon more positive fight and challenge.
3. Retain a feeling of control: Do Something!
4. Anchor meaning and value to your struggle.
5. Get physical.

---

lenge, and control. Corporate athletes, who are afforded health protection as a result of the hardiness factor, are those who have developed a strong commitment to their work, to their families, and to their friends. Rather than being alienated, they remain actively engaged and connected to the world around them. Hardy corporate athletes are also those who are challenged by the company's financial woes, the corporation's new downsizing directives, and the new, history-making sales quotas. Finally, hardy executives are those who retain a sense of control and continue to believe that they can make a difference. As Norman Cousins so aptly stated, "A weak body becomes weaker in a mood of total surrender."[9]

Stress and Your Immune System

Have you ever noticed that you don't come down with as many colds and flu attacks when you're exercising regularly? There's a reason for it. Even your immune system can be strengthened in response to periodic stress exposure. Every time you work out, your immune cells are literally bathed in the toxic by-products associated with energy expenditure. Exercise is a powerful biochemical event. Every time you exercise, you give your immune system a workout as well. Immune cells become more robust and vigilant in response to periodic stress exposure from exercise.

12. *Stress exposure is one of the only research-supported anti-aging agents we know of.* At Tufts University Center for Aging, researchers have identified a number of markers that are related to the aging process, and many of these same variables are influenced by exercise stress. The general conclusion is that exercise, when done properly, slows the aging process. In just about all areas of stress exposure, the aging process is significantly slowed when the hormones and the forces exerted by stress are intermittently stimulated. Among the markers that are used to determine aging are: lean body mass, overall strength, basal metabolic rate, body fat, aerobic capacity, blood pressure, blood sugar tolerance, cholesterol level, bone density, and body temperature regulation. Lean body mass and overall strength are considered to be the most important of the entire group. And, all of these aging markers can be influenced in a significant way by exercise.[10]

In a research study at Tufts University, 12 men, ages 60 to 72, lifted 80 percent of their repetition maximum 3 times a week for 3 months. (A repetition maximum is the maximum amount of weight a person can lift with one repetition.) During the experiment, their quadriceps more than doubled in size, their hamstrings tripled, and they could lift heavier boxes than 25-year-olds working in the lab. No matter what age you are, it's possible to continue to improve your strength and muscles and to significantly slow the aging process.

Researchers have linked a number of consequences to lack of exercise in adulthood. Increases in depression, moodiness, anxiety, fatigue, insomnia, and muscle weakness, and decreases in immunity, self-esteem, self-confidence, emotional stability, and frustration tolerance can all result from lack of exercise. Researchers now suspect that many age-related changes in the body, such as decrease in cardiac output, cholesterol increase, bone and muscle loss, and disturbances in balance and mobility are the result of sedentary factors rather than the aging process itself. An abundance of evidence now shows that regular physical activity can delay and even prevent many so-called aging problems. Potentially debilitating conditions such as osteoporosis, osteoarthritis, diabetes, and obesity have been shown to be positively affected by exercise stress.

Some additional changes occur in the body as we grow older:

1. Muscle mass decreases; without exercise, we lose approximately 10 percent of our muscle strength every decade.
2. A 1 percent to 3 percent loss in bone mass occurs after age 35.
3. Joints degenerate.
4. Blood pressure increases.
5. Maximum heart rate decreases.
6. Lung capacity decreases.

All of these age-related declines in functional capacity have been positively impacted by regular exercise. And the older you are, the more important is your continued exposure to exercise stress. The familiar maxim—the older you are, the less you should do—can have tragic consequences. More appropriate advice is: the older you get, the more important to use it or lose it.

Exercise stress is clearly one of the most powerful anti-aging agents ever discovered.

13. *Some forms and types of exercise are far superior to others in terms of toughening for business.* Years of experience in attempting to accelerate the toughening process through exercise exposure has led us to a series of highly specific exercise recommendations for corporate athletes. The Toughness Training exercise program consists of the following components:

- Expose yourself to abdominal stress.
- Expose yourself, at intervals, to heart and lung stress.
- Increase your general muscle strength.
- Train to stay flexible.

Expose Yourself to Abdominal Stress

This recommendation comes as quite a shock to most businesspeople. Why would applying doses of stress to your abdominals and obliques (muscles on the side of your lower abdominals) receive the highest priority? The reason is that the foundation of all strength in the body is in the abdominals; the ability to exert and resist force comes from the core of the body. Weak abdominals and poor fitness go hand-in-hand. Problems with movement, lower back pain, poor posture, and shallow breathing can be linked to abdominal weakness. Weak abdominals increase the chance for a wide diversity of lower back injuries. To become a great mental, physical, and emotional fighter in life, you've literally got to have the stomach for it.

The best way to strengthen abdominals and obliques is by doing abdominal curl-ups, not sit-ups. Our recommendation is that you do a minimum of 100 curl-ups daily.

Expose Yourself, at Intervals, to Heart and Lung Stress

Your ability to expend energy to drive behavior and emotions in targeted directions is largely a function of your heart-and-lung capacity. Most corporate athletes are familiar with aerobic steady-state (continuous) forms of exercise. Although 20 to 30 minutes of aerobic exercise 3 to 5 times weekly has been clearly shown by researchers to reduce the risk of coronary heart disease, we believe that the preferred heart-and-lung stress for corporate athletes interested in world-class toughening is not primarily aerobic exposure. We have found that a mixture of aerobic and anaerobic exposure has distinct advantages over steady-state exercise alone, from a toughening perspective.

Figure 7.1 traces a typical aerobic exercise protocol. Exercising aerobically means continuously stressing your heart and lungs at an intensity of from 65 percent to 85 percent of your maximum heart rate. This form of exercise exposes you to a level of stress that you can maintain without running out of breath. Aerobic means "with oxygen."

Exercising anaerobically means stressing your heart and lungs in a way that exceeds the body's capacity to supply enough oxygen to meet energy demands through breathing. You exercise at an intensity that cannot be maintained with respiration.

One of the most important principles in exercise physiology is that of *specificity*—the more similar a training activity is to the actual demands of the real-life situation you are training for, the greater the likelihood that the training effect will transfer into real life. Nothing in the life of a corporate athlete looks like a steady-state aerobic exercise session. Corporate life is stop and go. You race to catch a cab, and then you sit for 35 minutes until you arrive at your destination. You run to the bank and wait endlessly for the line to clear. You argue your point vehemently for ten minutes and

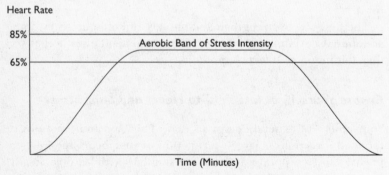

Figure 7.1   Standard Aerobic Model

then wait patiently for others to voice their opinion. The pattern of corporate stress is dynamic and pulsating, not static and uniform. Your exercise programs should mirror those demands for maximum impact.

Figure 7.2 depicts our recommended interval-type model. Note that the stress exposure is intermittent and oscillatory. Heart and lungs are exposed to the full range of stress intensities, and each cycle of stress is paired with a corresponding cycle of recovery. Stress and recovery are biochemical events, and interval training provides opportunities for training the mechanisms of recovery, as well as those of stress. Interval training, as we recommend it, also challenges both the aerobic and anaerobic energy systems.

Here is how exercise for interval training works. If you're a walker, warm up, walk fast for a period of time, and then **walk slow.** If you're a jogger, run, and then **walk slow.** If you're a runner, run fast—maybe even occasionally sprint—and then **walk slow.** Follow the same pattern whether swimming, cycling, biking, roller blading, or participating in any other sport. It's very important to walk, bike, or swim slowly—very slowly. Don't stop; keep moving at a very slow pace. Remember, the goal is to facilitate maximum recovery. You are to *walk slow—not jog slow*—if you're a runner or jogger. The same alternating speed applies to swimming, cycling, and so on. The goal is to contrast stress and recovery as dramatically as possible. During the recovery cycle, try to maintain a look of poise and confidence. Don't look tired and done in, even if that's how you

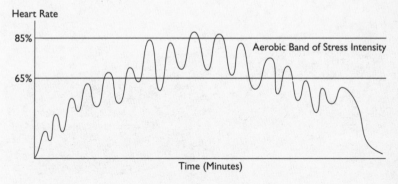

Figure 7.2   Model for Interval Stress Exposure

feel. We call this process TRAINED RECOVERY. There is nothing sacred about the length of the stress or recovery cycles. Tune into your body and follow your body's signals. Remember, the "No Pain, No Gain" principle is DEAD. If today is a toughening day, you'll venture into feelings of discomfort but not PAIN. If today is simply maintenance, feelings of discomfort should be minimized. By far the most important consideration is that you enjoy your workout and use the time to tune into your body—to come back home. Exercise in ways that reconnect your body, mind, and spirit. No spacing out or going dead emotionally just to get through your workout. The spirited mentality of a sprinter is much more in keeping with our IPS model than the endurance mindset of a marathoner.

The most exciting aspect of this exercise regimen is that it can be used as a dress rehearsal for how you intend to deal with stress throughout each day. In the stress cycle of your interval exercise, simply say the letters "I-P-S," and then consciously attempt to summon the chemistry of IPS as you take on the stress. This is precisely what you try to do so often in your business life—stay relaxed, challenged, and positive as the storms descend. This is a perfect time to work on your acting skills. Pull your shoulders back; take on a look of confidence. Then, when you're ready, give yourself the directive to RECOVER. Now disengage and let go; recapture lost energy. To reinforce the message of recovery, we recommend that you place your thumb and forefinger together as a trigger to begin the recovery cycle. In time, simply putting your thumb and finger together can become a conditioned stimulus for triggering a trough of recovery anywhere.

Anchor

Repeated short exercise sessions have the same physiological or metabolic effect in a weight-loss program as a single long workout with the same caloric cost.

Steven Blair, MD
Director of Epidemiology,
Cooper Institute for Aerobics Research

Be sure to check with your physician before launching your interval program, particularly if you intend to take your heart above your aerobic band. Only experienced exercisers in good health should work the higher levels of exercise intensity. We recommend a minimum of 3 to 4 interval sessions per week, with each session 20 to 30 minutes in duration. Optimal toughening results when exercise exposure occurs on a daily basis and uses several different kinds of exercise: walking, swimming, biking, and tennis, for example. Hard days should be followed by easy days. If you're exercising in intervals for more than 20 to 30 minutes, you're training for something other than business or life. A maximum of 30 minutes is all you need. Remember, the most important consideration is that you create a state of fun and enjoyment during your exercise exposure.

Dr. Angelo Trembley, a researcher at Laval University in Ste. Foy, Quebec, found that high-intensity interval training resulted in nine times greater fat loss than steady-state stress exposure, and raised metabolic rate for up to 15 hours after the exercise. The intense exercise appeared to cause fat burners to be turned up for as much as two-thirds of the day.

Increase Your General Muscle Strength

Strengthening your muscles strengthens your spirit. Increasing your physical capacity for exerting and resisting force translates into your mental and emotional activities as well. Reaching and protecting your full potential requires strong, well-conditioned muscles. You can use machines, free weights, flexible rubber tubing, or your own body resistance, as in pull-ups or push-ups. Adults naturally lose about 10 percent of their functional strength every decade after age 30. Strength training at any age completely reverses that age-related change.

Muscles should be challenged on alternate days because recovery requires a minimum of 48 hours (the only exceptions are your abdominals and your obliques). As an example, challenge your lower body with free weights or machines on Mondays, Wednesdays, and Fridays, and your upper body on Tuesdays, Thursdays, and Saturdays. For achieving optimal strength gains, we recommend a 5 to 7 RM (repetition maximum) for 3 sets. A 5 to 7 RM is the equivalent of the maximum amount you can lift 5 to 7 times without pain or loss of technique. Two to 5 minutes of recovery is the time recommended between sets. When you can perform the exercise 10 times, add 5 to 10 pounds to the resistance. Exercising with rubber tubing or bands is a very safe form of resistance training and is convenient for corporate athletes who travel a great deal. Having them readily available in your home, office, and travel bags means that, no matter what your day looks like, you can still apply doses of stress to your muscles.

I highly recommend that you start your resistance training with a qualified personal trainer. This ensures that you'll do it right and on time (because you've made the appointment). Always begin your strength work with a proper warm-up.

Train to Stay Flexible

The older we get, the more inflexible we become mentally, physically, and emotionally. Maintaining muscle flexibility helps to protect corporate athletes from injury when the forces of life heat up. Inflexibility and a lack of toughness are closely connected. Always begin your stretching exercises with 5 to 7 minutes of warm-up. Never purposely extend your muscles beyond their normal range of motion when they are cold. Set aside 10 to 15 minutes each day for your flexibility training.

14. *Physical stress exposure does not, by itself, ensure adequate stress capacity for life or business.* Although high levels of physical fitness contribute substantially to the capacity for tolerating stress, it is clearly not the whole answer. We've all known highly fit individuals who possessed low tolerances for life stress. And we've also known individuals who, for whatever reason, were relatively unfit but nonetheless possessed remarkable toughness. Toughness can be achieved from exposure to mental, emotional, or physical stress. The important point is that toughness and personal strength are

directly linked to stress exposure, regardless of the source. Of the possible sources of stress, exercise exposure is generally the easiest to apply in measurable doses and has the most profound effects on energy mobilization.

> I started exercising in my mid-forties, out of an increasing sense of mortality. In a few short weeks, I started to feel so much better. I lost weight and gave up smoking, started sleeping better, and had more energy at the end of the day for my family. But the most remarkable thing was that my capacity for work increased. The impact of exercise on my productivity and ability to deal with stress has been dramatic. I only wish I had started much earlier in my career. It's the easiest part of the whole puzzle.
> Troy Shaver
> Executive Vice President,
> State Street Research and Management

"Taking
High-Quality Breaks"

THE ART OF WORLD-CLASS RECOVERY

CHAPTER 8

THE SPEED WITH which you recover from physical stress is not only a measure of physical toughness but can be used as a barometer of your mental and emotional toughness as well. Conversely, inability to recover quickly from episodes of mental and emotional stress can signal a lack of physical toughness. When a breakdown occurs, the conclusion is often drawn that excessive stress was the cause; the real culprit, however, was the failure of recovery mechanisms.

BETWEEN-POINT TIME IN TENNIS

One of the greatest breakthroughs in my career with tennis players occurred when I realized that the between-point time in tennis is actually a period of trained recovery for the best competitors. Far from being simply 25 seconds of wasted downtime, the between-point time can be a critical variable in both match outcome and IPS control. Tough competitors use the between-point time to gain as much recovery as possible before the start of the next point, and poor competitors invariably throw the opportunity away. Top competitors follow precise rituals of thinking and acting that facilitate a brief but critical wave of mental, physical, and emotional recovery. Precision thinking and acting in the 25 seconds between points keep IPS within reach and allow the competitors to stay mentally and physically balanced during episodes of prolonged stress.[1]

The use of sophisticated telemetry to track top competitors' heart rates during match play has revealed how troughs of between-point recovery are used to balance spikes of during-point stress. Compared to poor competitors, top competitors were much more skillful oscillators during competition. The rhythmic increases in heart rate during points, and decreases in heart rate between points, meant that a competitor was adapting to the stress. Poor competitors perpetuated cycles of stress by becoming upset with line calls, by self-destructing with negative and pessimistic thinking, or by becoming engulfed in fear and anxiety. All of these served to block the between-point recovery process and prevented effective adaptation from occurring.

Once the importance of between-point time is fully understood, the next step is to apply to poor competitors the principles learned from top competitors. Could between-point recovery be trained, so poor competitors could learn to become better oscillators? Did successful competitors in tennis use similar recovery strategies, and , if so, could these be used to accelerate the adaptation process for poor competitors? The answer to all three questions was Yes.

Comparative studies of the top male and female players revealed remarkable similarities in how they managed the between-point time. Thought patterns, breathing patterns, posture, eye movements, facial expressions, and even the way they carried their racquets told the story. The differences between poor and great competitors were dramatic. Because great competitors were recovery experts, they were able to thrive on the competitive stress.

From 2½ years of collecting data on between-point patterns of thinking and acting has come a four-stage training system that has influenced the training of tennis players worldwide. It proved essential to my work in helping Gabriela Sabatini win her only Grand Slam victory, at the U.S. Open in 1990, Arantxa Sanchez-Vicario's climb to number one in the world in both singles and doubles, Jim

Courier's successful transition from the juniors to the professional ranks, and Sergi Bruguera's climb from number 55 in the world rankings to number 4 and honors as a two-time French Open Champion. But the new insights regarding the importance and significance of Trained Recovery went well beyond tennis. They had a dramatic impact on every area of application I was involved with. From Olympians like Dan Jansen to hockey stars Eric Lindros and Mike Richter, the recovery insights were at the core of my successful intervention. But, by far, the most exciting and impactful areas of application have been outside the boundaries of sport. Trained Recovery completely changed my effectiveness with surgeons, law enforcement officers and FBI agents, pilots, and corporate athletes from every level and dimension of business.

WHAT IS RECOVERY?

As a corporate athlete, what comes to mind when you think of recovery? Alcohol and drug rehabilitation programs? Long, lazy days at the beach? Wilderness vacations with your family? In the context of Toughness Training, recovery has a highly specific meaning. The word that captures the most important dimension of recovery is *relief*. [2] Both stress and recovery are biochemical events. Stress is energy expenditure and recovery is energy restoration. Recovery processes are healing, and they provide periodic relief from episodes of linear stress. Recovery is not a passive event; it is an active process that occurs mentally, physically, and emotionally. Relief from stress can be achieved through passive strategies such as meditation, prayer, sleep, and naps, or through active strategies such as running, talking, stretching, yoga, and recreational sports activities. Recovery does not mean "without movement." Both active and passive forms of *healthy recovery* result in highly distinct and familiar feelings of RELIEF FROM STRESS.

Here's an example. Let's say I ask you to start walking and keep walking for a prolonged period of time. Eventually, walking will become very painful. The energy you expend while walking is *stress*, and the pain becomes *distress*. Now I ask you to sit down. Sitting down instantly brings relief. The pain of walking dissolves very quickly. Sitting down is recovery. Electrochemical changes in the muscles used for walking are immediately altered; heart rate and blood pressure drop; breathing slows; and a host of other energy restoration processes are put into motion. If, however, I make you sit for a prolonged period, sitting will eventually become as painful as did the nonstop walking. Getting out of your chair brings immediate relief. Now, walking becomes recovery. The contracted muscles required to keep you in a sitting position produce stress, and breaking the linearity by walking brings recovery.

KAROSHI

Karoshi is a Japanese word meaning death from overwork. Japan's Institute of Public Health has witnessed an alarming increase in the incidence of *karoshi* during the past decade. Endless hours of work, high pressure to meet expectations, insufficient sleep, too much alcohol, too much smoking, too little time for family, fierce financial pressures, never-ending traffic, little or no exercise, and no recovery time are the markers on a typical playing field for millions of Japanese workers. The tragic consequences for such sustained overwork appear in the form of heart attacks, strokes, high blood pressure, suicide, cancer, and a host of stress-related degenerative and autoimmune diseases.

Japanese health officials have identified five primary work factors leading to the fatal *karoshi* syndrome:

1. Extremely long hours that interfere with normal recovery and rest patterns.
2. Night work that interferes with normal recovery and rest patterns.
3. Working without holidays or breaks.
4. High-pressure work without breaks.
5. Extremely demanding physical labor and continuously stressful work without relief.

Of significance was the discovery that inadequate recovery was a significant factor in all five patterns associated with *karoshi*.

But one need not to look to Japan to understand the tragic consequences of insufficient recovery in high-stress arenas. The costs are painfully evident throughout every sector of American business life. Wounded minds and bodies are strewn across the corporate landscape in the wake of downsizing, rightsizing, reengineering, and pressures to perform and make things happen. The message comes through loud and clear:

STRESS UNABATED BY RECOVERY CAN BE LETHAL.

But remember, the culprit is rarely the stress itself; rather, it is the failure or absence of life-giving recovery. The words of Erik Henriksen, president and CEO of Trader Navigation, go right to the point:

I'm about as hard driving a person as they come, and I always have been. I expect a lot from those who work for me, but I demand even more from myself. My job is so all-pervasive, so all-consuming, that it's not a job, actually, but a lifestyle. I live and breathe it. As the head of Trader Navigation, I spend a lot of time flying all over the globe—to Monaco, the former Soviet Union, Singapore, and the United States, to name just a few of our business loci. Trader Navigation is responsible for the commercial activities of many shipping lines in these and other countries, and I am in charge of international finance, international commodities trading, international investment, and the overseeing of the staffs in these countries.

A few years ago, I was diagnosed with atriofibrillation—a rapid, irregular heartbeat that can have serious health consequences. The doctors told me it was stress-related and that I should cut back on all my activities. I was appalled at the advice—it was like asking a sea turtle to stay away from salt water.

It was a relief to hear that stress reduction is not the answer and that stress exposure is not a problem as long as you balance it with enough time for healing.

Right then, I made a decision to keep a daily log to find and keep that balance. I haven't missed a single daily entry in the past 54 weeks. Now, when I have, say, a 13-hour flight, I find all kinds of ways to recover. I have my music tapes, my meditation, and a series of exercises I can do while cooped up in a plane. I don't sit there stewing about what I could be accomplishing if I wasn't sitting there.

Have I lost my intensity in the process? Most emphatically, No! But I am more relaxed and more focused than I used to be. I am still hard on myself but at the same time I've learned to laugh at myself. Other people aren't any more or less perfect than I am, and I've learned to accept their imperfection just as I'm trying hard to accept my own. I know I'm still a bit of a slave driver, but I'm no longer Simon Legree. I'm more understanding and more patient.

I still suffer from atriofibrillation, but the condition has improved and I'm confident that one day it will go away all together. I still drive myself. I still race fast cars. I still want to find at least 30 hours in each day. But I use every opportunity I have to build in recovery to balance my high stress. I have the same stress in my life—maybe more—but recovery has given me a way to deal with it.

LIMING

The antithesis of "no recovery" is the Carribean practice of *liming*—the art of doing nothing, guilt-free. It is the culturally approved art of periodically breaking away from the stress of time-watching. Liming can take the form of any healthy pleasure that provides mental relief from the relentless stresses of everyday work. In their book, *The Power of Five,* Harold Bloomfield and Robert Cooper describe liming in the following way:

> Time off is not the same as time out. The basic idea with liming is to shift yourself—as completely and deeply as you can—out of the rat race for at least five minutes, allowing your body to release tension at the same time your mind, senses, and emotions savor the moment.[3]

They issue a stern warning about habitually pushing deeper and deeper into fatigue and overtiredness.

Harvard Medical School researcher Raymond F. Flannery discovered that "escape time" was a critical factor in people who developed a high degree of stress resistance.[4] Levels of emotional distress and rates of illness were lowest in the individuals who regularly engaged in relaxation breaks lasting as long as 15 minutes. Included in the break times were activities such as listening to music, exercising, meditating, playing games, or going for a walk.

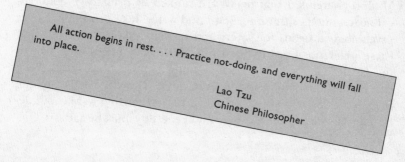

All action begins in rest. . . . Practice not-doing, and everything will fall into place.

Lao Tzu
Chinese Philosopher

Call it liming, recovery, escape time, or relaxing, staying tough and healthy in high-stress environments requires a deep appreciation of and a commitment to properly executed cycles of periodic relief and repair.

Six months after Tony, a district sales manager for a large pet-food company, attended a two-day Toughness Training program, we received a letter from him. He had recently accepted his company's offer to be relocated to corporate headquarters and take responsibility for administrative leadership of a sales region that spanned roughly half of the United States. He wrote:

> For nearly four years, I suffered from agonizing headaches and colitis. I've always been good at what I do, but the stress I had to face day after day gradually started to eat me alive. The breakthrough insight for me was linking toughness with recovery. I've always associated recovery with weakness and wasting time. Helping me understand the role and importance of recovery reorganized my life. Simply taking periodic high-quality breaks throughout the day has changed the whole equation for me . . . people at work ask me what's happened. My distress is levels below where it was. . . . Walking, listening to music, and eating often have been the most powerful for me . . . I haven't suffered a headache in nearly five weeks and my colitis is the best it's been in three years.

THE HIERARCHY OF RECOVERY NEEDS

Some recovery needs are clearly more urgent and important than others. Recovery and need fulfillment are one and the same. The urge associated with a need is stress, and fulfillment of the need is recovery. Abraham Maslow's Hierarchy of Needs is one of the best known and most practical theories of motivation ever developed.[5] Maslow contended that needs are ranked by priority. Physiological needs, such as those for food and water, take precedence over psychological needs for safety and security. Maslow also felt that these priorities were divided into deficiency needs and growth needs. Deficiency needs, such as hunger, thirst, and safety, have the highest priority and survival value. Growth needs include love, self-esteem, and self-actualization. According to Maslow, deficiency needs are more urgent and generally must be satisfied before growth needs.

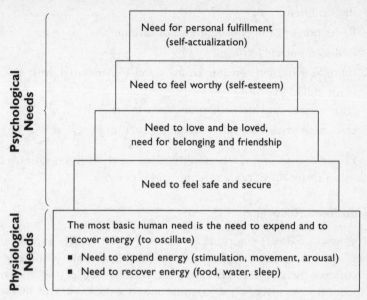

Figure 8.1 The Hierarchy of Needs[6]

In the context of Toughness Training, the most basic human need is to expend and recover energy (see Figure 8.1). Described another way, the need to oscillate between cycles of stress and recovery assumes the highest priority. The most essential forms of stress involve movement of the muscles of the body, and the most important forms of recovery involve eating, sleeping, and drinking. Failure to meet these basic oscillatory needs eventually blocks the fulfillment of all other needs. This is precisely why the establishment of daily rituals of eating, sleeping, drinking, and exercising is so important. After basic oscillatory needs are met, needs for safety, love, friendship, self-esteem and self-realization can be addressed.

WHAT RECOVERY FEELS LIKE

Physical Recovery

Physical recovery can be achieved through anything that provides relief from a bodily need; examples are: food, water, rest, or movement. The most common signals of physical recovery are:

Physical Relief.

Reduction of hunger, sleepiness, or fatigue.

Reduced muscle tension.

Increased muscle tension from exercise associated with relief from inactivity.

Declining heart rate (except for recovery exercise).

Declining breathing rate (except for recovery exercise).

Physical recovery is commonly associated with sensations of physical restoration, reenergizing, and renewal.

Emotional Recovery

The most powerful emotional stressors are *fear*, which stems from perceived threats to our physical or psychological safety, and *anger*. Emotional needs are expressed via various degrees of *distress*. Needs for love, affection, recognition, and self-esteem can surface in widely diverse ways. Feelings of depression, guilt, low energy, sadness, hopelessness, personal doubt, and confusion are examples. The most common signals of emotional recovery are:

Emotional relief.

Fun and enjoyment.

Increase in positive emotions.

Decrease in negative emotions.

Reduced distress.

Increased feelings of safety.

Increased feelings of self-worth.

Increased feelings of love.

Mental Recovery

Intense mental work can be very stressful and consumes a significant amount of energy. The sheer volume of the paperwork most corporate athletes must contend with in a single day is mind-boggling. Writing, reading, preparing, and reviewing endless reports, white papers, contracts, sales projections, and task force summaries can create a seemingly endless cycle of mental stress.

Relief from mental stress can take many forms. Allowing one's mind to drift away to some faraway place, to fantasize about going fishing, taking a nap, or vacationing brings momentary relief. The most common signals of mental recovery are:

Mental relief.

A feeling of mentally slowing down.

Increased calmness.

Broadening of attention.

Increased fantasy.

Increased creativity.

Increased imagery.

TRAINING THE MECHANISMS OF RECOVERY

Corporate athletes know well the relationship between training and stress. What is not so familiar, however, is the connection between training and recovery. From my work with between-point time in tennis, the importance and potential impact of that connection became fully understood. The foundation of Toughness Training rests squarely on the platform of *Trained Recovery*.

Employees cannot sustain peak performance 24 hours a day, week after week. It's just impossible, physically, mentally, and emotionally. We sponsor a "corporate wellness" program that includes company golf leagues and softball teams, healthy discounts at area gyms and health clubs, and outings like Laser Quest games. We reimburse health club fees in hotels for employees on the road. We encourage managers and other employees to manage stress by personalizing their offices and cubicles. For example, I keep a CD player on my desk that plays music all day long, while many companies don't allow such things. I ask myself: Why? Your office, after all, is your home away from home. It's important to make it work for you. These periods of relaxation, or recovery, from the usual grind are what help to maintain a high level of performance.

John Hawks
Vice President, Hawks Communication

The impact and importance of recovery were clearly evident to Kristen Lindelow:

> I had just returned to work from a nine-month maternity leave (my first child). My husband was working full-time at a rather stressful job and all his spare time was spent working on a Master's degree. And to add to the stress load, there were changes pending at my workplace that threatened to drastically change all our jobs—naturally, downsizing was part of it.
>
> A typical workday for me included:
>
> - Juggling nonstop telephone calls for myself, the president, and the executive vice president of our company;
> - Scheduling meetings and travel for two executives and rescheduling said meetings and travel, then scheduling them again;
> - Hours of creating, typing, and editing correspondence, spreadsheets, and databases;
> - Working with six different builders, each of whom had very positive ideas about why his or her particular project should receive priority—"Just this time, please";
> - Working with numerous consultants (architects, engineers, attorneys), relaying information to them and receiving information from them for my superiors—that is, taking reports, lengthy faxes, and messages, and summarizing them quickly in order to explain the "gist" of the information without their having to read tomes;
> - Performing a variety of special projects—from selecting cellular telephone service and equipment for the corporation to coordinating a professional international golf tournament to rewriting a design guideline manual or coordinating tee times for visiting royalty.
>
> I was responsible for a number of these jobs each day—in an environment where several staff were very suspicious and negative toward management and speculation was the favorite pastime; in an open— no walls—office where it was very difficult to keep confidential information confidential; and where all telephone calls were overheard in a not-so-subtle manner.
>
> I started giving myself recovery time by making sure I left my office at lunch and got outside. I went on mundane errands, browsed in a nearby bookstore, visited my infant daughter at her nursery, and took walks. This gave me nearly an hour of time to myself that I was

otherwise missing—time to regroup, recover, and return to the office to finish the day as strong as I had started it that morning.

Soon after starting my lunchtime escapes, I realized I had nearly an hour of alone drive-time in my car each morning and afternoon—time I used to resent and dread. I would leave work or the house at the last possible minute, then drive faster than was safe, curse out the other drivers, lights, and so on, for making me late! I realized this was a stressful part of my day and dimly realized, too, that I wasn't handling it well. I decided to go to the library for some more books-on-tape, and now regularly listen to a variety of books—fiction and nonfiction—during my "captive" time. That way, I reduce my bad, unproductive stress by learning to use those special intervals.

As another form of recovery, I started taking my daughter on an evening stroll through the neighborhood—not the "power walking" I do for active exercise.

Sleep was the most difficult change for me to make. I was in the habit of taking my worries and stresses to bed with me. But now that I'm keeping regular hours and practicing certain breathing rituals of relaxation, both my personal and professional lives have become more positive. Since we get up rather early, we now go to bed early. For some months, this was difficult; I fought it. Family and friends were in the habit of calling long-distance late in the evening. They now understand that we will be asleep so they call earlier. Also, I had a lifelong habit of getting everything done before I allowed myself to stop. All the laundry had to be washed, folded, and put away; the kitchen immaculate; the house picked up, swept and vacuumed. This—what I now call linear craziness—was the hardest to let go, but now that I'm no longer sleep-deprived I have the energy to go all day and I'm able to get everything done by my realistic bedtime.

The combination of these small changes in my life has resulted in my being able to handle stress much better than I thought possible a year ago. I may not be an important business leader, but in this world, with all of its attendant responsibilities and lack of time, we all have to think and act with executive mentality. There's business, there's home, there are children, there are relationships—all of these have to be balanced, negotiated and dealt with. How I ever lived without understanding the importance of recovery is beyond my comprehension. Recovery has given me more hours in the day, and infinitely better ways of coping with those hours.

In the remainder of this chapter, the most important areas of recovery will be explored from a training perspective. They are:

1. Sleep.
2. Nutrition.
3. Exercise.
4. Humor.
5. Music.
6. Active and passive rest.
7. Need fulfillment.

SLEEP

Apart from eating, drinking, and breathing, sleeping is unquestionably our most important recovery activity. It is also the largest and most powerful of our circadian rhythms (biological rhythms that rise and fall every 24 hours). Disruption of this biological clock will eventually have serious health and performance consequences.

If you live to be 70, you will have spent over 200,000 hours sleeping! For thousands of years of evolution, the human sleep cycle was regulated by light and darkness. Since its invention roughly a century ago, electric light has played havoc with humans' essential biological rhythms. Prior to Thomas Edison's light-extending invention, people slept an average of 8 to 9 hours per night. Today's corporate athletes often get by on less than 7 hours, and a full 20 percent of our corporate audiences report that they sleep only 5 or 6 hours each night.

The real question is: How much sleep do we need? Was Edison correct in his contention that sleep represents nothing more than a bad habit which should and could be eliminated? Most sleep experts strongly disagree with Edison's position. Considerable consensus exists among experts that 7 to 8 hours of sleep are required for optimal functioning in the human species. Findings by Dan Kripke and his team or researchers is typically supportive of the 7 to 8 hours recommendation.[7] Kripke and his colleagues monitored the health of more than a million adults over a 6-year span to determine whether any relationship existed between sleep habits and mortality rates. The evidence indicated that mortality rates from nearly all causes of death were lowest among people who slept between 7 and 8 hours nightly. Mortality rates were 2½ times higher for those sleeping less than 4 hours, and 1½ to 2 times higher for those sleeping more than 10 hours. Either too little or too much sleep appears to increase health risk factors in an important way. Studies strongly indicate that poor health and poor or inadequate sleep go together. Sleep-deprived individuals suffer considerably more fatigue and average twice as many doctor visits annually. They also average twice as many infectious incidents, signaling a potential link between sleep deprivation and immune impairment.

All mammals show a sleep pattern. Opossums and bats sleep as much as 20 hours per day, and horses and donkeys sleep as little as 3 hours daily. Our closest relatives, chimpanzees and monkeys, sleep 9 to 10 hours daily.[8]

The precise amount of sleep one needs is highly individual and depends on a number of factors, including age, volume of physical activity, and levels of mental and emotional stress. Infants and children can require as much as 16 to 20 hours of sleep daily, adults between 7 and 9 hours, and elderly persons, as little as 6 to 7 hours. Remember that growth actually takes place during recovery. We grow the most during the sleep cycle, which explains why children require considerably more sleep than adults. Growth hormones and repair enzymes are released most abundantly during sleep as are various chemical restoration processes.

When placed in time isolation, the average adult will sleep approximately 8 hours out of every 24-hour period. Every 90 to 120 minutes during those 8 hours, the body passes through an ultradian rest–activity cycle. Even newborns follow the same sleep rhythms. Each of the cycles has several stages.

Stage 1 is a transitional phase between waking and sleeping. It lasts only a few minutes in healthy sleep. Eyes are quiet and muscle tension levels are significantly lower than in the waking state. Stage 2 accounts for more than half of total sleep time and is signaled by the occasional appearance of slow, long brain waves called K-complexes. Scientists use the appearance of these K-complexes to mark the actual beginning of sleep. Stages 3 and 4 are termed "delta sleep" or slow-wave sleep. These stages appear in the first two 90-minute cycles and occur briefly or not at all as sleep progresses. Slow-wave sleep accounts for 15 to 20 percent of total sleep time. Sometimes referred to as the healing frequency, this is the most important sleep phase for energy restoration, recovery, and rejuvenation. During delta sleep, metabolic rate and muscle tension reach their lowest levels, and brain waves fall to less than 4 cycles per second. The amplitude of brain waves is highest and their frequency is lowest at this time. Growth hormones and cell division are most active. If you spend the right amount of time in stages 3 and 4, you awaken feeling rested and rejuvenated. Disruptions in slow-wave sleep are associated with daytime tiredness, fatigue, and sluggishness.

Stages 1 through 4 are collectively referred to as non-REM sleep. REM stands for rapid eye movement. Stage 5, called REM sleep, accounts for 20 to 25 percent of total sleep and first occurs roughly 90 minutes after the onset of sleep. REM first appears for only a few minutes initially but its duration progressively increases as the waking cycle approaches. During REM sleep, the muscles are frozen as a protective measure, breathing quickens, blood pressure and heart rate become irregular, and brain waves increase to 13 to 35 cycles per second. This is when we enter a dream state; the brain processes information gathered during the day.

Stanley Coren, a psychologist and author of *Sleep Thieves*, believes that depriving yourself of sleep is analogous to depriving yourself of food. A number of studies demonstrate how sleep deprivation negatively impacts performance factors. Sleep debt of as little as 3 hours has been shown to significantly reduce (1) physical strength in weight lifters and (2) the ability of competitive cyclists to utilize oxygen. Sleep debt of 8 hours produces significant changes in mood, energy, fatigue, and vigor, and is associated with increases in depression, irritability, and negativity.

More than fifty studies have shown how mental performance steadily declines as sleep debt increases.[9] Reaction time is reduced by as much as 45 percent with only 4 hours of sleep loss. Significant declines in attention control, concentration, memory, and logical/ analytical reasoning have been documented by researchers.

Factors Affecting Sleep

1. *Age.* The younger you are, the greater your need for sleep. Sleep cycles become more fragile among older age groups. The quantity of delta sleep decreases as age increases.

2. *Fitness.* Fit persons require less sleep than nonfit persons. The fitter you are, the faster you recover. Fit subjects require less sleep because, compared to unfit subjects, they extract more delta

sleep from the same time interval (faster speed of recovery). Lean body mass is positively correlated with delta sleep.

3. *Exercise type.* Aerobic and anaerobic exercise, as well as strength training, have been shown to reduce sleep latency and increase delta sleep. Sleep cycles are healthiest and delta sleep is highest in those who remain most physically active.

4. *Timing of exercise.* Exercising too close to the sleep cycle can be very disruptive in terms of both sleep latency and depth. Many of the chemicals produced during exercise are powerful stimulators and promote central nervous system arousal. Vigorous exercise within two hours of sleep can seriously disturb natural sleep rhythms.

5. *Diet.* Many foods contain stimulants that can be very disruptive to the sleep cycle. One of the most powerful stimulants is caffeine. The effects of caffeine peak within 30 to 45 minutes after ingestion and require as long as several hours to completely clear the system. A single cup of coffee can double the length of time required to fall into sleep. Chocolate contains both caffeine and another stimulant called theobromine. The darker the chocolate, the greater the dose of caffeine.

Nicotine is also a central nervous system stimulant. Both reduced sleepiness and increased alertness are associated with its use. Adrenaline and noradrenaline are indirectly released in response to nicotine exposure.

Alcohol consumption can be very problematic from a sleep perspective. Alcohol reduces the length of time it takes to fall asleep, but disruptions in both slow-wave and REM sleep are common, particularly in the second half of nighttime sleep.

The size and timing of meals also impact sleep effectiveness. Large meals consumed close in time to sleep periods, particularly meals high in fats and protein, can be very disruptive.

A light supper and a good night's sleep have sometimes made a hero of a man who, by indigestion and a restless night would have proved a coward.
Lord Chesterfield, 1748

6. *Other factors.* Additional factors impacting sleep integrity include anxiety, overall stress levels, room temperature (cooler temperature promotes better sleep), noise, altitude, sunlight, and travel across time zones.

Training Recommendations

- Develop a specific sleep ritual and follow it, particularly during stressful times.
- Go to bed and get up at the same time as often as possible.
- If possible, establish an early-to-bed, early-to-rise sleep rhythm.
- Exercise daily but not within two hours of bedtime (for some people, a longer restricted time is needed).
- Exercising in the late afternoon or early evening (rather than in early morning) has a more positive impact on the sleep cycle for many people. Exercising later reduces stress levels built up throughout the day, paving the way for improved sleep.

Are You Sleep-Deprived?

1. Do you have trouble getting up in the mornings?
2. Do you wake up tired and longing for more sleep?
3. Are you tired and fatigued during the day?
4. Do you get sleepy when you drive?
5. Do you find it *very difficult* to stay alert and focused between 2:00 and 4:00 in the afternoon?
6. Do you have difficulty staying awake in long meetings and classes?
7. Do you get sleepy when you are forced to sit still for extended periods of time?
8. Do you frequently fall asleep watching television or movies?
9. Do you find yourself frequently thinking about sleep?
10. Do you constantly require caffeinated beverages to stay alert and focused?

If you answer "Yes" to five or more questions, a red flag should be raised. You are likely suffering from sleep deprivation.

- Take no caffeine or chocolate around bedtime, and be very cautious about the use of alcohol, nicotine, and central nervous system stimulants.

- Get a half-hour of sunlight within 30 minutes of awakening, whenever possible. Turn all the lights on in your house immediately upon rising. Exposure to light is a primary biological clock regulator. Light causes sleep hormones to be deactivated and replaced with hormones of arousal.

- Keep your bedroom at a cool temperature, well ventilated, and dark whenever possible.

- Employ specific relaxation strategies such as tensing and relaxing muscles, deep breathing, and sleep images to assist you in your efforts to gain control over the sleep cycle.

- Resist the temptation to become angry, frustrated, or upset when you can't sleep. Negative emotions increase arousal and decrease the likelihood of sleep. Relax and enjoy the quiet time.

Tough Napping

The human species enters a trough of circadian vulnerability between roughly 2:00 and 4:00 in the afternoon.[10] That simply means that you have the urge to rest during that time span. This oscillatory rhythm is apparently hard-wired into humans' makeup. Some cultures have decided not to fight it. It's called *siesta* in Central and South America. In present-day China, office and factory workers routinely lie down for naps following lunch. The Chinese offer two primary reasons for allowing the workforce to nap in the afternoon: (1) the Chinese Constitution specifically states that "the working population has a right to rest," and (2) there is a strong belief that resting improves employee productivity. The Federal Aviation Administration has recently permitted "controlled napping" by airline pilots on certain designated long-distance flights. Co-pilots take the controls during these time-out naps. Napping is permitted as a way to increase pilot alertness, decision making, and concentration.

But don't expect corporate America to move in this direction anytime soon. The survival of corporations today mandates increasing, not decreasing, productivity. The very notion of "corporate napping" has a nearly heretical sound to most industry leaders. But the cost to corporate America for productivity declines associated with this ultradian rhythm is in the billions of dollars. Over 90 percent of those attending our Toughness Training programs acknowledge a significant reduction in productivity in early afternoon. When combined with alcohol, large meals, and high-fat or high-sugar menus, the urge to sleep can completely erode focus and concentration.

Napping has been widely practiced in professional sport as a performance booster. Professional hockey is a good example. Napping on a game day is a sacred performance ritual for most players. It's viewed as an essential component in pregame preparation.

What can be done to diminish the productivity decline associated with this troublesome ultradian rhythm? Here are our training recommendations for corporate athletes:

1. No alcohol during lunch. No exceptions. Even small amounts can make the trough irresistible. All the two-martini hard-liners were swept out in the first wave of downsizing.

2. Always have lunch, but make it small. Having lunch stabilizes blood sugar, but a large meal creates digestive stress that increases the urge to sleep.

3. Avoid foods high in sugar, and make sure your meal contains both carbohydrates and protein. Pure carbohydrate lunches are trouble for most people. Carbohydrate intake stimulates the production of the neurotransmitter serotonin, which can make you sleepy. Consumption of protein has been linked to increases in epenephrine and dopamine, both of which contribute to alertness and arousal. Rather than pure pasta lunches, combine pasta with chicken, turkey, or fish. Foods high in sugar can lead to blood sugar spikes, resulting in a powerful insulin response.

4. Avoid high-fat lunches at all costs. The more fat you consume, the more you are seduced into sleep.

5. Ritualize the 2:00 P.M. to 4:00 P.M. time so that tasks requiring precise concentration are routinely done at other times. This is a good time to do your walk-through of the plant, return

phone calls, have team meetings, and consult with your executive staff.

6. Learn to take power naps. We call them tough naps. Close your office door, hold your calls, put your head on your desk, and take a 5- to 10-minute dive into the ultradian pool. Taking a brief plunge completely eliminates the sleepy, groggy feeling for a large number of people. A 10-minute tough nap can literally return an hour and fifty minutes of high productivity. Not a bad exchange on the corporate books.

NUTRITION

Consuming adequate amounts of food and water is a recovery strategy of the highest priority. If nutritional and hydration needs are not sufficiently met, all stress eventually becomes excessive, and all recovery mechanisms fail. Only a few of the most important training considerations regarding nutrition can be covered here. A complete nutritional program can be reviewed in Dr. Jack Groppel's *The Anti-Diet Book*.[11] Here are the basics:

- Develop a consistent, regular routine of eating. The consistency of meals helps to synchronize a number of biological rhythms. Stabilizing the timing and regularity of food and water intake represents an important contributor to overall stress-recovery.

- Eat often and light. From a performance perspective, this is one of the most important nutritional strategies discovered in two decades. Eating many small meals throughout the day (roughly, every two hours)—raises metabolic rate, stabilizes mood and energy levels, and reduces any obsession with food.

- Always start your day with breakfast. To stabilize your blood sugar level, the one meal you should never miss is breakfast. Eat light, but always start your day with nutritious food.

- Never eat a large meal. Eating large meals virtually guarantees sluggish, less-than-optimal performance. The safest frequency guide to follow is *never*. Eating small meals eventually causes your stomach to shrink, protecting you against overeating.

- Eat a wide variety of foods. One of the best ways to meet all of your nutritional needs is to eat as wide a variety of foods as possible. Constantly eating the same foods significantly increases the risk of nutritional deficiencies.

- Stay away from diets. A diet is a temporary change in your customary habits of eating to accomplish some goal. The problem with diets is that as soon as you go back to your normal dietary habits, the old dysfunctional patterns reappear. Any changes in dietary habits should be permanent and should take into consideration the long-term view.

- Combine protein with carbohydrates to boost alertness. Protein consumption stimulates norepinephrine an dopamine production, two brain hormones associated with activation and alertness.

- Reduce fat intake. Nearly every nutritional expert agrees that excessive fat in your diet poses significant health and performance risks. If possible, no more than 20 percent of your daily caloric intake should come from fats. A gram of fat is twice as dense in calories as a gram of carbohydrate or protein. Fat is hidden in a variety of prepared foods. Be sure to READ LABELS.

- Substitute baking, broiling, or grilling your foods for frying. Frying foods makes the 20 percent fat guideline just about unreachable. Eventually, baked, broiled, or grilled foods will taste better than the unhealthier fried choices.

- Select unprocessed, nutrient-dense foods whenever possible. Even foods that are fortified or enriched cannot replace the full range of nutrients lost in processing. Examples of processed foods are white bread, mayonnaise, and bologna.

- Avoid alcohol and caffeine around performance times. Even small quantities of alcohol can impair judgment and reduce alertness and focus. Caffeine increases arousal but is associated with edginess and loss of calmness. The effects of both alcohol and caffeine in high-stress situations are highly unpredictable.

- Avoid simple sugars. Refined carbohydrates often have virtually no nutrients left after they have been processed. Simple sugars are also more likely to spike your blood sugar level, causing insulin to be produced. The end result is less energy and reduced focus.

- Consume foods high in fiber. Many studies have confirmed that a high-fiber diet reduces the incidence of colon cancer. Fruits and whole-grain foods are high in fiber. A link has also been made between high-fiber diets and control of blood sugar.

- Drink eight glasses of water daily. Most corporate athletes don't consume enough water. Contamination of public water systems presents a real problem in some areas of the country. Water purification systems and purchased purified water are important considerations for increasing numbers of people.

- Take a multivitamin, multimineral supplement daily. This supplement is just for insurance. No matter how good you think your diet is, you're probably missing some essential vitamins and minerals.

Eat and Drink More:

Fruits

Low-fat protein

Leafy green vegetables

Salads, pasta, rice, whole-grain breads, oatmeal, cereals that have no sugar added

Egg whites, plain yogurt, turkey, and chicken

Meats and vegetables that have been broiled or grilled

Fruit juices and water

Eat and Drink Less:

Fried meat

Fried vegetables

Margarine, mayonnaise

Creamy salad dressings: Ranch, French, Blue Cheese, Thousand Island, Creamy Italian

Egg yolks (the yellow part), ice cream, doughnuts, Danish pastries, cookies, candy

Soft drinks and alcoholic beverages

- Consume only a low to moderate amount of salt each day. The standard American diet contains excessive levels of salt. For some people, particularly those having problems with high blood pressure, salt intake should be carefully monitored.

- Reduce consumption of cholesterol. Diets high in cholesterol can be a significant factor in coronary heart disease.

EXERCISE

Exercise is a mechanism of both stress and recovery. Exposing yourself to doses of physical stress can be useful both to stimulate recovery and to increase functional capacity. Exercise can be a powerful mechanism of mental and emotional recovery for corporate athletes. It's important to remember that exercise is a biochemical event that affects nearly every cell in your body. In a real sense, exercise washes the chemistry of distress away. The release of hormones like adrenaline and endorphin reshapes your internal architecture and brings relief from toxic emotions like anger, fear, sadness, guilt, and depression.

Here is a sampling of our core exercise recommendations to enhance recovery:

- Exercise in the late afternoon if possible. Corporate athletes are very immobile during the day, and mental and emotional stress continues to build as the day progresses. Late afternoon exercise brings relief both physically and psychologically.

- Do some type of exercise daily. The exercise should continue for 20 to 30 minutes, at a minimum. Anything from gardening to walking qualifies.

- Use interval exercise three to four times per week. Walk fast and then slow. Use the same pattern when you're swimming, cycling, or running. Constantly contrast stress with recovery.

- Use vigorous exercise to get relief from highly toxic episodes of mental and emotional stress. To change your body chemistry, you've got to get the juices flowing. Exercise safely and comfortably, given your medical and fitness limitations, but try to get a sweat going. Longer and more vigorous exercise sessions typically provide more relief than shorter and less vigorous ones do.

- Vary your exercise routines as much as possible. Boredom kills the recovery value and eventually undermines your willingness to exercise at all. Also, the broader your range of exercise options, the higher the level of functional fitness you'll typically have.

- Create a play frame around the exercise. Fun is emotional recovery. Combining fun and exercise is unbeatable from an emotional recovery perspective. Remember, exercising for recovery should not involve feelings of discomfort or pain. The dominant feeling should be relief.

- Any exercise is better than no exercise at all. Use stairways instead of elevators, keep moving forward on escalators and walking sidewalks. Use the exit stairways inside hotels when no other exercise options are available. Go up four flights and down four flights, then do it again. Be creative in finding ways to get your recovery in safely and consistently. Don't make excuses for failing to exercise.

- Get a thorough medical checkup before you start. If you're not an experienced exerciser, know your medical risks. Whenever possible, get started properly with a personal trainer. It will be some of the best and smartest money you'll ever spend.

The two most important strategies I have for controlling stress in my life are daily exercise and keeping my priorities straight. I exercise 6 days a week for 45 minutes to an hour. I do a combination of running and weight training. . . . I've found that if I act in ways that are consistent with my priorities, my stress is infinitely less. My family comes first.

Jim Stern
Chairman of the Cypress Group, LLC
(equity investment fund)

HUMOR

In the context of recovery, humor is serious business. Every laugh is a wave of recovery. In a real sense, laughter is a form of internal jogging. Laughter breaks stress up from the inside. Jane Evans, President and Chief Operating Officer of Smart TV, puts it this way:

> Humor has helped me think clearly under pressure and remain calm—inside and out. It keeps me flexible and open during difficult times, which I believe is an important part of my leadership. Humor has been absolutely critical in helping me lead my team through troubled times.

A good laugh is a powerful biochemical event. A whole collection of physiological changes have been documented both during and following a hearty laugh episode.[12] Changes in heart rate, blood pressure, skin temperature, brain wave activity, muscle tension, and norepinephrine and endorphin production have been linked to the humor response. Increasing evidence suggests that laughter is good medicine for both the body and the mind.[13]

Here are some of our most important training recommendations:

- Constantly work to improve your sense of humor. In the context of recovery, your sense of humor has nothing to do with your ability to tell jokes or make others laugh. Instead, it is your ability to access the chemistry of humor through laughter *yourself*. Don't wait for others to make you laugh. Look for and find humor in daily happenings.

    Get yourself to laugh.

- Learn to laugh at yourself, and invite others to do so as well. Learn not to take yourself too seriously. When you can laugh at yourself, you're in control. The ability to laugh at oneself and see humor in times of great stress is a life-saving skill.

- Look for funny things everywhere during periods of high stress. Learn to be responsive to others' attempts to be humorous, and quick to see funny things in life. Exaggerate and overstate reality until you break into laughter. Begin your day with a minute of forced laughter just to get your juices flowing.

> I try to find a reason to laugh under high stress. It's an important part of everything I do. When things get rough, I actually look for funny things, particularly in myself. The more stress I have, the more I use humor to break me up and then refocus.
>
> Charles L. Peifer
> President and CEO, Prince Sports Group

- Laugh at least 50 times each day. The average number of laughs per day for adults is 25. The average for children is 400! What did we lose when we grew up? The ability to see humor in things is learned, but humor has never been encouraged in corporate life. Humor is considered appropriate only for parties on weekends. Work is serious! Lighten your workload by noticing contrasts, juxtapositions, and other elements of humor that are present.

- Make it easy to laugh. Environmentalize your home, car, and office so that humor comes easily. Set the stage for laughter. Develop an audio and video *funny tape library* that is always there to help you decompress with laughter.

- Resist negative humor. Gallows humor, making fun of others, or throwing punches with humor reflects insecurity or insensitivity—or both. These have no place in the arena of recovery.

Recovery and Your Heart

Myer Friedman and Diane Ulmer found that Type A cardiac patients who were instructed to walk more, eat more slowly, smile more, enjoy more, and laugh more, experienced half as many repeat heart attacks over a three-year period as those not receiving the instruction.[14]

MUSIC

Music is a great recovery enhancer. It's no accident that athletes are constantly listening to music just prior to important competitions.

As early as the 6th century B.C., Pythagoras used music to cleanse the soul and body and reestablish harmony and health in his patients. When people were sick, he prescribed a regimen of music to wake up by, to work by, to relax and fall asleep by. Historical records show that early physicians used music to regulate heart rate. And from the Renaissance period to the 19th century, music and singing were used to lift people's spirits and enhance the flow of positive emotion.[15]

Modern medicine has also seen the value of music for healing and bringing about calm. In the 1930s, dentists used music to augment the less-than-satisfactory pain relievers of the day, as well as to reduce fright and fear in patients. Starting after World War II, there has been widespread use of music in psychiatric care. Therapists in veterans' hospitals, for example, added music to the treatment of emotionally disturbed veterans.

Since 1975, a number of studies have demonstrated the effect of music on human functioning. Music results in breathing changes. Loud music has a tendency to speed up breathing rate (frequency) and to decrease regularity (rhythm); soft music slows the breathing rate and increases regularity. Music also brings about various biochemical changes in the neocortex (the "thinking brain") and in the limbic system (the "emotional brain"). Music even affects the most primitive part of our brain, where regulation of our heart rate, respiration, and muscle tension occurs.

In 1985, Mark Ricker found that the mean level of circadian amplitude (a measure of the level of stress hormones) significantly decreased during music.[16] In 1989, Valerie Pfaff, Karen Smith, and Darryl Gowan studied the effects of music to assist relaxation in distressed cancer patients.[17] The music provided a statistically significant reduction in fear and pain. In 1990, Stephen Boutcher of the University of Virginia reported significantly lower perceived exertion levels during exercise or work while music is being played.[18]

As does sleep, music has a marked effect on learning. According to a study by Ron Woods, the addition of popular music positively influences the mood of learners. Not only are positive moods enhanced, but negative moods can become more positive as a result of music. The attitudes of learners improve dramatically and, therefore, their performance improves when music is present in the environment. Music seems to relieve the effect of boredom and the fatigue of doing repetitive work.

Here are some specific recommendations for using music as a tool for accelerating the processes of recovery from stress:

- Use music to facilitate recovery from distressful emotions. Record onto an audiotape the best music you have for changing your negative moods into positive ones. Use the tape regularly to help you alter your mood state. Tune into how each piece of music affects you emotionally.

- Develop your own music tape for relaxation. The right music can dramatically accelerate your ability to shut down. All you have to do is find the music that moves your physiology in that direction. For some, it's classical music; for others, it's Kenny G or Yanni or Enya. Find out which works best for you and keep it handy.

- Develop your own IPS tape. Find music that stimulates your positive energy, determination, confidence, and focus. For most people, the music that works best to move their emotions is selected from the soundtracks of movies. Soundtracks are powerful because they were specifically written to move the film audience's emotions in the direction of the script. More than one executive has called a tough meeting to order with the Indiana Jones theme replaying in his or her head.

- Use selected music to reduce the distress of daily commuting to work. Traffic is a source of significant distress for millions of corporate athletes. The right music can completely alter your body's response to this aspect of the playing field. Get the right tunes flowing in traffic, and the traffic shrinks in significance.

- Learn to play a musical instrument or sing, to balance world-class stress. Think of playing a musical instrument as PURE RECOVERY. Playing an instrument or singing is mental and emotional therapy for corporate athletes. As a recovery activity, it offers high functional value for almost everyone.

- Think of music as an important part of your overall training. Constantly search for music that moves you in positive, healing directions.

ACTIVE AND PASSIVE REST

Active rest refers to cycles of physical, emotional, and mental stress that *involve movement of the physical body*. Examples of active rest include:

- Yoga.
- Tai-chi.
- Stretching.
- Fishing.
- Walking.
- Noncompetitive tennis, biking, jogging, golf, and swimming.
- Gardening.
- Sex.

Passive rest refers to activities that break normal cycles of physical, emotional, and mental stress and *do not involve movement of the physical body*. Examples of passive rest include:

- Prayer.
- Massage.
- Viewing peaceful places or scenes.

> Workers with a view of nature felt less frustrated and more patient, found their job more challenging and interesting, expressed greater enthusiasm for their work and reported greater overall life satisfaction and health.
>
> David Sobel, M.D. and Richard Ornstein, Ph.D.
> The Mental Medicine Update[19]

- Naps.
- Meditation.
- Deep breathing.

> **Deep Breathing and Recovery**
>
> One of the most powerful, time-tested tools for controlling physiology is breath control. The stress–recovery relationship is fully understandable in a single breath. Breathing in is stress and breathing out is recovery. If we breathe more air in than we recover, the results are hyperventilation and increased mental and physical arousal. If we exhale longer and more fully than we inhale, the consequence is decreased mental and physical arousal. Breathing in to a count of four and breathing out to a count of eight can lead to a profound state of relaxation and recovery. A single diaphragmatic (belly) breath, wherein the out-breath is long and slow, can stimulate significant recovery. The more you practice, the better you get.

- Reading.
- Watching movies, TV.
- Listening to music.
- Talking about feelings.

> People most at risk for illness are those who experience a trauma, continue to think about it, but don't talk about it.
> David Myers, Ph.D.
> Author of *The Pursuit of Happiness*[20]

NEED FULFILLMENT

It's important to know that all recovery is need fulfillment. The urge associated with a need is stress and fulfillment of the need is recovery. The healthiest people are those who know *what they need* and know *best how to fill their needs*. For example, the urge associated with the need is to sleep is stress, and the relief that comes from satisfying the urge by sleeping is recovery. The same is true for hunger, thirst, love, safety, security, and self-esteem. All we have to do is recognize the need and then respond accordingly. Sounds simple enough. Unfortunately, it isn't. People get lonely or depressed and attempt to fill the need by eating; they get tense and nervous and seek relief in alcohol and drugs. They feel insecure and threatened and respond by putting people down and becoming aggressive.

Here is a sampling of our core training recommendations regarding need fulfillment:

- Learn to listen to needs. Needs are expressed via feelings and emotions. One of the primary purposes of negative emotions is to alert you to your unmet needs. The more intense the negativity and discomfort, the more urgent the need.

Creative Recoveries*

1. Read comics.
2. Write or read poetry.
3. Say a prayer.
4. Browse through your favorite bookstore.
5. Go for a brisk walk at sunset.
6. Plan a surprise party for someone.
7. Take the longer, more peaceful route home from work.
8. Eat lunch at a nearby park.
9. Plan a practical joke on a favorite colleague.
10. Browse through travel books and maps to plan your next vacation.
11. Review photos from last year's vacation.
12. Visit the zoo.
13. Play games you haven't enjoyed since childhood—checkers, dominoes, and so on.
14. Visit a historical landmark or museum.
15. Plan a bicycle trip.
16. Go rock climbing.
17. Take an astronomy class.
18. Attend a concert.
19. Try to learn juggling.
20. Wash and detail your car.

---

*An excellent resource for creative recoveries is Ann McGee-Cooper, *You Don't Have to Go Home from Work Exhausted*, Dallas: Bowen and Rogers, 1988.

- Become skillful in identifying your needs and responding in ways that drive real recovery. Matching the right recovery activity with the right need is a lifelong learning process. Self-understanding is the key. Matching appropriate recovery to specific needs is the most important building block in the achievement of high levels of health and happiness.

- When unmet needs are being expressed that cannot be immediately satisfied, take the message and move on. Acknowledge the need, commit to taking care of it as soon as possible, then get back to business. Don't bask in your sea of negativity and pull everyone down with you. Take the message that you're feeling insecure or tired, and respond as soon as you can. But don't wallow.

"Every So Often I Go Over the Edge"

RIDING THE WAVES OF STRESS AND RECOVERY

OVER THE YEARS, we came to a critical understanding: our healthiest, happiest, and most
productive performers were invariably the best
wave makers. Wave making has nothing to do
with surfing or trouble making. Here's what it
means for corporate athletes:

To work hard and play equally hard.

To go and then let go.

To be active and then idle.

To make it happen and then let it happen.

To maintain healthy work–rest ratios.

Either too much stress without recovery or
too much recovery without stress ultimately
becomes dysfunctional. It's as
much a mistake to link humans'
search for happiness and health
with complete tranquility and
the absence of stress as it is to link it with stress
alone. We suffer from stimulus hunger as much
as stimulus overload. Recovery is half the formula, and arousal, stimulation, and challenge

CHAPTER 9

are the other half. The real key to achieving sustained happiness, health, and productivity at the highest level is contained in a single word—*oscillation*.

Nearly every phenomenon in nature is periodic. Darkness follows daylight, winter follows autumn. All living things are creatures of oscillation. In physiological systems, oscillation invariably means cycling between episodes of stress and recovery, between periods of activity and rest. And oppositional to the rhythms of oscillation are the forces of linearity. Linearity is too much rest without activity or too much activity without rest. Linearity breeds disharmony and disorder in living organisms wherever it is found. And corporate athletes are no exception.

Linear stress causes energy stores in the muscles, adrenal glands, endocrine system, and nervous system to become depleted. Stress without intermittent recovery leads to chronically elevated levels of stress hormones, which become highly toxic over time. Failure to detoxify with restorative periods of recovery and healing can have tragic consequences for corporate athletes who are pushed to achieve at record-breaking levels. Everything from suppression of immune function to depression, and from eating disorders to ulcers can be the consequence.

Linear or excessive recovery, on the other hand, causes one's capacity for energy expenditure (stress) to erode. Protracted recovery simply undermines functional capacity, be it mental, physical, or emotional. We simply lose our ability to tolerate stress wherever and whenever periods of sustained protection from stress occur.

BUILT-IN RHYTHMS

Every bodily rhythm has its own wave form, amplitude, and frequency. Rhythms that pulse within us on a 24-hour cycle are called circadian (*circa - dies,* "about a day"). These rhythms change in concert with the rotation of the earth. Changes in temperature and light that occur as the earth moves in relationship to the sun serve as timers for synchronizing the biological clocks. The most important circadian rhythm is the sleep–wake cycle.

Collectively, the myriad rhythms of the body form a complex stress–recovery matrix. They are referred to as Basic Rest–Activity Cycles (BRAC). Energy, mood, alertness, emotional state, muscle strength, resistance to disease, and performance are affected by the timing, frequency, and strength of such cycles.

Psychobiology researcher Ernest Rossi contends that we wreak havoc on our bodily systems when we disturb our built-in rhythms.[1] Rossi argues that when we override the body's natural cycles of stress and rest, we become vulnerable to a wide range of physical and emotional problems, including everything from chronic fatigue to depression.

He contends that we must break cycles of stress every 90 to 120 minutes with 15 to 20 minutes of recovery. These small rest breaks, he says, restore the proper ultradian rhythms, and are critical to physical and psychological rejuvenation, not to mention long-term health. If we ignore this need to renew, we risk depleting the body's hormonal messenger molecules, glucose and insulin, as well as a host of other adaptive biochemical mechanisms. In Toughness Training, we refer to the oscillation principle as wave making.

DISEASE AS A FAILURE TO OSCILLATE

A number of researchers now conceive disease as a result of altered rhythmic functions.[2] An ideal oscillatory pattern exists for every bodily system. Health at the highest level clearly follows a nonlinear dynamic. From nearly every perspective, human physiology and behavior are patterned and rhythmic. The human organism functions as an integrated whole, and the unifying principle throughout appears to be oscillation. Within this context, optimal health is characterized in oscillations that are rhythmic, patterned, and stable. Altered rhythms can be easily seen in widely varied illnesses and disease—sleep disorders, hypertension, gastrointestinal disorders, asthma, and eating disorders, to mention just a few.

A useful analogy is to view the human body as a vast reservoir of oscillating pendulum clocks held together by a resonating, vibrating wall of skin. When the rhythms are properly synchronized and harmonious, the consequence is health and vitality. When any one or more of the major clocks gets out of phase, eventually the rhythms of all systems become affected. When all clocks are in phase, the result is similar to the music that is produced when all the instruments in an orchestra are properly synchronized and harmonized. In the human body, the result is higher levels of health, happiness, and productivity.

When one or more of the body's major biological rhythms are disturbed, the rhythms of all other systems will eventually be affected. Our "large clocks" include such things as sleep cycles, eating cycles, respiration rate, and rhythms of the heart. Disturbances in any of these clocks typically have profound consequences for the entire organism. The rhythms of all systems are influenced by the rhythms of all other systems. Blood pressure, for example, is influenced by respiration rate, timing of meals, and the volume and timing of sleep and exercise. And although blood pressure appears to be nonrhythmic (linear), it too has its own daily oscillatory mode. In fact, blood pressure oscillates in both its systolic and diastolic levels more than 65 times per minute.

 Synchronization of the myriad rhythms in our lives is called entrainment—we are in harmony with the world around us. Our body's internal rhythms are in sync with the rhythms of our lives. To put it another way, the waves of stress and recovery in our external world are in harmony with those of our internal world.

A good analogy for understanding the corporate athlete's role in the entrainment process is Gerry Griffin's notion of being a conductor leading a world-class symphonic orchestra. The conductor's responsibility is to get all the independent musicians in harmony and in sync with everyone else. To be successful, all rhythms must be perfectly synchronized in ways that bring the

---

Important Understandings

1. The more intense the pressure situation, the more important the need to oscillate.

2. Recovery and oscillation are not the same. Recovery is only half the oscillation cycle. Stress is the other half.

3. Excessive recovery eventually undermines the ability to expend energy and seek stress.

4. Too much recovery is as disruptive and harmful as too much stress.

5. Synchronizing your daily stress/recovery cycles with your body's built-in natural rhythms should be a constant goal.

---

music to life. For corporate athletes, the music is performance at maximum capacity without compromising health or happiness. We must find ways to mesh the rhythms of corporate life with our natural biological rhythms. The forces of linearity and disharmony in the corporate world are very powerful. Making music there is no simple task.

THE LANGUAGE OF LINEARITY

Failure to attune to the body's natural variations produces effects that become increasingly more evident over time. Ernest Rossi has identified a four-stage progression that occurs when we don't fulfill our body's need for restorative breaks every 90 to 120 minutes. The first stage of linearity brings poor concentration, sharp drops in performance, careless errors, distracting fantasies, and memory lapses. These are first-line signals that an oscillatory break should be taken.

When ignored, stage-two signals of disharmony take form. They include feelings of irritability, hyperactivity, sudden anger, and impatience. Commonly witnessed in workaholics, failure to oscillate leads to mounting muscle tension, hostility, aggressiveness, and resentment. This imbalance makes things like coffee, cigarettes, alcohol, and drugs particularly inviting.

Stage-three signals invariably evolve around declines in performance. The continued linearity shows up in accident proneness, bad decisions, mistakes of all kinds, poor reaction time, and missed appointments.

Stage four involves health. Eventually, the sustained linearity undermines the body's capacity for repair and healing. The immune system eventually breaks down in the face of the chronically high level of stress hormones. Opportunistic infections such as flus and colds become common as do illnesses such as ulcers, high blood pressure, headaches, and respiratory difficulties.

Examples of linearity in corporate life include the three scenarios described below.

1. **Sitting at your desk all day.** Hours on the phone, hours pounding away at your computer, hours of meetings in your office

represent business-as-usual for many corporate athletes. The forces of linearity in such situations are very powerful. Building in a few oscillatory rituals can make a world of difference. Here are our recommendations for wave making:

- Spend at least 50 percent of your time on the phone standing or moving around. Use hands-free phones whenever possible, to give you more freedom of movement and less sustained neck stress. You can even do some stretching exercises during your phone conversations.

- Do regular finger-and-hand stretching exercises when you must do sustained work on your computer. Periodically, shake your hands vigorously to break up the tension. Take a break at least every 90 minutes, and go for a walk outside in the fresh air whenever possible. Do wrist-and-hand strengthening exercises regularly.

- Never allow meetings in your office to run continuously. Insist on breaks every 1½ to 2 hours. Move, drink liquids, and consume nutritious snacks that are low in fat. Get fresh air into the room regularly, and be sure room temperature does not become too warm.

2. **Thinking about work-related problems every waking minute.** Shutting down the juices and shifting gears is a major problem for many corporate athletes. Once problems get into your brain, they just get recycled over and over, particularly if they pose a serious

> Our brain, like the whole cerebral mechanism and the body in general, works better when it respects a certain biological rhythm. If we force it to work at an excessive rate for too long, it causes mental strain.[3]
>
> Monique LePoncin, PhD
> Brain researcher

threat. At the office and at home, your brain remains in the ON position. Try these recommendations for wave making:

- Develop a highly specific ritual for changing mental gears and setting aside all your worry and perseverating. Getting physical is an important step for most corporate athletes. Running, weight lifting, tennis, or walking will start a new oscillatory pattern. Hitting a bucket of balls at the golf driving range on the way home from work, or stopping to shoot baskets for 30 minutes before returning to the home front can help tremendously. You simply can't simultaneously think about the problem of the day and hit golf balls or play a three-on-three pick-up game of basketball. Any physical activity that requires your undivided attention can be very helpful in breaking patterns of linearity.

- Adopt strict policies about doing work at home, conducting business on your home phone, or talking business 24 hours a day. If job-related work must be done at home, put specific boundaries around the time. "I'll work between 7:30 and 8:30 P.M., but that's it."

- If you have children, spend time getting totally out of your world and into theirs. Do fun things together. Play laugh tapes. The point is to leave your workday by becoming completely absorbed in another time and space. If you have no children, depend on a hobby, a pet, or a specific mental ritual to decompress and change gears.

3. **Sustained anger, fear, or hostility on the job.** Unethical power moves, brutal office politics, failed mergers, and broken promises can cut deeply into a corporate athlete's psyche. The deeper the wounds, the longer the healing process. The anger, hostility, and resentment will generally not pose a serious health or performance threat so long as you learn to periodically shut down the highly toxic emotions and get intermittent relief.

- For the majority of corporate athletes, the most effective strategy for breaking negative emotional states is *exercise*. And generally, the more intense the exercise, the better. Working out

Making Waves

Stress: Push. Try harder. Charge forward. Never let up. Win. Achieve. Accelerator to the floor. Make something happen. Go for it. Don't be lazy. Work hard. Sacrifice. Fight on. Never quit!

Recovery: Chill. Shut down. Turn off. Take a break. Smell the roses. Hang out. Let go. Relax. Rest. Time out. Just be. Recover. Rejuvenate. Fill your well. Heal.

and getting sweaty, however, may not be possible in your work environment. If that's the case, other rituals must be explored. Any strategies that help teach you how to better maintain a present focus can be extremely valuable. Anger and hostility stem from focusing on the past, and fear is rooted in the future. Meditation, deep breathing, and progressive relaxation are all present-centered activities and therefore can be very helpful in fighting this type of linearity.

LINEARITY AND PRESSURE

The greater the pressure, the more difficult it is to oscillate. But that's precisely why corporate athletes train for toughness. Without well-established rituals in sleeping, eating, exercising, recovering, and preparing, you'll stop oscillating whenever crunch time rolls around again and you're pushed to your limits. There will be no synchronization of biological clocks, no stress–recovery balance, no harmony. Your genius will dry up like the dust of the Serengeti. When you need it the most, your ability to perform and maintain a sense of order and rhythm in your life will fade away.

It's important to understand that, unless you're properly trained to preserve them, the rhythms of recovery, such as sleeping, eating, and exercising, tend to fail under conditions of extreme stress. Just when you need sleep the most, you can't sleep. When you should be eating, you don't feel hungry. You don't feel like exercising, laughing, spending time with your family, or socializing with friends when the forces of linearity are the greatest. The point is: you can't trust the natural rhythms of your body to keep you in balance when the pressures of life and business start peaking. If, however, you've been training properly, you'll adhere to your balancing and oscillatory rituals even more precisely as the pressures and demands on you mount. You won't have to rely solely on nature's instincts to guide you; all your training will be there to protect you. Your health and happiness remain intact because you continue to oscillate, regardless of the demands of your playing field.

The forces of linearity are greatest for accountants during tax season; for attorneys during high-profile, high-stakes trials; for salespeople in their scramble to make year-end quotas; for executives who have only two months remaining to reverse a loss of market share. The temptation here is to live out-of-balance temporarily, in order to achieve the goal: just tough it out, work harder and longer, forget the sleep, eat when you can, no time for exercise, family and friends don't exist. Get the damned job done and then you'll have time for all those things later. Sounds good, but don't forget Rossi's stages. Out of balance eventually means mistakes, bad decisions, poor judgment, and missed opportunities. Even when the answers to your dilemma are right in front of you, you're likely to miss them. Your ability to get along with other people, to work as an effective member of a team also becomes compromised. Your most precious asset, your personal health, is placed in serious jeopardy.

What's the answer? Push like hell but keep oscillating. Guard your sleep, your intake of food, your exercise routines, and recovery opportunities. Get the job done, do it right, and get it done on time, but STAY IN BALANCE. The key to this dual performance is training. The tougher the corporate life gets, the more you need to use your training to oscillate.

In his own way, Theodore Roosevelt was referring to wave making:

Far better it is to dare mighty things, to win glorious triumphs, even though checkered by failure, than to rank with those poor spirits who neither enjoy much nor suffer much, because they live in the gray twilight that knows not victory nor defeat.

BURNOUT AS FAILURE TO OSCILLATE

In a real sense, burnout is nature's way of forcing you to oscillate. When you burn out, you shut down. You don't feel like doing anything, so you don't. You go dead, mope around, sleep, get lazy, and veg. This "I don't want to do anything" feeling is protective. It's exactly what you need. Burnout is a forced *time out* because you wouldn't take the time voluntarily. Remember, it's not stress that causes burnout, it's your failure to periodically seek relief. High stress rhythmically balanced with intermittent recovery is no problem. But a combination of high stress, poor sleep, inadequate nutrition, no exercise, no humor, too much alcohol, too little (or no) personal time, and alienation from friends and family is lethal. In a real sense, burnout is an emergency call for restorative powers of oscillation.

The banking industry provides a good analogy for understanding the relationship between stress and recovery. Stress is analogous to writing checks. It's much more difficult to make deposits than it is to spend. Big-time spenders must make big-time deposits. Chronically spending more money than you deposit eventually spells financial disaster. The outcome in the banking industry is bankruptcy. In the stress/recovery world, it's called burnout. The volume of recovery has not kept pace with the level of stress. Bankruptcy forces you to adopt new patterns of spending and saving. Low motivation has the same effect; it leads to "not doing so much," which automatically increases the volume of recovery. After sufficient deposits are made, your motivation and enthusiasm come racing back. The motivational crisis was a wake-up call that your patterns of oscillation needed changing. Chronically failing to heed the message to change your spending habits can permanently alter your ability to write checks at all.

COACHES CALL IT PERIODIZATION

The training of all elite athletes is done in cycles. The technical word for it in sports is *periodization*[4]—the practice of scheduling episodes of stress and recovery in a predetermined ratio to achieve optimal training effects. A good periodization plan specifies when to push and when to shut down. It addresses issues of how hard to

Linear Stress

Here are some examples of excessive stress:

Linear Physical Stress

- Pounding away for hours on your computer keyboard without a break.
- Attending meeting after meeting without breaks.

Linear Emotional Stress

- Worrying about the loss of market share for days, without relief.
- Feeling constant pressure to reach quotas day after day, without relief.
- Feeling chronically frustrated and angry over senior management's lack of integrity and honesty.

Linear Mental Stress

- Reviewing annual report figures for extended periods, without relief.
- Constantly rethinking and reviewing upcoming sales conferences, without relief.
- Sustaining an intense problem-solving focus, for hours on end.

Linear Recovery

Here are some examples of excessive recovery:

Linear Physical Recovery

- Sitting at your desk for extended periods of time, without movement.
- Traveling on planes or in cars for extended periods of time, without movement.
- Prolonged TV-watching, without periodic physical stress exposure.

Linear Emotional Recovery

- Protecting yourself emotionally by repeatedly avoiding pressure situations.
- Persistently refusing to invest emotional commitment and energy.
- Constantly avoiding responsibility and emotional risk taking.

Linear Mental Recovery

- Not taking on new challenges that push you mentally.
- Allowing your mind to wander from the reality of a crisis for extended periods.
- Extended fantasy thinking.

push (intensity), how often (frequency), and how long (duration). Cycles of stress and recovery, work–rest ratios, and specific training objectives are carefully detailed in the plan. Experienced coaches clearly understand the consequences of failure to properly periodize. Too much stress relative to recovery leads to overtraining. Too much recovery relative to stress results in undertraining. And issues of overtraining and undertraining are just as pertinent to corporate athletes as they are to Olympic athletes. The following descriptions illustrate the similarities.

A professional tennis player (ranked 35th in the world at the time) describing an overtraining episode:

I was impossible to deal with. No matter what my coach said, I would take an opposing view. I became super-defensive. I couldn't accept even the slightest criticism, no matter how true or constructive it was. Every mistake made me furious. I was negative about everything and had serious problems concentrating. Crazy thoughts would go through my head, like "I hate tennis" or "I'm wasting my time on the circuit" or "I'll never become a success." I kept thinking, "I should quit this game," which is really strange for me. I really love tennis, and the weird thoughts, my foul language, the abuse of my coach were so wrong, but I simply couldn't stop it. I took three weeks off, never touched a racquet, and the whole thing turned around. Every time I push too much, the feelings start coming back again.

A plant manager for a Fortune 500 food manufacturing company:

Every so often, I just go over the edge. Not enough sleep, too many late nights, too much pushing to make deadlines. First I start getting very quiet and I don't want anyone around me. Then I develop a real attitude problem. I get very rough on people. I have zero patience and zero tolerance for wasting time and small talk. Word gets around at the plant when my monster personality shows up. Those are the times I really hate my job and everyone around it. That's when I know I've pushed too much. I recognize when it starts happening much sooner now.

Both of the preceding examples of overtraining were the result of failure to oscillate. The problem was not excessive stress in itself, but the volume of stress relative to the volume of recovery. The flood of negative, toxic emotions is simply a message of imbalance.

For a Formula I race car driver, it's the instrument panel with red lights going off everywhere—change tires, refuel, shift gears. Among the most common symptoms of overtraining are:

Boredom	Irritability
Eating and appetite problems	Low enjoyment
Exaggerated fears and doubts	Low motivation
Fatigue and low energy	Moodiness
Impaired immunity	Negativity
Insomnia	

Ironically, the symptoms of overtraining and undertraining are nearly identical. When you are undertrained, you are always being pushed beyond your limits. You are, in fact, always in a state of overtraining.

Here are the bottom-line lessons to be learned in this context:

1. Overtraining is a reality of corporate life just as it is in sport.
2. Overtraining is the consequence of failure to oscillate. The culprit is typically not the high stress but the insufficiency of periodic recovery.
3. Undertraining is also a consequence of inadequate oscillation. The culprit is lack of periodic stress exposure.
4. Messages of overtraining and undertraining are typically sent via negative emotions. An important toughness skill for corporate athletes to learn is how to recognize the signals before serious imbalances materialize. Using the race car analogy, check all the indicators on your instrument panel, and take corrective action before any real emergency occurs.
5. Corrective action for both overtraining and undertraining is BETTER OSCILLATION. Improved wave making usually brings immediate relief. Failure to listen, however, makes it increasingly difficult to break long-standing patterns of linearity. The longer the imbalance, the greater the potential for serious harm and the harder it will be to reestablish healthy rhythms.

6. When corporate athletes cease to oscillate properly, the best Performer Skills in the world won't save them. Eventually, even the best acting and mental preparation skills will fail to move their chemistry in empowering directions. That's precisely why toughness requires a partnership of world-class Performer Skills (to drive emotions) and world-class Life Skills (to keep you in balance and constantly oscillating).

YOU'RE GOING TO OSCILLATE— ONE WAY OR ANOTHER!

There's healthy oscillation and unhealthy oscillation. Failure to oscillate in natural, healthy ways doesn't mean you won't oscillate. The urge to oscillate is so powerful in the human species that, one way or another, you *will* do it. Unhealthy oscillatory patterns are painfully evident everywhere in corporate life. One of the most tragic is the use of drugs to get up and down the wave forms. Caffeine, amphetamines, cocaine, heroin, and the like, bring arousal, excitement, and energy. Alcohol, barbiturates, marijuana, valium, librium, xanax, and sleep medication bring you back down. "Uppers" and "downers" in the drug scene are artificial oscillators. As the forces of linearity increase, the seductive power of these unhealthy alternatives steadily increases. When the excitement and thrills can be achieved from such things as athletic competition, mountain climbing, or breaking new performance records on the job, or when relief can be achieved with exercise, meditation, or humor, the unhealthy seduction dies.

Phebe Farrow Port, currently the Vice President of Retail Sales Development Worldwide for Estée Lauder, Inc., is a world-class corporate athlete. Her global responsibilities include assessing specific foreign countries, or cities in the United States, for potential market share growth, and developing a plan of action that includes sales, marketing, and training. Her other responsibilities encompass the Estée Lauder at Vassar College program and the Estée Lauder International Leadership Summit at Oxford University in England. These are strategic professional development programs that impact the Estée Lauder companies' executives worldwide, at all levels of senior and middle management.

Phebe, however, is the first to admit that she was at one time a seriously undertrained corporate athlete. She says:

There are two key concepts that have had an enormous impact on my professional (and personal) life. The first is to "savor the moment and love the battle" more than the actual results. This was a huge change for me as I am extremely results-driven and had a hard time savoring the process. To step back and learn to enjoy and love the process as much as the actual results has enabled me to actually produce more and higher-quality results as well as enhanced productivity. As organizations are required to do more with less, this is a key skill or mindset needed at every level of business—that is, if the business hopes to be successful. To see the analogy of sport in this concept helped me understand the "how to" so that I could execute the toughness concepts and make them active in my daily life.

The second most important change for me was in the area of recovery. It was truly an eye opener to discover how linear my life was during a typical 12- to 14-hour workday. Understanding that recovery is your true growth period—and that it can be done in 30 seconds and in small, sound bites frequently throughout the day—was a tremendous awakening. Learning how to oscillate added to my energy store and to my ability to relax and think quickly on my feet. As I look back, it's amazing to me that I survived all the bad and unnecessary stress of my linear days as well as I did. The Mentally Tough program taught me how to increase my capacity to actually welcome *more* stress, not just manage or try to decrease the impact of stress on my life. This is the reality of business into the year 2000.

The phrase I use most during my business day is *IPS!* Learning how to change my chemistry in a matter of seconds, through acting skills coupled with a brief moment of recovery, has been an invaluable lesson. Now if I encounter an "emotional hit in the face" minutes before I must conduct a meeting, or address an audience, I have the tools required. I'm stronger now, I'm in training. I can deliver performance on demand, when I need it, 100 percent of the time.

"Fatigue Makes Enemies of Us All"

THE NEED FOR ENERGY

TAKE A MINUTE to describe how you feel in terms of energy right now. Your description will likely lead you directly to whatever emotional state you're experiencing at the moment. Your emotional state and your energy state are nearly synonymous. Emotions mobilize you to respond to changing situations by turning on and off your body's various energy systems.

Emotions and energy are rooted in the same physiology and chemistry. Learning to manage emotions, learning to manage energy, and learning to manage stress are all closely interconnected.

CHAPTER 10

Let's return again to your energy state right now. How would you describe it? If you're like the hundreds of people I interviewed in the course of building a model of energy used in the training of emotions, you will characterize your energy along two lines.[1] One will be intensity. You will describe your energy in terms of *how much* you're feeling, ranging from very low to very high. The second characteristic will be the affective quality of the energy. You will begin to describe how the energy makes you feel—comfortable or uncomfortable, pleasant or unpleasant, positive or negative. The relationship between energy intensity and energy affect is depicted in Figure 10.1.

Combining energy intensity with energy affect creates four distinct energy cells. In the upper left-hand quadrant is High Positive. This is the feeling of high energy fueled from a source that is pleasant and enjoyable. The distinction between positive and negative emotion is essentially one of affect. You experience positive emotions as pleasant and negative emotions as unpleasant. When you are in the High Positive energy state, you feel challenged, inspired, energetic, alive, engaged, connected, psyched, and pumped up. This is the energy of the IPS.

In a Low Positive energy state (lower left-hand quadrant), what little energy you have is still pleasant. Feelings of being peaceful, free, relaxed, and relieved, along with a sense of recovering, coasting, letting go, and reenergizing, are characteristic of this cell.

High Negative, in the upper right-hand quadrant, is the fight-or-flight cell. Feelings center around one of the two powerful emotions—anger or fear. The intensity is high, but the feeling state is very unpleasant and unenjoyable. Feelings of being afraid, fearful, anxious, angry, frustrated, vengeful, jealous, hateful, and defensive are characteristic. Such feelings are highly distressful.

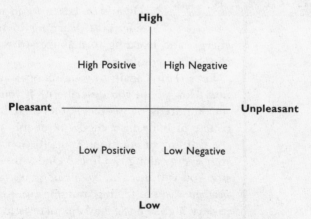

Figure 10.1 A Two-Dimensional Model of Energy

In the Low Negative cell (lower right-hand quadrant), what little energy is present is clearly unpleasant. The most common feelings are those of depression, sadness, loneliness, hopelessness, and helplessness. We descend into this energy state when we are feeling burned out, helpless, or sad, or when we are grieving.

One of the most helpful things we do, when we are getting people started in the Toughness Training program, is called an Energy Audit. Its purpose is to have our trainees tune into the kinds of energy they experience throughout the day. They are asked to estimate how much time they spend in each of the four cells shown in Figure 10.2. Once we know their current energy estimates, we'll gain real insights into how happy, healthy, and productive they're likely to be.

In the energygram shown in Figure 10.3, you can estimate what percentage of your time you spend in each of the four cells. The total percentages of all four quadrants should equal 100%. (Refer to the descriptions in Figure 10.2 in making your estimates.)

The second part of the energy audit involves a five-day sampling of personal energy on a systematic basis. Approximately every two

Figure 10.2   How You Feel—The Energy Audit

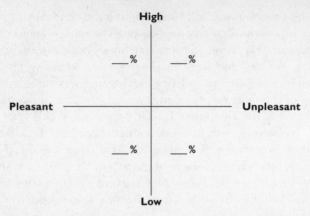

Figure 10.3 Energygram—Estimates of Personal Energy Expenditures

hours, estimate your energy level for the two hours just completed, using a 1-to-10 scale for both Intensity (low to high) and Affect (Unpleasant to Pleasant), as shown in Figure 10.4.

Start your energy recording as soon as you get up on the morning and make entries approximately every two hours thereafter. Here is a sample chart for one day:

Time	Intensity	Affect	Cell*
1. 7:00 A.M.	2	4	LP
2. 9:00 A.M.	3	5	LP
3. 11:00 A.M.	5	5	LN
4. 1:00 P.M.	6	3	HN
5. 3:00 P.M.	3	7	LP
6. 5:00 P.M.	6	7	HP
7. 7:00 P.M.	7	2	HN
8. 9:00 P.M.	2	6	LP
9. 11:00 P.M.	2	6	LP
Totals	36	45	
Average Energy (Divide by 9)	4	5	LP

* Refer to Figure 10.1 for cell labels.

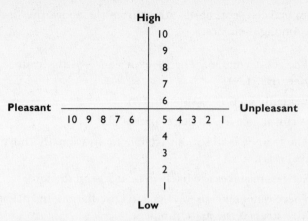

Figure 10.4   Rating Scales for Intensity and Affect

Here are just a few things that can be learned from the above one-day energy audit:

- The trainee has very little energy in the mornings.
- The trainee spends most of his or her time in Low Positive (LP).
- Virtually no time is spent in IPS.
- Performance is well below potential.
- There is not enough wave-making oscillation. The main problem is insufficient positive stress.

A five-day sampling provides the most accurate profile. We summarized the same trainee's five-day data as follows:

Day	Average Intensity	Average Affect
1	4.0	5.0
2	3.6	4.2
3	6.1	3.0
4	4.0	5.0
5	3.6	5.0
Totals	21.3	22.2
Average Energy (Divide by 5)	4.2	4.4

We can make several observations from the above five-day energy audit. Among them are:

- The most common energy experience of the trainee is Low Negative (LN).
- Virtually no time is spent in IPS.
- Performance is well below potential.
- The trainee is in serious trouble motivationally (burnout is a real risk).
- Serious mistakes are likely to be made on the job.
- There is not enough wave-making oscillation. Insufficient positive stress is the main problem.
- The trainee's health, happiness, and productivity are seriously in jeopardy.

Forms for a five-day audit are provided in Appendix C.

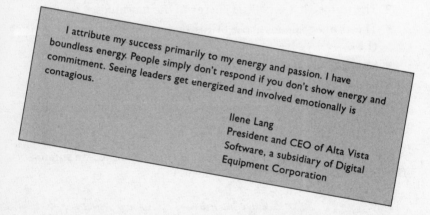

I attribute my success primarily to my energy and passion. I have boundless energy. People simply don't respond if you don't show energy and commitment. Seeing leaders get energized and involved emotionally is contagious.

Ilene Lang
President and CEO of Alta Vista
Software, a subsidiary of Digital
Equipment Corporation

Here's what we've learned from our work with the energygram over the past 15 years:

- Achievement of full performance potential requires entry into the High Positive energy cell.
- The worst performances will typically occur in either the Low Positive or the Low Negative cell. Better to be nervous or angry than without energy at all.

- Too much time in either the High Positive or the High Negative cell will eventually force you into the Low Negative cell. Too much timne in the High Negative cell will get you into the Low Negative cell much faster.

- The Low Positive and Low Negative cells are *Recovery Cells*. Low Positive is *natural recovery* and Low Negative is *forced recovery*.

- Entry into Low Negative is a *red alert*. Except when someone is grieving the loss of a loved one or sadness is tied to a specific event, Low Negative is a painful message of imbalance. Low Negative is often the body's way of protecting against the dangers of further overtraining. Repeated entry into Low Negative typically signals that important needs are not being met.

- Healthy wave making means oscillating between High Positive and Low Positive energy states. Sustained peak performances requires skillful oscillation between the High Positive energy associated with the Ideal Performance State (IPS) and the Low Positive energy associated with the Ideal Recovery State (IRS).[2] (See Figure 10.5.)

- The more time you spend in negative energy states, the greater the risk to your personal health. The chemistry of negative emotion can be highly toxic to immune cells. Chronic anger,

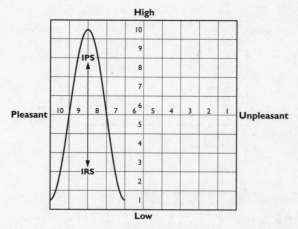

Figure 10.5   Healthy Wave Making: Oscillating Between the IPS and IRS

fear, and hostility can seriously compromise your immune function. The risk factors associated with Type A behavior and coronary heart disease have also been linked to chronic levels of distress associated with negative energy states.

- Low Positive energy stimulates healing and repair. The more stress in your life, the more important Low Positive becomes.

- High Negative energy states are, from time to time, appropriate and necessary. The key, however, is to make sure that they are appropriate and necessary. The price paid for High Negative energy can be very high.

- A major component of Toughness Training is converting High Negative stressors such as traffic jams, important clients, incompetent bosses, nightmare coworkers, speaking in front of

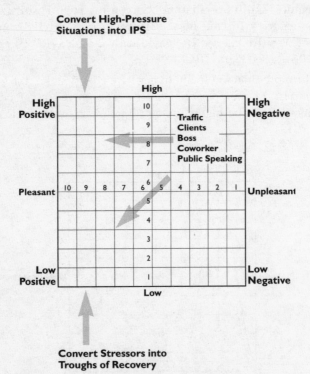

**Figure 10.6   Converting Stressors into Positive Energy:
The Toughness Training Effect**

groups, and so on, to High Positive or Low Positive stressors (Figure 10.6). Rituals, acting skills, and mental preparation are the available tools.

- A close relationship exists between energy states and tension. High Positive, for example, is high energy without tension (Figure 10.7).

- Each energy cell has its own distinctive chemistry, and each emotion within each cell has its own unique physiologic signature in the body. The energygram in Figure 10.8 represents a sampling of this type of relationship.

- Getting control of stress means getting control of and managing energy cells more effectively.[3] Increasing your awareness of ongoing energy states is the first step in accelerating control. Linking patterns of sleep, diet, exercise, rest, recovery, and need fulfillment to various energy states is fundamental to taking control. Important also is identification of the stressors in your life that require reconditioning so that they no longer stimulate inappropriate responses. After you've been on the Toughness Training program for thirty days, do another five-day energy audit. The dynamics of your energy will be very different and will positively impact every dimension of your life.

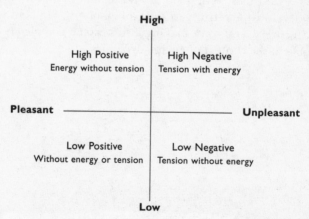

High

High Positive
Energy without tension

High Negative
Tension with energy

Pleasant ——————————————— Unpleasant

Low Positive
Without energy or tension

Low Negative
Tension without energy

Low

Figure 10.7 The Tension–Energy Relationship

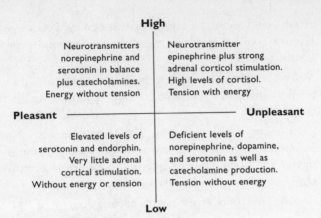

High

Neurotransmitters norepinephrine and serotonin in balance plus catecholamines. Energy without tension	Neurotransmitter epinephrine plus strong adrenal corticol stimulation. High levels of cortisol. Tension with energy

Pleasant ———————————————— **Unpleasant**

Elevated levels of serotonin and endorphin. Very little adrenal cortical stimulation. Without energy or tension	Deficient levels of norepinephrine, dopamine, and serotonin as well as catecholamine production. Tension without energy

Low

Figure 10.8   The Chemistry–Energy Relationship

CONCLUSION

Energy and emotion are intimately connected. Understanding the dynamics of energy takes you to the heart of the Toughness Training system. As Vince Lombardi said so aptly, "Fatigue makes cowards of us all." Take away energy and our empowering emotions collapse. Anything that affects our energy affects us emotionally. A fighting spirit requires powerful energy. Our happiness, health, and ability to perform all depend on our ability to mobilize and utilize energy. Rituals, acting skills, and mental preparation impact energy levels as powerfully as they do emotions. Skills in seeking stress, recovery, and wave making also become completely understandable in the context of energy dynamics.

Coming Home

A Daily Journey
Without End

I USE THE metaphor of **COMING HOME** to summarize the most important understandings about *Stress for Success* and Toughness Training. The following guidelines are for your own personal toughening journey.

- **COMING HOME** *is reordering your life so that the highest levels of health, happiness, and productivity are in fact attainable.* Toughness Training is based on the premise that when your life becomes properly synchronized and adapted to the forces around you, you need not compromise health and happiness in order to achieve maximum levels of productivity.

- **COMING HOME** *is facing the truth about your most profound weaknesses and making a commitment to do something concrete and tangible about them.* Taking responsibility for who and what you are right now is an essential step in facing the truth. No excuses. No defensiveness. No hiding. No denial.

223

- **COMING HOME** *is accepting the reality that every day is a battle for control, not of the world around you but of your response to it.* Who you are and what you become is not so much the result of what happens in your life as of how you respond to what happens. The forces of corporate life boggle the imagination. In the final analysis, the ultimate battleground is emotional. Victory requires a remarkably resilient, strong, flexible, and responsive warrior spirit.

- **COMING HOME** *is increasing your capacity to respond to the forces of life in the most adaptive, emotionally intelligent ways possible.* The issue here is your ability to drive the right emotions, particularly the IPS response, at the right time. Expanding and deepening your emotional capacity is not an option for you as a corporate athlete. It is an ongoing, never-ending reality of corporate life. It is the heart of Toughness Training.

- **COMING HOME** *is connecting what you do every day to your deepest and most enduring values and beliefs.* Your greatest strength flows from your deepest convictions. Passion, fight, commitment, drive, courage, and spirit are always linked to your core values and beliefs. Living a life that is inconsistent or out of sync with the core of who you are is a form of stress that simply cannot be balanced. Without meaning and purpose, your warrior spirit eventually fades into personal surrender.

> Dwell as near as possible to the channel in which your life flows.
> Henry Thoreau

- **COMING HOME** *is getting comfortable with change—the only real constant of corporate life.* The landscape changes on a daily basis for corporate athletes. Get comfortable or get overwhelmed. As Charles Darwin put it, "It is not the strongest of the species that survives, nor the most intelligent, but the one most responsive to change." Getting comfortable is emotional!

- **COMING HOME** *is acknowledging and respecting the interconnectedness of all things.* What you eat and how you sleep; your thoughts, feelings, beliefs, and values; your habits of exercise and recovery; your sense of humor; and your health, happiness, and productivity are all intimately bound together. Affect one and all are affected. Your mind and body are inseparably linked. Acknowledging this unity is fundamental to achieving balance and harmony in your life.

- **COMING HOME** *is realizing that all time is sacred time.* Life, however long or short, is essentially a gift of time. Your time is finite. Your chance to change, to grow, to connect, to make a difference is finite. There is no time to waste, no second to throw away. Take the time. Make time.

- **COMING HOME** *is fully acknowledging the importance and significance of past and future while understanding that life is lived to the fullest in the present.* Life becomes more precious and real in the present moment. When you step into the present, life pours in.

> The present is where life happens. . . . In truth, paradise is where you are right now. Period.[1]
>
> Stephan Rechtschaffen
> Author of *Time Shifting*

- **COMING HOME** *is fully understanding the connection between a sound mind and a sound body.* Hardy spirits inhabit strong bodies. Seeking stress physically deepens your capacity for life in general. The energy demands of corporate life exceed those placed on Olympic athletes. Actively seeking physical stress is fundamental to winning the energy battle.

- **COMING HOME** *is developing rituals in your life that keep you in rhythm with the world around you and enhance your ability to perform to your fullest potential in high-stress arenas.* The right rituals bring order and structure to the chaotic stage of corporate life. Rituals in eating, sleeping, and exercising, in family time, spiritual time, and personal time, are protective. They ensure that your most important needs will be met. Rituals mobilize your emotions and physiology so that your talents and skills remain within reach, regardless of the level of pressure!

- **COMING HOME** *is precision thinking and acting in high-stress performance arenas.* As a corporate athlete, one of the most powerful tools you have for controlling your emotional response to crisis is precision thinking and acting. What you think, the images you carry, and the way you act with your physical body have profound emotional consequences. Accept the reality that you can act and think your way into a new way of feeling.

- **COMING HOME** *is becoming a seeker of stress for a lifetime.* Staying young, retaining functional capacity, experiencing personal growth, and maintaining maximum health all require intermittent stress exposure. Protection from stress erodes the very foundation of all growth. Without stress, high levels of health, happiness, and achievement are simply unattainable.

- **COMING HOME** *is structuring your life to allow sufficient recovery time to adequately balance your high volume of stress.* It's not stress that's taking you apart; it's the lack of healing time to balance the stress. World-class stress requires world-class recovery. Your goal is to establish world-class stress–recovery balance in your life.

- **COMING HOME** *is acknowledging the fundamental importance of making waves in every sphere of your life—mental, physical, and emotional.* The principle of oscillation is deeply woven into the fabric of human nature. The relentless stresses of corporate life create powerful forces of linearity. All linearity eventually becomes dysfunctional and the price is paid by your health, happiness, and ability to perform.

- **COMING HOME** *is acknowledging that emotions do in fact run the show.* When all is said and done, your bottom-line need is GETTING RIGHT EMOTIONALLY. When you feel right, you can perform right. When you feel right, maximum health and happiness are attainable. Getting right emotionally is the core issue in Toughness Training.

- **COMING HOME** *is learning to love the battle—all of it!* Maxim Gorky captured it best when he said, "When work is a pleasure, life is a joy! When work is a duty, life is slavery!" Loving the battle is an acquired emotional response that must be strengthened and honed daily. Finding enjoyment in the simplest of tasks gets the process started.

- **COMING HOME** *is understanding that toughness, for a corporate athlete, is a forever journey.* You can't stand still. You can't go back. You must keep moving forward with a constant commitment to rebirth, to change, to personal growth. Just as companies must downsize, rightsize, and reengineer to survive and thrive into the future, so must you. You must constantly work to train away your mental, physical, and emotional baggage. You will then become stronger and more resilient than you have ever been before.

It's a tough corporate world we live in and it's not likely to get any easier in the next century. We live with stress but we don't have to die from it. Enlightened business practices are going to have to learn to pass that message on. Work hard, laugh, live, enjoy. If you can do those things and mean them, stress can be handled. I had to learn these lessons the hard way, but once I learned them I could do twice as much work in a day, twice as effectively.

John Hawks
Vice President, Hawks Communication

YOUR PERSONAL TOUGHNESS CHECKLIST

_____ I can sleep anywhere, anytime.

_____ I can take a nap whenever and wherever I need it and wake up feeling fresh and alert.

_____ I wake up in the morning without an alarm.

_____ I wake up feeling rested and energized without the help of caffeine.

_____ I consistently go to bed and get up at the same time every day.

_____ I eat often and light.

_____ I function best as an early bird (morning person) rather than as a sleep-deprived night owl.

_____ I laugh easily and often (more than 50 times per day).

_____ I use humor that's noncynical, nonaggressive, and playful.

_____ I can laugh easily at myself.

_____ I exercise a minimum of three times per week for 20 to 30 minutes each time.

_____ I regularly work to strengthen my stomach muscles (daily curl-ups).

_____ I routinely do some form of interval exercise to improve my cardiovascular function.

_____ I routinely do some form of strength training.

_____ I stretch daily.

_____ People tell me that I'm a happy person.

_____ I can change my mood states when necessary.

_____ I've acquired excellent IPS acting skills.

_____ I'm a seeker of stress.

_____ I'm challenged during tough times.

_____ I work hard and play equally hard.

_____ I listen to my negative emotions but am not controlled by them.

_____ I have a keen sense of personal awareness.

_____ I can generally trace negative emotions to their source.

_____ I am a High Positive energy person.

_____ I recover quickly from stress.

_____ I have a deep capacity for tolerating stress of all kinds.

_____ I can perform at high levels, on demand, regardless of the circumstances.

_____ My needs and wants are pretty much the same.

_____ My lifestyle would be described as healthy.

_____ My lifestyle meets most of my needs.

_____ I have an accurate perception of my strengths and weaknesses.

_____ I train every day to get stronger and tougher.

_____ I am always exploring new personal frontiers.

_____ I have a strong will to live and a passionate relationship with life.

_____ The way I live my life is consistent with my deepest values.

_____ I have a strong connection with family and friends.

_____ I am a courageous fighter when others need me most.

_____ I assume complete responsibility for the direction and structure of my life.

_____ I never surrender my spirit.

_____ I keep a daily record of my efforts.

APPENDIX A

Face-the-Truth Profiles

Toughness Training Profile™ for Coworkers

Make four copies of the TTP below and give them to coworkers who know you well. Forms should be filled out and returned to you anonymously.

Please fill out the form below on _____. You are to answer each item according to how you see this person responding under pressure.

	1	2	3	4	5	6	7	8	9	10	
Rigid	○	○	○	○	○	○	○	○	○	○	Flexible
Nonresponsive	○	○	○	○	○	○	○	○	○	○	Responsive
Nonenergetic	○	○	○	○	○	○	○	○	○	○	Energetic
Nonresilient	○	○	○	○	○	○	○	○	○	○	Resilient
Fearful	○	○	○	○	○	○	○	○	○	○	Challenged
Moody	○	○	○	○	○	○	○	○	○	○	Even-tempered
Noncompetitive	○	○	○	○	○	○	○	○	○	○	Competitive
Dependent	○	○	○	○	○	○	○	○	○	○	Self-reliant
Uncommitted	○	○	○	○	○	○	○	○	○	○	Committed
Unfriendly	○	○	○	○	○	○	○	○	○	○	Friendly
Passive	○	○	○	○	○	○	○	○	○	○	Assertive
Insecure	○	○	○	○	○	○	○	○	○	○	Confident
Impatient	○	○	○	○	○	○	○	○	○	○	Patient
Undisciplined	○	○	○	○	○	○	○	○	○	○	Disciplined
Pessimistic	○	○	○	○	○	○	○	○	○	○	Optimistic
Not Open to Change	○	○	○	○	○	○	○	○	○	○	Open to Change
Unmotivated	○	○	○	○	○	○	○	○	○	○	Motivated
Poor Problem Solver	○	○	○	○	○	○	○	○	○	○	Good Problem Solver
Poor Team Player	○	○	○	○	○	○	○	○	○	○	Team Player
Unwilling to Take Risks	○	○	○	○	○	○	○	○	○	○	Risk Taker
Physically Unfit	○	○	○	○	○	○	○	○	○	○	Physically Fit
Negative Body Language	○	○	○	○	○	○	○	○	○	○	Positive Body Language
Not Playful at Work	○	○	○	○	○	○	○	○	○	○	Playful at Work
Defensive	○	○	○	○	○	○	○	○	○	○	Open
Poor Sense of Humor	○	○	○	○	○	○	○	○	○	○	Great Sense of Humor

Team Building Perceptual Assessment

Date _____ Person to be Profiled _____

☐ Self-Profile   ☐ Not Self-Profile

	1	2	3	4	5	6	7	8	9	10	
Defensive	O	O	O	O	O	O	O	O	O	O	Open
Unfriendly	O	O	O	O	O	O	O	O	O	O	Friendly
Poor Sense of Humor	O	O	O	O	O	O	O	O	O	O	Good Sense of Humor
Critical of Others	O	O	O	O	O	O	O	O	O	O	Accepting of Others
Negative Attitude	O	O	O	O	O	O	O	O	O	O	Positive Attitude
Unmotivated	O	O	O	O	O	O	O	O	O	O	Motivated
Nonenergetic	O	O	O	O	O	O	O	O	O	O	Energetic
Thinks "Me"	O	O	O	O	O	O	O	O	O	O	Thinks "We"
Constantly Seeks Praise	O	O	O	O	O	O	O	O	O	O	Rarely Seeks Praise
Poor Communicator	O	O	O	O	O	O	O	O	O	O	Good Team Player
Moody	O	O	O	O	O	O	O	O	O	O	Even-tempered
Poor Team Player	O	O	O	O	O	O	O	O	O	O	Good Team Player
Distant	O	O	O	O	O	O	O	O	O	O	Caring
Uncooperative	O	O	O	O	O	O	O	O	O	O	Cooperative
Poor Listener	O	O	O	O	O	O	O	O	O	O	Good Listener
Suspicious	O	O	O	O	O	O	O	O	O	O	Trusting
Threatens Others	O	O	O	O	O	O	O	O	O	O	Challenges Others

Sample Daily Ritual

5:30 A.M. Get Up (Same Time Every Day)

- Turn on all the lights (to stimulate flow of cortisol).

- Get outside if the sun is up.

- Exercise for 10 to 30 minutes. Go for a walk, jog, do some mild stretching. You can skip the exercise if you feel alert and fully awake without caffeine or wish to exercise at another time.

- Drink a small glass of orange juice to raise your blood sugar.

- Perform your personal hygiene ritual.

- Perform your personal dressing ritual.

- Eat a small breakfast.
  Example: Slow cooked oatmeal (10 minutes), small juice, skim milk, half a banana, slice of whole wheat toast with low-calorie jam.

- Take a vitamin/mineral supplement with 6 to 8 ounces of bottled water.

- Review yesterday's mail (take home all mail on the previous day) and all important notes from yesterday's priority list. Construct today's priority list. Place reminders, numbers, and affirmations in your time management planner.

- Prepare a snacking brown bag.
  Examples: apples, oranges, raisins, cereal, bagels, veggies, pretzels, and so on.

- Organize your inner resources via spiritual time (15 min.).

- Spend 10 minutes in a mental rehearsal of how you intend to bring IPS to life today and why it's important to do so. Use music to enhance the effectiveness of your thoughts.

- Bring workout gear for exercise, if appropriate.

Commute to Work

- If driving, listen to music, books on tape, or motivational, humor, or language tapes. If riding on subways, buses, or trains, focus on some reading materials to minimize any travel distress. Your goal is to convert travel distress into either positive stress or additional recovery.

- For subway, bus, or train travel, if additional sleep is needed, learn to nap lightly.

Arrival at the Office

- Arrive a minimum of 15 minutes before you are scheduled to begin work or take appointments. Perform your start-up ritual. Take no calls or visitors until your ritual is complete. Place your priority list at the assigned corner of your desk, have your daily planner opened and ready, put away the files taken home for review, set out the folders and materials needed for the day. Place them appropriately, with reminders and phone numbers ready.

- Set a specific time in your afternoon schedule to return phone calls.

First Recovery Break

- Occurs after 1½ to 2 hours of work.
- Lasts 10 to 15 minutes.
- Contains both a nutritional and an exercise component.
  Nutritional examples: ½ orange, ½ plain bagel, pretzels, 6 ozs. of bottled water. Exercise examples: walk outside and around building, walk up and down four flights of stairs, perform rubber tubing exercises, stomach crunches.

Recovery Midday Meal

- Work out for 15 to 30 minutes.
  Examples: walk outside, in-company gym, up and down stairs, exercise with rubber tubing.

- Light meal (carbohydrate and protein combination).
  Examples: turkey sandwich on dark bread with mustard (no mayo), lettuce, and tomato; fruit, nonfat yogurt, juice, bottled water.

2:00 to 4:00 P.M.   Circadian Trough

- Save this time for tasks not requiring intense, focused concentration.

- A good time for telephone calls, meetings, travel time, activities requiring movement. Avoid scheduling detail work, writing projects, and similar tasks during this time.

- A 10- to 15-minute power nap or an IPS music break will return 1 hour and 45 minutes of alertness and focus. When your playing field allows, utilize this opportunity to drive productivity, staying in sync with your body's natural rhythms.

Telephone Time Oscillation

- Spend at least 50 percent of your telephone time standing and moving. This is a great time to do stretching exercises. Hands-free phones provide the opportunity for exercise-band work.

Regular Afternoon Recovery Breaks

- Break after every 1½ to 2 hours of work. Take 10 to 15 minutes of recovery oscillation.

- In each break, completely cease whatever you are doing and replace it with activities that provide a wave of genuine recovery.
  Examples: walking, stretching, stomach crunches, laughter, listening to music, calling home to connect with loved ones, time alone.

- In each break, introduce some type of nutritional recovery. Juice and water intake should be adapted to heat and humidity conditions, exercise levels, and so forth. At least 6 to 8 ounces of bottled water should be consumed during the afternoon.
  Examples of snacks: carrots, properly balanced energy shakes, low-fat energy bars, fresh fruit.

Late Afternoon Exercise

- Best time to reduce mental, emotional, and physical stress.
- Do 20 to 30 minutes of interval exercise followed by 10 minutes of stretching. Do strength training with machines, free weights, or exercise bands every other day.
- If you are unable to set aside late afternoon time, exercise whenever you can establish a regular, reliable exercise time.
- Do not exercise within 2 hours of your sleep cycle. Hormonal changes from exercise can be very disruptive to entry into sleep.

Recovery Evening Meal

- Light, low-fat items—consistent with overall dietary theme (small portions).
  Examples: baked chicken, brown rice, fresh vegetables, fruit, bottled water, and juice.
- A glass of wine or one beer with dinner is optional. Not recommended for anyone with sleep problems. Even small amounts of alcohol can be very disruptive to some people's sleep cycle.
- Complete your meal before 8:00 P.M. whenever possible.
- Center the meal around the family if possible.

Family Time

- Set aside a certain block of time daily to connect with loved ones. The important issue is the quality, more than the quantity, of the time spent together. Uninterrupted, focused listening, talking, and communicating should be enjoyed.
- When traveling, set aside a daily telephone time for loved ones.
- Carefully plan weekends, holidays, and vacations to reconnect emotionally with family and close friends.

Non-Work-Related Hobbies

- Spend more time (however short) working on your hobby, playing a musical instrument, painting, writing, doing anything creative. Such activities provide powerful recovery mentally and emotionally.

Evening Snack

- Carbohydrates only. No protein or fat.
- Facilitates sleep for some people.

10:30 to 11:00 P.M.   Begin Sleep Ritual

- Sleep ritual should begin approximately 30 minutes before you wish to be asleep. Can include such things as hot shower, TV watching, reading, music, meditation.
- Goal is to be asleep by 11:00 P.M.

General Considerations

- Follow nutritional guidelines for the day: 55 percent carbohydrates, 25 percent proteins, 20 percent fats (explained in detail earlier).
- Eliminate all caffeine over time.
- As soon as possible, establish a consistent routine for making waves and staying balanced throughout your day.
- Controlling the way you use your time is the key to staying in control in high-stress arenas.

Five-Day Energy Audit Form

DAY 1

Time	Intensity (1–10)	Effect (1–10)	Cell
1. _____	_____	_____	_____
2. _____	_____	_____	_____
3. _____	_____	_____	_____
4. _____	_____	_____	_____
5. _____	_____	_____	_____
6. _____	_____	_____	_____
7. _____	_____	_____	_____
8. _____	_____	_____	_____
9. _____	_____	_____	_____
10. _____	_____	_____	_____

Totals _____ _____

Average Energy _____ _____ _____
(Divide by number of entries)

DAY 2

Time	Intensity (1–10)	Effect (1–10)	Cell
1. _____	_____	_____	_____
2. _____	_____	_____	_____
3. _____	_____	_____	_____
4. _____	_____	_____	_____
5. _____	_____	_____	_____
6. _____	_____	_____	_____
7. _____	_____	_____	_____
8. _____	_____	_____	_____
9. _____	_____	_____	_____
10. _____	_____	_____	_____

Totals _____ _____

Average Energy _____ _____ _____
(Divide by number of entries)

DAY 3

Time	Intensity (1–10)	Effect (1–10)	Cell
1.			
2.			
3.			
4.			
5.			
6.			
7.			
8.			
9.			
10.			

Totals

Average Energy
(Divide by number of entries)

DAY 4

Time	Intensity (1–10)	Effect (1–10)	Cell
1.			
2.			
3.			
4.			
5.			
6.			
7.			
8.			
9.			
10.			

Totals

Average Energy
(Divide by number of entries)

DAY 5

Time	Intensity (1–10)	Effect (1–10)	Cell
1. _____	_____	_____	_____
2. _____	_____	_____	_____
3. _____	_____	_____	_____
4. _____	_____	_____	_____
5. _____	_____	_____	_____
6. _____	_____	_____	_____
7. _____	_____	_____	_____
8. _____	_____	_____	_____
9. _____	_____	_____	_____
10. _____	_____	_____	_____

Totals   _____   _____

Average Energy   _____   _____   _____
(Divide by number of entries)

5-DAY SUMMARY

	Average Intensity	*Average Effect*
Day 1	_____	_____
Day 2	_____	_____
Day 3	_____	_____
Day 4	_____	_____
Day 5	_____	_____
Totals	_____	_____
Average Energy (Divide by 5)	_____	_____

Meditation Resources

Benson, Herbert. *The Relaxation Response.* New York: Avon, 1976.
The best single source for understanding what relaxation means and its connection to meditation.

Goldstein, J., and Kornfield, J. *Seeking the Heart of Wisdom: The Path of Insight Meditation.* Boston: Shambhala, 1987.
A variety of essays on meditation practice.

Kabat-Zinn, J. *Full Catastrophe Living: Using the Wisdom of Your Body and Mind to Face Stress, Pain and Illness.* New York: Delacorte, 1991.
A step-by-step approach to learning meditation. An outstanding resource.

Thich Nhat Hanh. *The Miracle of Mindfulness: A Manual on Mediatation,* 2nd ed. Boston: Beacon, 1988.
An elegant introduction to meditation practice.

Notes and
Related Readings

PART I: The Corporate Athlete

Chapter 1. "In Today's Corporate World, You Either Perform to the Max or Don't Play": Learning How to Be Tough

1. Jansen, D. *Full Circle.* New York: Random House, 1994.
2. Loehr, J.E. "The Ideal Performance State." *Sports Science Periodical on Research and Technology in Sports* (Canada), Jan. 1983.
3. Loehr, J.E. *Mental Toughness Training for Sports.* New York: Penguin, 1986.

Chapter 2. "Without Balance, We Shut Down Our Ability to Perform": Facing the Truth

1. Items for the assessment of emotional intelligence were provided by Rose, M.R., Prange, M.E., and Hall, N.R. "The Measurement of Emotional Intelligence," manuscript in preparation, 1996. Used with permission.
2. Salovey, P., and Mayer, J. "Emotional Intelligence." *Imagination, Cognition and Personality* 9 (1990): 185–211.
3. Items for the Toughness Training Profile were abstracted from *The Mentally Tough® Corporate Training Workbook: (Mentally Tough Coach),* published by LGE Sport Science, Inc., 1995.
4. Items for the Team Building Perceptual Assessment were abstracted from the source given in note 3.
5. Items for the Mentally Tough Test were abstracted from the source given in note 3.

Chapter 3. "It's the Heart, Guts, and Determination": Emotions Run the Show

1. Netland, D., and Yocom, G. Interview with Lee Trevino. *Golf Digest,* Sept. 1996: 96.

2. Joseph, R. *The Naked Neuron: Evolution and the Language of Brain and Body.* New York: Plenum, 1993.

3. Millman, D. *The Warrior Athlete.* Walpole, NH: Stillpoint Publishing, 1979.

4. Jansen, D. *Full Circle.* New York: Random House, 1994.

5. Welles, E.O. Interview with Phil Jackson. *Inc. Magazine,* Sept. 1996: 35.

6. Salovey, P., and Mayer, J. "Emotional Intelligence." *Imagination, Cognition and Personality* 9 (1990): 185–211.

7. Goleman, D. *Emotional Intelligence.* New York: Bantam, 1995.

8. LeDoux, J. "Emotion and the Limbic System Concept." *Concepts in Neuroscience* 2 (1992): 135–176.

9. Konik, M. Interview with Corey Pavin. *Sky Magazine,* June 1996.

10. Loehr, J.E. *Mental Toughness Training for Sports.* New York: Penguin, 1982.

11. Loehr, J.E., and McLaughlin, P.J. *Mentally Tough: The Principles of Winning at Sports Applied to Winning in Business.* New York: Evans, 1986.

12. Csikszentmihalyi, M. *Flow.* New York: Harper Perennial, 1990.

13. Maier, S.F., and Seligman, M.E.P. "Learned Helplessness: The Theory and Evidence." *Journal of Experimental Psychology* 105 (1976): 3–46.

14. Miller, S.M., and Seligman, M.E.P. "The Reformulated Model of Helplessness and Depression: Evidence and Theory." *Psychological Stress and Psychopathy,* ed. R.W.J. Newfeld. New York: McGraw-Hill, 1982: 149–179.

Related Readings

Damasio, A.R. *Descartes Error.* New York: Avon, 1994.

Patterson, C. "Learned Helplessness and Health Psychology." *Health Psychology* 1, 2 (1982): 153–168.

Seligman, M.E.P., and Maier, S.F. "Failure to Escape Traumatic Shock." *Journal of Experimental Psychology* 74 (1967): 1–9.

PART II: Performer Skills and the Toughening Process: Targeting the Stress Response

Chapter 4. "Keep Things Simple and in the Same Routine": The Rituals of Success

1. Black, E., and Roberts, J. *Rituals for Our Times.* New York: Harper Perennial, 1993.

2. Johnson, J. "Despite Game's Magnitude, Preparation Remains the Same." *The Dallas Morning News,* Jan. 15, 1993.

3. Loehr, J.E., and McLaughlin, P.J. *Mentally Tough: Winning in Sports Applied to Winning in Business.* New York: Evans, 1986.

4. Loehr, J.E. *The New Toughness Training for Sports.* New York: Penguin, 1994.

5. Rechtschaffen, S. *Time Shifting.* New York: Doubleday, 1996: 48.

Related Readings

Cohen, D. *The Circle of Life: Rituals from the Human Family Album.* San Francisco: HarperCollins, 1991.

Cunningham, N. *Feeding the Spirit: How to Create Your Own Rites, Festivals and Celebrations.* San José, CA: Resource Publishing, 1988.

Flinstein, D., and Mayo, P. *Rituals for Living and Dying.* New York: HarperCollins, 1990.

Mumm, S. *Rituals for a New Age: Alternative Weddings, Funerals, Holidays.* Ann Arbor, MI: Quantum Leap Publishing, 1987.

Tuleja, T. *Curious Customs: The Stories Behind 296 Popular American Rituals.* New York: Harmony Books, 1987.

Chapter 5. "It's Showtime Every Day": Learning to Create Emotion on Demand

1. LeDoux, J. "Emotional Memory Systems in the Brain." *Behavioral and Brain Research* 58 (1993).

2. Ekman, P., et al. "Autonomic Nervous System Activity Distinguishes Among Emotions." *Science* 221 (1983): 1208–1210.

3. Hall, N.R.S., and Goldstein, A.L. "Thinking Well: The Chemical Changes Between Emotions and Health." *The Sciences.* New York Academy of Sciences (1986): 34–41.

4. Hall, N.R.S., et al. "Personality Transformation and the Immune System." *Advances,* Sept. 1994.

5. Moore, S. *The Stanislavski System.* New York: Penguin, 1984.

6. Imrie, D. *Good-Bye to Backache.* New York: Fawcett, 1983.

7. Ekman, P. "An Argument for Basic Emotions." *Cognition and Emotion* 6 (1992): 169–200.

8. Duclose, S.E. "Emotion-Specific Effects of Facial Expressions and Postures on Emotional Experience." *Journal of Personality and Social Psychology* 57 (1989): 100–108.

Related Readings

Frijda, N.H. "The Laws of Emotion." *American Psychologist* 43 (1988): 349–358.

Hall, N.R.S., and Kvarnes, R. "Behavioral Intervention and Disease: Possible Mechanisms." *International Perspectives in Self-Regulation and Health,* eds. J.G. Carson and A.R. Seifert. New York: Plenum, 1991.

Keleman, S. *Emotional Anatomy.* Berkeley, CA: Center Press, 1985.

Leibowitz, J., and Connington, B. *The Alexander Technique.* New York: Harper Perennial, 1991.

Myers, D. *The Pursuit of Happiness.* New York: Avon, 1992.

Zajouc, R.B. "Emotion and Facial Efference: A Theory Reclaimed." *Science* 228 (April 5, 1985): 15–21.

Chapter 6. "It's About Being Right Upstairs": Getting a "Head" Start on Your Day

1. Patrick, D. Interview with Bob Kennedy and Sam Bell. *USA Today,* July 17, 1996.
2. Kosslyn, S., Alpert, N.M., Thompson, W.L., Malijkovic, V., Weise, S.B., Chabris, C.F., Hamilton, S.E., Rauch, S.L., and Buonanno, F.S. "Visual Mental Imagery Activates Typographically Organized Visual Cortex: PET Investigations." *Journal of Cognitive Neuroscience* 5 (1993): 263–287.
3. Karni, A. "When Practice Makes Perfect." *Lancet,* 345 (1995): 395.
4. Jansen, D. *Full Circle.* New York: Random House, 1994.
5. Pennebaker, J.W., Kiecolt-Glaser, J.K., and Glaser, R. "Disclosure of Traumas and Immune Function: Health Implications for Psychotherapy." *Journal of Consulting and Clinical Psychology* 56 (1988): 239–245.
6. Loehr, J.E. *The New Toughness Training For Sports.* New York: Plume, 1994.
7. Rechtschaffen, S. *Time Shifting.* New York: Doubleday, 1996: 64.
8. Murphy, S. *The Achievement Zone.* New York: G.P. Putman's Sons, 1996: 89.
9. Davidson, R.J. "Emotion and Affective Style: Hemispheric Substrates." *Psychological Science* 3 (1992): 39–43.
10. Lieber, J. Interview with John Smoltz. *USA Today,* June 19, 1996.
11. Benson, H. *Timeless Healing.* New York: Scribner, 1996.

Related Readings

Loehr, J.E. *The New Toughness Training For Sports.* New York: Plume, 1982.

Thayer, R.E. *The Origin of Everyday Moods.* New York: Oxford University Press, 1996.

Weinberg, R.S., and Gould, D. *Foundations of Sport and Exercise Psychology.* Champaign, IL: Human Kinetics Publishing, 1995.

PART III: Life Skills and the Toughening Process: Targeting Stress Exposure

Chapter 7. "The Things That Pushed Me the Most Were the Things That Helped Me the Most": Becoming a Stress Seeker

1. Selye, H. *The Stress of Life.* New York: McGraw-Hill, 1976.

2. Dienstbier, R., et al. "Catecholamine Training Effects from Exercise Programs: A Bridge to Exercise–Temperament Relationships." *Motivation and Emotion* 2 (1987): 297–318.

3. Weiss, J.M., et al. "Effects of Chronic Exposure to Stressors on Avoidance–Escape Behavior and on Brain Norepinephrine." *Psychosomatic Medicine* 37 (1975): 522–533.

4. Lee, I-Min, and Paffenbarger, R. "Do Physical Activity and Physical Fitness Avert Premature Mortality?" *Exercise and Sport Science Reviews* 24 (1996): 135–172.

5. Holmes, T.H., and Rahe, R.H. "The Social Readjustment Rating Scale." *Journal of Psychosomatic Research* 11 (1967): 213–218.

6. Singer, M.T. "Vietnam Prisoners of War, Stress and Personality Resiliency." *American Journal of Psychiatry* 138 (3) (1991): 345–346.

7. Dimsdale, J.E. "The Coping Behavior of Nazi Concentration Camp Survivors." *American Journal of Psychiatry* 131(7) (1974): 792.

8. Kobasa, S.C. "Stressful Life Events, Personality and Health: An Inquiry into Hardiness." *Journal of Personality and Social Psychology* 37 (1984): 1–11.

9. Cousins, N. *Head First: The Biology of Hope.* New York: Dutton, 1989.

10. Rejeski, J.W., et al. "Physical Activity and Health-Related Quality of Life." *Exercise and Sport Science Reviews* 24 (1966): 71–108.

Related Readings

Beall, B. "The Overtraining Syndrome." *American Rowing,* April–May (1986): 40–42.

Charney, D., et al. "Psychobiologic Mechanisms of Post-Traumatic Stress Disorders." *Archives of General Psychiatry* 50 (April 1993): 294–305.

Claytor, R.P. "Stress Reactivity: Hemodynamic Adjustments in Trained and Untrained Humans." *Medicine and Science in Sports and Exercise* 23 (1991): 873–881.

Cousins, N. *Anatomy of an Illness as Perceived by the Patient.* New York: Norton, 1979.

Dienstbier, R. "Arousal and Phsysiological Toughness: Implications for Mental and Physical Health." *Psychological Review* 96 (1989): 84–100.

Dienstbier, R. "Behavioral Correlates of Sympathoadrenal Reactivity: The Toughness Model." *Medicine and Science in Sport and Exercise* 23 (1991): 846–852.

Eliot, R.S. *From Stress to Strength: How to Lighten Your Load and Save Your Life.* New York: Bantam, 1994.

Fergley, D.A. "Psychological Burnout in High-Level Athletes." *The Physician and Sports Medicine* 12 (1984): 109–119.

Sacks, M.L. "Psychological Well-Being and Vigorous Physical Activity." *Psychological Foundations of Sport,* eds. J.M. Silva and R.S. Weinberg. Champaign, IL: Human Kinetics Publishing, 1984.

Weiss, J.M., et al. "Coping Behavior and Stress-Induced Behavioral Depression: Studies of the Role of Brain Catecholamines." Reported in *Psychology of Depressive Disorders,* ed. R.A. Depue. New York: Academic, 1979: 125–160.

Chapter 8. "Taking High-Quality Breaks": The Art of World-Class Recovery

1. Loehr, J.E. "The Development of a Cognitive-Behavioral Between-Point Intervention Strategy for Tennis." Paper presented at the 8th World Congress of Sport Psychology; Lisbon, Portugal, June 1993.

2. Loehr, J.E. *Toughness Training For Life.* New York: Penguin, 1994: 71.

3. Bloomfield, H., and Cooper, R. *The Power of Five.* Emmaus, PA: Rodale Press, 1995: 44.

4. Flannery, R.F., Jr. "The Stress Resistant Person." *Harvard Medical School/Health Letter,* Feb. 1989: 5–7.

5. Maslow, A.H. *Motivation and Personality.* New York: Harper & Row, 1970.

6. Adapted from Maslow's "Hierarchy of Needs," 1970. Reproduced from Loehr, note 2 above.

7. Kripke, D.F., et al. "Short and Long Sleep and Sleeping Pills: Is Increased Mortality Associated?" *Archives of General Psychiatry* 36 (1979): 103–116.

8. Coren, S. *Sleep Thieves*. New York: Free Press, 1996.

9. Monk, T.H. *Sleep, Sleepiness and Performance*. Chichester, UK: Wiley, 1991.

10. Stampi, J.H. *Why We Nap: Evolution, Chronology and Functions of Polyphasics and Ultrashort Sleep*. Boston: Bukhauser, 1992.

11. Groppel, J.L. *The Anti-Diet Book*. Provo, UT: Executive Excellence, 1995.

12. Nezer, A.M., et al. "Sense of Humor as Moderator of the Relation Between Stressful Events and Psychological Distress: A Prospective Analysis." *Journal of Personality and Social Psychology* 54 (1988): 5220–5225.

13. Cousins, N. *Anatomy of an Illness: Reflections on Healing and Regeneration*. New York: Bantam, 1981.

14. Friedman, M., and Ulmer, D. *Treating Type A Behavior—and Your Heart*. New York: Knopf, 1984.

15. Stor, A. *Music and the Mind*. New York: Ballantine Books, 1992.

16. Ricker, M.S., et al. "The Effect of Music, Imagery and Relaxation on Adrenal Corticosteroids and the Re-entrainment of Circadian Rhythms." *Journal of Music Therapy* 22 (Spring 1985): 45–58.

17. Pfaff, V.K., Smith, K.E., and Gowan, D. "The Effects of Music on the Distress of Pediatric Cancer Patients Undergoing Bone Marrow Aspirations." *Journal of Children's Health Care* 18 (Fall 1989): 232–236.

18. Boutcher, S.H. et al. "The Effects of Sensory Deprivation and Music on Perceived Exertion and Affect During Exercise." *Journal of Sport and Exercise Psychology* 12 (June 1990): 167–176.

19. Sobel, D., and Ornstein, R. *The Mental Medicine Update* 2 (Fall 1993).

20. Myers, D. *The Pursuit of Happiness*. New York: Avon, 1992.

Related Readings

Benson, H. *Timeless Healing*. New York: Scribner, 1996.

Berkman, L., et al. "Social Networks, Host Resistance and Mortality." *American Journal of Epidemiology* 109 (1979): 186–204.

Blair, J. *Who Gets Sick*. New York: G.P. Putnam's Sons, 1987.

Blumenfeld, E., and Alpern, L. *Humor at Work*. Atlanta: Peachtree Publishers, 1994.

Borbely, A. *Secrets of Sleep*. New York: Basic Books, 1996.

Carskadon, M.A. *Encyclopedia for Sleep and Dreaming*. New York: Macmillan, 1993.

Dinges, D.F., and Broughton, R.J. *Sleep and Alertness: Chronological, Behavioral and Medical Aspects of Napping*. New York: Raven Press, 1989.

Dotto, L. *Losing Sleep: How Your Sleeping Habits Affect Your Life*. New York: Morrow, 1990.

Goldstein, A. "Thrills in Response to Music and Other Stimuli." *Physiological Psychology* 8 (1980): 126–129.

Goodwin, J., et al. "The Effect of Marital Status on Stage, Treatment and Survival of Cancer Patients." *Journal of the American Medical Association* 258 (1987): 3125–3130.

Hirshberg, C., and Ian Barasch, M. *Remarkable Recovery*. New York: Riverhead Books, 1995.

House, J., et al. "Social Relationships and Health." *Science* 241 (1988): 540–545.

Kavussanu, M., and McAuley, E. "Exercise and Optimism: Are Highly Active Individuals More Optimistic?" *Journal of Sport and Exercise Psychology* 17 (1995): 246–258.

Kennedy, S., Kiecolt-Glaser, J., and Glaser, R. "Immunological Consequences of Acute and Chronic Stressors: The Mediating Role in Interpersonal Relationships." *British Journal of Medical Psychology* 61 (1985): 77–85.

Kiechel, W. "Executives Ought to be Funnier." *Fortune,* Dec. 12, 1983.

Lefcourt, H.M., and Martin, R.A. *Humor and Life Stress*. New York: Springer-Verlag, 1986.

McGee-Cooper, A. *You Don't Have to Go Home from Work Exhausted!* Dallas: Bower and Rogers, 1990.

Peter, J.H., et al. *Sleep and Health Risk*. Berlin: Springer-Verlag, 1991.

Sobel, D., and Ornstein, R. *Healthy Pleasures*. Reading, MA: Addison-Wesley, 1989.

Spiegel, D. "Facilitating Emotional Coping During Treatment." *Cancer* 66 (1990): 1422–1426.

Spiegel, D. *Living Beyond Limits*. New York: Time Books, 1993.

Thayer, R.E. *The Biopsychology of Mood and Arousal*. New York: Oxford University Press, 1989.

Thayer, R.E. *The Origins of Everyday Moods*. New York: Oxford University Press, 1996.

Wurtman, J.J. *Managing Your Mind and Mood Through Food.* New York: HarperCollins, 1987.

Chapter 9. "Every So Often I Go Over the Edge": Riding the Waves of Stress and Recovery

1. Rossi, E.L. *The Twenty-Minute Break.* Los Angeles: J.P. Tarcher, 1991.
2. Weiner, H. *Perturbing the Organism.* Chicago: University of Chicago Press, 1992.
3. LePoncin, M. *Brain Fitness.* New York: Fawcett, 1990.
4. Loehr, J.E. *The New Toughness Training For Sports.* New York: Penguin, 1995: 121–129.

Related Readings

Heller, J., and Henkin, W.A. *Bodywise.* Los Angeles: J.P. Tarcher, 1986.

Rossi, E.L. "The Eternal Quest: Hidden Rhythms of Stress and Healing in Everyday Life." *Psychological Perspectives* 22 (1990): 6–23.

Chapter 10. "Fatigue Makes Enemies of Us All": The Need for Energy

1. Loehr, J.E. *Mental Toughness Training For Sports.* New York: Penguin, 1982.
2. Abstracted from *The Mentally Tough® Corporate Training Workbook: (Mentally Tough Coach),* published by LGE Sport Science, 1995.
3. Loehr, J.E., and McLaughlin, P.J. *Mentally Tough: Winning in Sports Applied to Winning in Business.* New York: Evans, 1986.

Related Reading

Thayer, R.E. *The Origin of Everyday Moods.* New York: Oxford University Press, 1996.

Epilogue Coming Home: A Daily Journey Without End

1. Rechtschaffen, S. *Time Shifting.* New York: Doubleday, 1996.

Related Readings

Covey, S., et al. *First Things First.* New York: Fireside, 1994.

Frankl, V. *Man's Search for Meaning: An Introduction to Logotherapy.* Boston: Beacon Press, 1962.

Hendriks, G., and Luderman, K. *The Corporate Mystic.* New York: Bantam, 1996.

Kabat-Zinn, J. *Wherever You Go There You Are.* New York: Hyperion, 1994.

Pritchett, P. *Mind Shift*. Dallas: Pritchett and Associates Publishing, 1996.

Schwartz, T. *What Really Matters*. New York: Bantam, 1995.

Smith, H. *The 10 Natural Laws of Successful Time and Life Management*. New York: Warner Books, 1994.

Index

acting skills, 95–96, 101, 102–104, 107–108, 117
active rest, 194
adrenal hormones, 60–61
aerobic exercise, 159–63
  model for interval stress exposure (Figure 7.2), 161
  standard model (Figure 7.1), 160
affirmations, 121–23, 124, 137–38
age/aging:
  changes/markers, 157, 158
  and sleep, 180
  and stress (anti-aging factor), 146, 157–59
airline pilots, and approved napping, 183
air turbulence story (example, summoning emotion on demand), 114–16
alcohol, 80–81, 181, 184, 186, 196, 211
alone time, 87–88, 134
amygdala, 99–100, 101, 102, 107, 115–16, 128
anger, 50, 52, 95, 174
  summoning on demand, 104–105
Apollo 13, 108–109, 129, 148
areta, 19
axons, 144

balance, 5, 29
Basic Rest–Activity Cycles (BRAC), 199
Bell, Sam, 118
Benson, Herbert, 140
beta-endorphin, 61
biochemical mechanisms, 51–52, 60–61, 62–63, 149, 154, 186, 190, 199, 200, 222
  see also brain; physiological mechanisms
biological clocks, and rituals, 92
Blackstone Group, 55
Blair, Steven, 162
Bloomfield, Harold, 171
Bogart, Humphrey, 80
Boutcher, Stephen, 192
Bowman, Scotty, 79
brain:
  amygdala, see amygdala
  biochemistry of, see biochemical mechanisms

evolution of, 57–58
exercise of, and growth/rewiring, 119–20, 144
neuromotor circuits, 128
scanning technology, 120
brainwashing, positive, 123
breakfast, importance of, 185
breathing exercises, 16, 194, 195
Bristol-Myers Squibb, 5
Bruguera, Sergi, 4, 168
burnout, as failure to oscillate, 207

caffeine, 181, 183, 186, 211, 237
Captain Tom (firefighter's story), 73–75, 135
Carey, Jim, 79
catecholamines, 61
challenge, 50, 52, 54, 61
chemistry-energy relationship (Figure 10.8), 222
  see also biochemical mechanisms
Chesterfield, Lord, 181
children, 204
  see also family time
China, and napping, 183
chocolate, 181, 183
choking in sports, 125
cholesterol, 188
Christmas rituals, 81
cigarettes, see smoking/nicotine
circadian rhythms, 199
circadian trough, 235
Clinique, 5
clocks, pendulum (analogy), 200–201
coffee, as negative ritual, 81
  see also caffeine
coffee breaks, traditional, 87
"Coming Home" metaphor, 223–27
computed tomography (CT), 120
Connors, Jimmy, 23
control, importance of, 61–63, 157
Cooper, Robert, 171
Coren, Stanley, 180
corporate athlete, 5, 14, 23–26, 58
  vs. professional athlete, 23–26
  training, see Toughness Training
cortisol, 60, 155
Courier, Jim, 4, 168

Cousins, Norman, 157
creative recoveries (list), 196
creative time rituals, 87
curl-ups, 159

daily preparation plan, 133–39
daily ritual, sample (Appendix B),
    233–37
daily training log, 6–9, 33
    IPS Acting skills, 117
    and rituals, 94
    samples, 8, 21, 33, 94, 117, 122
    themes in, 33
Dalai Lama, 85
Darwin, Charles, 224
Davidson, Richard, 130
dendrites, 144
diet, see nutrition/diet
Dimsdale, Joel, 156
disciplined thinking/acting, 101,
    106–108, 117
disease, see health
"Dive into the present" ritual, 89–90
dopamine, 184, 186
drugs, 81, 196, 211

eating habits, 181, 185–88, 234–35, 236,
    237
    see also nutrition/diet
eating disorders, 81
Eckerd Corporation, 5
Edison, Thomas, 175
Eisner, Michael, 23
Ekman, Paul, 101
emotion(s), 46–64, 95–117, 226
    control of, 95–117
        steps, 106–107
    and energy state, 215
    and evolution, 57–58
    importance of, 46–64
    and linearity (recovery/stress), 208
    and perception, 149–51
    physiology of, 50–51, 56, 101–102, 104,
        105–106, 113–14, 130–33
        hemispheric specialization, 130–33
        see also limbic system (emotional
            brain)
    triggers for, 101
emotional intelligence, 34–38, 55–57
    handling relationships, 37–38
    knowing one's emotions, 34–35
    managing emotions, 35
    motivating oneself, 36
    recognizing emotions in others, 37
emotional recovery, 174, 208
emotional toughness, four primary
        indicators of, 47–50
    flexibility, 48
    resiliency, 50

responsiveness, 49
    strength, 49–50
energy, 213–22
    audit, 215–18, 238–43
    model of, two-dimensional (Figure
        10.1), 214
entrainment, 201
epenephrine, 184
escape time, 171
Esposito, Phil, 79
Estée Lauder cosmetics company, 5, 211
Evans, Jane, 190
Evert, Chris, 112
evolutionary forces, 52, 55
    emotional vs. rational capacity, 57–58
Execunet, 15
exercise, see physical exercise

Faldo, Nick, 4, 54
family time, 84, 204, 236
Farrow Port, Phebe, 211–12
fatigue, 153–54, 213–22
FBI undercover agent (ritual success
        story), 70–72
fear, 50, 51, 52, 100, 174
    desensitizing, 124–26
    of flying, 95
    military toughening for controlling,
        109–10
fight-or-flight, 52, 57, 214
fitness, and sleep, 180–81
Flannery, Raymond F., 171
flexibility:
    emotional, 48
    physical, 164
focus, mental, 129–30, 134
food, as negative ritual, 81
    see also eating habits
Frankl, Victor, 135–36
Friedman, Myer, 191

gardening, 194
Gates, Bill, 23
"Get-you-moving" sayings, 123
Glaser, Janice, see Kiecolt-Glaser, J. K.
Glaser, Ronald, 125, 248
Goleman, Daniel, 55, 58
golfers, and affirmations, 124
Gorky, Maxim, 226
Gowan, Darryl, 192
Griffin, Gerry, 108–109, 129, 148, 201
Groppel, Jack, 185

Harbaugh, Jim, 4
Hawks, John, 145, 174, 227
hazing, 148
health:
    disease, as failure to oscillate,
        200–202

and energy states, 219
and linearity, 202
and stress, 155, 156
Heffernan, John, 30–32
helplessness, 155
learned, 63–64
hemispheric specialization, 130–33
Henriksen, Erik, 170
Hippocrates, 155
hobbies, 236–37
holiday rituals, 81
Holmes and Rehe Readjustment Rating
Scale, 155
home, working at, 204
home recovery rituals, 87
"How fortunate I am" ritual, 88–89
humor, and recovery, 190–91

IBM, 5
Ideal Performance State (IPS), 4, 20
accessing, 20, 22–23, 108
and control, importance of, 61–63
on demand, 108
descriptors of, 60
emotional component of, 51
important understandings about, 60
physiological and neurochemical
events, 60
research into, 59
and rituals, 78
in Toughness Training roadmap, 7
Ideal Recovery State (IRS), 219
illness, see health
immune system, 51
and stress, 157
Imrie, David, 106
intermittent stress exposure, 154–55
interval exercise/training, 161–63, 188
IPS, see Ideal Performance State (IPS)
IRS, see Ideal Recovery State (IRS)
"Is this an intelligent response?" ritual, 89

Jackson, Phil, 54
James, William, 52
Jansen, Dan, 4, 17–18, 19–22, 23, 28,
52–54, 121–23, 136–37, 146, 168,
245, 246, 248
Japanese karoshi, 169
jet lag, sample flying ritual to prevent, 86
Johnson, Jimmy, 68–69, 246
Jurassic Park and physiology of fear, 100

Kaiser Permanente, 5
karoshi, Japanese, 169
Kennedy, Bob, 118, 119
Kiecolt-Glaser, J. K., 125
Knapp, Rob, 64, 136, 138
Kobasa, Suzanne, 156
Kripke, Dan, 175

Lang, Ilene, 63, 107, 218
Lao Tzu, 48, 171
laughter, biochemistry of, 190
leadership, and stress tolerance, 143
LePoncin, Monique, 203
Levenson, R. W., 101
life-and-death pressures, 108–109
Life Skills, 7, 28, 141, 211
energy management, see energy
recovery training, 166–97
see also recovery
stress seeking, 143–65
see also stress
in Toughness Training road map, 7
wave making, see oscillation
light, primary biological clock regulator,
183
limbic system (emotional brain), 57, 58,
99, 192
liming, Carribean practice of, 171–72
Lindelow, Kristen, 176
Lindros, Eric, 4, 168
linearity, 199, 202–206, 208
language of, 202–205
linear recovery, examples, 208
linear stress, examples, 208
and pressure, 205–206
Lombardi, Vince, 222
lymphocytes, 51

McGee-Cooper, Ann, 196
Maddi, Salvatore, 156
magnetic resonance imaging (MRI), 120
Maier, S. F., 63
Mancini, Ray, 4
mantra, 129
Martin, Todd, 125
Maslow, Abraham, 172
massage, 194
Mayer, John, 55–56
meals, see eating habits
medical checkup, 189
meditation, 16, 129–30, 171, 194
mental preparation, 118–40
affirmations, see affirmations
approaches (seven best), 121–33
daily plan, 133–39
fears, desensitizing, 124–26
focus, 129–30, 134
placebo effect of, 139–40
rehearsing mentally, 128–29, 138–39
thinking, negative (controlling), 124
thinking, positive (practicing), 130–33
in Toughness Training roadmap, 7
training for, 119–33
writing exercises, 126–28
mental recovery, 174–75
linear, 208
mental stress, linear, 208

mental toughness, test of, 41–45
Merrill Lynch, 5, 6
method acting, 102–104
military toughening, two-step process, 109–10
Miller, Neil, 61
Miller, S. M., 63
mistake ritual, 92
mob impersonator (ritual success story), 70–72
Morgan Stanley, 5
mortality rates:
  and exercise and stress, 154
  and sleep habits, 178
Murphy, Shane, 130
muscle strength, general, 163–64
music, 134, 171, 174, 191–93, 195, 234
  analogy for maximum performance capacity, 201–202
Myers, David, 195

napping, 183–85, 194
  tough naps/power naps, 185
  see also sleep
natural rhythms, 92
need fulfillment, 195–97, 221
  hierarchy of recovery needs, 172–73
negative thinking, controlling, 124
  with writing exercises, 126–28
neocortex (thinking brain), 57, 58, 128, 192
neurology, see biochemical mechanisms; brain
nicotine, see smoking/nicotine
Nieto, Augie, 15–16
Nilsmark, Katrin, 4
"No Pain, No Gain," 16, 162
norepinephrine, 154, 186
Norman, Greg, 125
Norway's training philosophy, 1994 Winter Olympics, 18
nutrition/diet, 16, 17, 184, 221, 237
  and recovery, 185–88
  rituals, 84
  and sleep, 181

office recovery rituals, 87
O'Meara, Mark, 4
Orlando Sentinel (toughness training at), 27
Ornstein, Richard, 194
oscillation, 87, 198–212, 226
  built-in rhythms, 199–200
  burnout as failure to oscillate, 207
  disease as failure to oscillate, 200–202
  healthy vs. unhealthy, 211–12
  linearity, language of, 202–205
  linearity and pressure, 205–206
  periodization, 207–11

overtraining, 209–10
overwork, 169

pain vs. discomfort, 152, 162
passive rest, 194
Pavin, Corey, 59
Pavlov, Ivan, 103
Peifer, Charles, 131, 191
Pennebaker, James, 125
peptides, 51
perception, and biochemistry, 149–51
performer self vs. real self, 97–99
Performer Skills, 7, 28, 211
  acting, see acting skills
  defined, 97
  mental preparation, see mental preparation
  rituals, see rituals
  in Toughness Training road map, 7
periodization, 207–11
personal toughness checklist, 227–29
personal trainer (recommended), 164
Pfaff, Valerie, 192
physical exercise, 153, 157–65, 188–89, 221
  interval training, 161–63, 188
  lack of, and consequences, 158
  recommendations, 159–64, 188–89
    abdominal exercises, 159
    flexibility training, 164
    general muscle strength, 163–64
    heart/lung stress, exercises for, 159–63
  and recovery, 188–89
  rituals, 84
  in sample daily ritual, 233, 234, 235, 236
  and sleep, 181
  as wave making, 204
physical recovery, 173–74
  linear, 208
physical toughness, vs. mental toughness, 118, 119
physiological mechanisms:
  biochemistry, see biochemical mechanisms
  brain, see brain
  and emotions, 50–52, 104
  and rituals as triggers, 68
placebo, mental training as, 139–40
positive thinking, 16, 123, 130–33
  see also emotion(s), control of; mental preparation
positron emission tomography (PET), 120
posture, 106
power naps, 185
prayer, 194, 196
preperformance rituals, 76, 85

present focus, in mental training, 129, 134
Price Waterhouse, 4
professional sports:
  vs. corporate arena, 23–26
  and napping, 184
  and periodization, 207–11
  and superstitions, 79
psychological hardiness, 156
psychological *vs.* nonphysical, 140
psychosomatic illness, 139–40
Puerner, John, 27
Pyles, Margaret, 93
pythagoras, 192

rat experiment (importance of control), 61–63
real self:
  in Ideal Performance State, 113–14
  vs. performer self, 97–99
Rechtschaffen, S., 89, 130, 225
recovery, 166–97, 219, 221
  defining, 168–69
  and energy audit, 219
  and exercise, 188–89
  and humor, 190–91
  inadequate (*karoshi*), 169–71
  linear:
    examples, 208
    liming (no stress), 171–72
  and music, 191–93
  natural *vs.* forced, 219
  and needs:
    hierarchy of recovery needs, 172–73
    need fulfillment, 195–97
  and nutrition, 185–88
  and rest, active/passive, 194–95
  signals of:
    emotional recovery, 174
    mental recovery, 174–75
    physical recovery, 173–74
  and sleep, 178–85
  see also sleep
  training, 175–78
Rehe, Richard, 155
rehearsal, mental, 128–29, 138–39
relaxation techniques, 16–17, 129, 171, 183
repetitive self-talk (affirmations)
  changing beliefs, 121–23, 124, 137–38
rest, active/passive, 194–95
rhythms, built-in, 92, 199–200
Richter, Mike, 4, 132, 168
Ricker, Mark, 192
rituals, 67–94, 173, 184, 225
  alone time, 83, 87–88
  breakthrough, 88–93
  creative time, 83, 87

designing your own plan, 93–94
"Dive into the present," 89–90
exercise, 83, 84
  see also physical exercise
family time, 83, 84
home recovery, 83, 87
"How fortunate I am," 88–89
identifying adaptive ones in your life, 82
important, twelve most, 83–88
"Is this an intelligent response?," 89
maladaptive, 80–81
mistake ritual, 92
nutrition, 83, 84
  see also eating habits
office recovery, 83, 87
preparation ritual in six parts, 91
preperformance, 83, 85
sample daily ritual (Appendix B), 233–37
sleep, 83
  see also sleep
spirituality, 83, 85
spontaneous ritual, 93
vs. superstitions, 78–79
telephone, 83, 86–87
travel, 83, 85, 86
value of (list), 68
"Yes, I can," 90–91
Roberts, J., 246
Roosevelt, Theodore, 206
Rose, M. R., 245
Rossi, Ernest, 200, 202, 206
Rotella, Bob, 133

Sabatini, Gabriela, 4, 167
sadness, summoning on demand, 104–108
Salovey, Peter, 34, 55–56
Sampras, Pete, 4
Sanchez-Vicario, Arantxa, 4, 167
Scheibel, Arnold, 144
Schumacher, Joel, 26
Schwartz, Tony, 76–78
Schwarzman, Steve, 55
Seles, Monica, 4
self evaluation, *see* tests for self evaluation
Seligman, M. E., 63
Selye, Hans, 145
senses, and mental rehearsal, 128–29
serotonin, 184
sex, 194
Shaver, Troy, 75–76, 164
Shaw, George Bernard, 147
Simorrov, R. V., 103
Singer, Margaret, 156
sleep, 15, 81, 83, 178–85, 221, 235, 237
  deprivation, self-test, 182
  factors affecting, 180–82
  napping, 183–85, 235

sleep (*cont'd*)
  recommendations, 182–83
  rituals, 81, 83, 182, 237
  stages, 179–80
Smith, Karen, 192
smoking/nicotine, 80, 164, 181
Smoltz, John, 132
Snowdon, David, 144
Sobel, David, 194
spiritual rituals, 85
spontaneous ritual, 93
sport science, 5, 144–65
Stanislavski, Konstantin, 103–104, 105, 106
Stern, Jim, 189
stretching, 194
stress:
  benefits of, 4, 144–45
  capacity, exceeding, 151
  conclusions about (fourteen), 146–65
  in corporate world, 13–17, 23–26
  and discomfort (*vs.* pain), 151–52, 162
  exposure to *vs.* response to, 4
    targeting exposure, *see* Life Skills
    targeting response, *see* Performer Skills
  and illness, caused by occurrence of traumatic life events, 155
  linear; examples of, 208
  management; paradigm shift in, 16–17
    see also Ideal Performance State (IPS); Toughness Training
  myths about, 3
  physical stress (exercise) increasing overall capacity for, 153–54
  and recovery, *see* oscillation; recovery
  remedies for typical stressors, 110–11
  seeking after, 143–65
  sport science and, 144–65
superstitions, 78, 79
Sydor, Alison, 85

tai-chi, 194
Team Building Perceptual Assessment, 40, 232
team player, 25
telephone rituals, 86–87
telephone time oscillation, 235
tennis, between-point time (as recovery), 111–13, 166–68
tension-energy relationship (Figure 10.7), 221
tests for self evaluation:
  emotional intelligence, 34–38
  energy audit, 215–18, 238–43

Mentally Tough Test, 41–45
  personal toughness checklist, 227–29
  rituals, 88
  sleep deprivation, 182
  Team Building Perceptual Assessment, 40, 232
  Toughness Training Profile, 38–40, 231
themes, 33–34, 45
thinking brain, *see* neocortex (thinking brain)
Thoreau, Henry, 224
time alone rituals, 87–88, 134
toughness:
  assessing your own, 32–34
  continuum, mind and body, 118
  redefinition of, 18
Toughness Training, 4–5
  caveat, 26–27
  identifying areas of weakness (four tools), 34–45
  new paradigm ("new way to fight"), 52–54
  overviews:
    "Coming Home" metaphor, 223–27
    roadmap (graph), 6, 7
  Toughness Training Profile, 38–40, 231
Toynbee, Arnold, 54
travel rituals, 85, 86
Trembley, Angelo, 163
Trevino, Lee, 51, 245
Trump, Donald, 76
Tzu, Lao, 48, 171

Ueshiba, Morikei, 50
ultradian rhythms, 184
undertraining, 152, 209, 210, 212

visualization/imaging, 101, 120, 128, 136
vitamin supplements, 187

war, and stress, 156
water, drinking, 187
wave making, *see* oscillation
weakness, identifying areas of, 34–45
weight training, 18
Weisman, Billy, 49–50
Weiss, J. M., 154
Westwood Squibb, 6
Woods, Ron, 192
writing (form of mental training), 126–28

"Yes, I can" ritual, 90–91
yoga, 16, 194